About the Authors

NEIL BIERBAUM (B.Com) has been a life and executive coach since 2005 and has practised and taught meditation for more than 25 years. He has worked with large corporates, SMEs, entrepreneurs and private clients—many of them looking to manage the enormous stress and increasing complexity in their professional and personal lives and make sure they achieve their potential in an uncertain world.

COLINDA LINDE (M.A. Clin. Psych., D.Litt. et Phil.) has been a clinical psychologist since 1993 and is the former chairperson of the South African Depression and Anxiety Group (SADAG). She specialises in cognitive behaviour therapy (CBT) for anxiety disorders (panic, social phobia), and works extensively in the areas of stress management, work-life balance, sleep issues, assertion and mindfulness. Colinda also practises and teaches meditation and founded the self-help CBT website thoughtsfirst.com.

Practical Mindfulness

Master yourself. Master your life.

A handbook for self-development, combining the best of mindfulness, coaching and CBT.

NEIL BIERBAUM

with

DR COLINDA LINDE

Alembic

Practical Mindfulness by Neil Bierbaum, with Dr Colinda Linde

Published by ALEMBIC (Pty) Ltd

Suite 350, Private Bag X31, Saxonwold, 2132,

Gauteng, South Africa

info@alembic.co.za

First Edition

Paperback ISBN: 978-0-6399246-2-5

e-Book ISBN: 978-0-6399246-3-2

Visit the authors' websites at

www.neilbierbaum.com
www.colindalinde.com
www.practicalmindfulness.co.za

Contents

Preface

THE PRACTICAL Mindfulness program was born out of a conversation that Neil and I had about how beneficial mindfulness and meditation has been for both of us. We both agreed that it had helped us, firstly, on a daily basis, with all that life in our colourful country—South Africa—tends to throw at a person. It also enabled us to navigate calmly and rationally through various upheavals in our lives. We both wondered how anyone gets by without it.

This gave us the idea of bringing mindfulness to everyone, in a practical way that could be used immediately. Out of the conversations that followed, the live workshop series took shape. We chose the key elements of mindfulness based on our years of reading and experience. Then we selected the main areas of life, or fields of application, where we've experienced its benefits for ourselves and many of our clients over the years. Our underlying goal was always to share something useful and beneficial, so that others could experience life differently as well.

We've run the programme several times now—more than 250 people have attended—and received knockout feedback about its benefits. Neil's take-home notes for each module proved even more popular and the request for a book came up more than once. Neil needed little prompting—he's not only an accomplished meditator but also an award-winning writer, and so he leapt into the task. After months of additional research, writing and editing of his own work, with some proofing and a few nods of approval from me, you're about to benefit from that output.

I feel obliged to emphasise that I really do mean it when I say there were just a few nods of approval from me. Although I'm the qualified psychologist, Neil's grasp of the subject is astonishing and most of the ideas and interpretations that you'll see here came from him.

In fact, watching Neil create this book felt a lot like observing a master craftsman. I think of a watchmaker, who has a single-pointed focus as every component is carefully placed, layer upon layer, connection point to connection point, until a fully functioning precision instrument is born. Every word has been deliberately chosen and placed, as has the evolution of each chapter from the component parts that have come before.

This book will take you through a similar process. If you follow it step by step it will enable you to turn your own mind into a precision instrument too.

And just as a bespoke watch needing a service or repair returns to the craftsman, this book can be taken along with you as a lifetime resource.

Dr Colinda Linde
Johannesburg
July 2018

SECTION A | Introduction

AS THE name suggests, this book will provide you with a practical path to develop personal mastery—and thereby improve your experience of life—by applying the principles and practices of mindfulness. These principles and practices go much further than just calming you down in order to deal with stress, or paying attention while you eat instead of being on your phone.

Most people will agree that the world is a pretty topsy-turvy place at the moment. Election results are unexpected. Terrorist attacks are unpredictable. New companies can scale to global proportions in astonishingly short periods of time, while historical giants—whether they be companies, government dictators, or celebrities—can crash to zero within weeks.

In truth, the world has always been a topsy-turvy place. As Winston Churchill said, "History is just one damn thing after another." The difference now is the pace of change and the degree of unpredictability. Even personal anchors, like having a steady career and a lifelong marriage, are fast becoming the exception rather than the norm.

The net effect of this is that the old reference points no longer apply. We can no longer be guided by firm, fixed and clear religious and social norms. The trust that people once placed in their leaders has been massively eroded. Who do we turn to? We have to figure it out for ourselves.

Mindfulness is capable of providing an important anchor. Yeah, right, you might say. Mindfulness is just a bunch of hippy crap that's been packaged for the social media age. Or you may have a more positive view of mindfulness, but see it as merely a good way to deal with stress. Much like yoga, or Pilates.

That may be fair comment, and we're here to say that mindfulness is also much more. We like to say it's the "salt in the mix". In the way salt brings out the flavours in a dish, we say that mindfulness, applied correctly, can raise individual—and, ultimately, collective—human consciousness.

That's a pretty lofty claim. To stay with the analogy we used, what can we say about salt? It brings up the other flavours of the dish. Have you heard the story of the king, the three sons and the salt? The king sends his three sons out on a mission to find something of the greatest value. The two eldest sons return with a jewel of sorts; the youngest son returns with a small bag of salt. The king is insulted and banishes him to the kitchen, and throws a banquet for the two older sons. Well, guess who wins when he withholds the salt from the food at the banquet and the king is embarrassed?!

What the king discovers about salt is that it's only needed in tiny proportions to make a big difference. One more thing we should recognise about salt is that it's incredibly abundant on earth, but not in its isolated form. For the most part, it has to be distilled from water.

Mindfulness is about becoming aware of the nature of one's mind and using that awareness to consciously direct one's mind, rather than be directed by it. As anyone who has practiced mindfulness will know, the mind is fairly unruly. We can say that "the mind has a mind of its own", and we have little control over it. Yet we allow this out-of-control mind to run our lives and direct our way in the world.

> *The mind has a mind of its own. Yet we allow this out-of-control mind to run our lives and direct our way in the world.*

For people who claim to be rational, that's not very rational. It's a bit like being at the steering wheel of a bus, but having no direct connection to the wheels. The wheels do their own thing. This is dangerous, because the mind is naturally reactive, which means that people are naturally reactive.

The consequences of this are obvious, and all around us in broad daylight. Political polarisation is perhaps the prime example. It's becoming so prevalent—fuelled by the trolling that social media makes possible—that the beer brand Heineken actually attempted to address the theme through its advertising.

Despite all our scientific knowledge and technology, we're apparently not improving our ability to manage our differences at the same rate as we're developing things like artificial intelligence. In fact, we can say that what we humans have is a kind of artificial intelligence—an intelligence that lacks awareness, mindfulness, wisdom.

As the global leader of *Vipassana* meditation, S N Goenka, says, "No wonder there's so much madness in the world!"

Fortunately, some sanity has prevailed, and science has been used to produce something other than weapons or other forms of competitive advantage: some scientists have shown that certain forms of meditation can actually change the brain. For example, studies showed that seasoned Vipassana meditators grew more physical connections between the amygdala (which controls the fight-or-flight response) and the prefrontal cortex (which controls reason). These people proved to be much less reactive—their brains recovered much more quickly from a fight-or-flight response—than non-meditators.

In our bus-driving analogy, this is like connecting the steering wheel to the wheels. Things feel a whole lot safer and in control that way—for you and for other people—and that's what mindfulness can do for your own life and, ultimately, for society.

When you practice mindfulness—and this book will show you how—you distil your own essential point of awareness from the sea of thinking and feeling that will have hitherto dominated and run your life. That tiny measure of awareness, like a tiny measure of salt, can infuse and transform your life.

This is why Colinda and I believe—and are able to state with confidence—that everybody can benefit, and everybody can learn to manage themselves to have a different, better experience of life. We also believe that if this reaches a tipping point, then the whole of humanity can benefit. If ever there was a time when people needed that, it's now.

My journey to this point has been primarily through journalism and coaching— and the daily practice of meditation for more than 25 years. I began with Transcendental Meditation in my mid-twenties and maintained that practice while learning many other forms, until I came across Vipassana ten years ago. Vipassana is the big daddy of meditations—I'll explain more in the book—and I've practiced that ever since. This dovetailed with the coaching modality I learned, which can be described as ontological and was strongly rooted in developing conscious awareness and mindful nonreactivity.

If this sounds like New Age hippy crap, it's not. In parallel to the above I've worked in corporates and with entrepreneurs—as well as having been an entrepreneur, partner and parent—and I've seen the impact, both in my own life and those of my clients.

This last point is particularly pertinent: my approach has always been to test what I have learned by throwing my whole life at it. (This was something my best man, who has known me my whole life, said at my wedding, so it's not only me saying it.) So I can say that my path has been more experiential. I've often referred to myself as "a gonzo journalist of the soul". To that extent, my coaching career has been as much about doing the research as it has been about helping people.

While I studied psychology at university, I was also a bit of a rebel and chose to get started with life rather than finish my post-grad studies. I have more recently started to incorporate a more scientific approach to my writing, life and work.

For this reason, I invited clinical psychologist and cognitive behaviour therapy (CBT) specialist Dr Colinda Linde to join me as a sounding board and kind of academic supervisor for this book. Colinda shares my belief, expressed earlier, that everybody can learn to manage themselves to have a different, better experience of life. She has also joined me as a co-founder of the Practical Mindfulness live and online learning program.

It's important to note that CBT is the branch of psychology that is anchored most strongly to the scientific method and yet it has begun to incorporate mindfulness as being central to its treatment methods. Colinda herself has practiced meditation since before it became popularised as mindfulness, and she, like me, has realised incredible benefits in her professional and personal life. She has also seen the impact that mindfulness has had on the lives of her clients when she has introduced it in combination with CBT.

We are both confident that CBT and coaching are two of the most powerful and effective modalities for causing personal transformation. We know that mindfulness can provide a lens through which those modalities can be simply and practically taught, learned, assimilated and applied.

By combining the best of those modalities and presenting them through a mindfulness lens, this book and online learning program offers a simple, replicable model that you can apply anytime, anywhere, even to complex life situations.

This points to the line by 15th century Indian poet Kabir: "Wherever you are, is the entry point." You can begin practising mindfulness anytime, anywhere, and you will instantly gain benefits. And you can bring mindfulness into any situation—it only takes a few seconds to presence yourself, and a couple of minutes to ground yourself completely—and instantly transform your experience of that situation and your performance within it.

In addition, the more you practice "off the field" by doing the meditation practices, the easier it will be to remain mindful "on the field" in those real-life situations. As with anything in life, the long-term benefits of consistent practice are exponential.

Finally, if you still need convincing that mindfulness is beneficial, there is a growing body of scientific research, with regards to meditation practices in particular, and I will point you to it throughout this book.

Acknowledgements go to Colinda for recognising the value of experience gained through years of having done the hard yards and for potentiating that through her unfailing support throughout the process. Also to my son, Luke, who, at four years old, said to me, "I know what the future is, it's just thoughts," and who has always set the gold standard for being present and powerful. Whenever I've needed inspiration, I've just reminded myself that I'm this guy's dad.

1 | The Benefits of Being Mindful

AT THE end of a year in my mid-forties when my life had turned upside-down, I found myself living in a friend's house, back in the town where I was born, with nothing but a car, some clothes and a laptop to my name. Oh, and an unbearably painful recent past and a very bleak-looking future.

Believing that things couldn't get worse, and yet not sure how they could ever get better, I sat down on my meditation cushion and did what I had been practising for years: I presenced and grounded myself, and let go of my ideas of how things should be, either now, or in the future.

It was one of the most powerful moments of my life. Powerful, not only because of what opened up for me (I noticed that I was in a beautiful, red-brick Victorian house, high on a ridge on the edge of a forest, with a view all the way to the ocean, with no day-to-day obligations and a host of possibilities as a result), but also because it was the point at which, I believe, many people would have given up.

It sounds so simple, doesn't it? Presence yourself. Ground yourself. Give up your ideas of how life should be, either now, or in the future. I'm sure you could do it right now, and there, you're mindful. Aha, but let one bit of information pierce your awareness that threatens your financial or social status, the future of your kids, or your country, and you'll be up and at 'em, unable to relax until you've dealt with that threat.

There's nothing wrong with that if the threat is real. However, in today's world, most of the threats are conceptual. We live in fear of—and in reaction to—political statements, market trends, corporate and personal brand reputation threats. It's only when you've actually lost everything, and survived, that you get to see how crazy and out of touch we've become—how neurotic, how reactive.

Equanimity, the ability to be with things as they are, and to move with life as it unfolds, has been held up as one of the most desirable traits by all the spiritual and philosophical traditions. Interestingly, as I'll discuss in this book, it's almost completely devoid from the modern corporate leadership lexicon. And where does most of our stress and anxiety come from? Go figure.

It's no wonder, then, that the most common understanding of the benefits of mindfulness is to do with "boosting how well people deal with stress" (Goleman & Davidson, p.85). This derives primarily from the popularity of the work of MIT graduate Jon Kabat-Zinn, who experienced a form of meditation called *Vipassana* back in 1974.

Kabat-Zinn saw how elements of this method—a whole body scan where one learns to not react to bodily sensations, whether pleasant or unpleasant—could be applied to people in pain clinics. He launched a successful program to this effect, and quite soon after that developed the program that is known as mindfulness-based stress reduction (MBSR), which is now taught globally and has garnered a hefty amount of scientific evidence to support its stated outcomes.

Another outcome of mindfulness that has received a lot of scientific validation is that of attention. More than 1,200 studies have been done to date and the evidence strongly supports the notion that mindfulness meditation improves attention. This is valuable in a world where technology and social media have fragmented our attention.

These benefits are important and necessary, and they make a massive difference to modern life. And they are the tip of the iceberg in terms of what mindfulness can deliver.

Science is now also supporting the notion that meditation doesn't just have a "state effect", but also a "trait effect": yes, by meditating you can shift your state temporarily—to be more relaxed in the moment, for example—but long-term measures are showing that with consistent long-term practice, you actually move in a positive direction along the spectrum of personality traits, towards traits that are seen as desirable for—and representative of—psychological wellbeing. These include traits such as equanimity and compassion.

So what? you might say. *I get along fine without those.* Well, do you? What is the impact on your life, that you may not be aware of, of operating at the lower end versus the higher end of the personality traits? How do you know you're not like that frog in the water, just comfortable enough as it slowly heats up, until one day it reaches boiling point?

There are so many things we take for granted about life. Possessiveness in relationships. Politics at work. Anxiety about the future. Our mission statement points to the belief—based on experience—that it doesn't have to be this way.

You can learn to manage yourself to have a *different* experience of life, one that is a whole lot better.

Here are four key benefits that being mindful and practicing mindfulness can have on your experience of daily life and on the outcomes that you get from your efforts in the world each day.

Benefit #1 | Getting Less Hung Up About Stuff That Doesn't Matter

Think about a situation where you spent a great deal of effort trying to control what would happen, and things still didn't turn out the way you wanted them to. Perhaps you organised a family holiday, or wedding, or planned certain career moves, or a business deal. There's nothing wrong with trying to direct the outcome of things like that, and at the same time, you probably created a lot of stress for yourself just worrying, scheming, arguing, as you tried to force things to go your way. Then, when they didn't, you may have spent a lot of time and energy in anger or regret. A lot of our time, energy and attention gets wasted in this way.

Now think about this: if it were up to you to beat your heart, breathe your lungs, work your spleen, stomach and liver, and so on, you'd be dead within minutes. You simply don't have the capacity for all of that. Even keeping your attention on any one of those functions for any length of time would be impossible. Thankfully you don't have to. Your autonomic nervous system takes care of those things for you, which frees up your attention to be able to do more meaningful tasks.

Despite this obvious limitation in terms of being able to manage our own bodily functions, if you're like most people, you probably live under the illusion that you can control events outside of yourself, and which involve other people. You can't. At least, not nearly as much as you think you can.

It's also a fallacy to think you can always predict which way events should go in order to benefit you. Have you ever got upset because you were delayed, for example, and then you figured out later that the delay quite possibly saved you from being in an accident? Often, things that seem "bad" for you, turn out to be not so bad.

Taken together, this means you probably spend a lot of your time, energy and attention trying to control outcomes when in fact, like your bodily functions, they are busy taking care of themselves. If that's the case, you'd be better off deciding where to put your attention.

By teaching you to observe your own mind and your own life in a more objective way, mindfulness enables you to see more clearly what you can and can't influence, and what does and does not matter. It enables you to see how little of what you worry and panic about actually does matter, and therefore lets you free up energy and attention for actions that will make a difference in terms of your most meaningful goals.

As you become more mindful, you become more aware of this fact. You start to move with life instead of trying to force it or resist it. You become more focused, make better decisions, get into flow more easily, and have a better experience of life. That makes it sound easy, it's not—it requires conscious effort, which may be experienced by some as hard work.

THE SCIENCE

Trait Effects Versus State Effects

THERE HAVE been many claims about the efficacy of mindfulness and meditation. Naturally, these need to be treated with due scepticism. A definitive book on this subject was released in 2017: *The Science of Meditation* by Daniel Goleman (he of *Emotional Intelligence* fame) and Richard J. Davidson.

These two highly respected research scientists collated all the research that has been done on meditation—6,838 articles—and categorised it according to its level of academic rigour and summarised the results.

One of the key features that the authors looked for was evidence for how mental training could lead to "highly positive altered traits" (eg. ongoing compassion, or equanimity), not just "altered states" (eg. feeling chilled out for a short while).

Clearly, when one has meditated, one emerges feeling relaxed and probably able to be less reactive, at least for a short period of time. This is likely to end abruptly when you're back in the traffic, for example. The goal, they insisted, is to establish these healthy states as predominant, lasting traits that you can sustain in your general, everyday life.

They found compelling evidence for this. Below are some statements quoted directly from the book:

- The amygdala, a key node in the brain's stress circuitry, shows dampened activity from a mere 30 or so hours of MBSR practice.

- Other mindfulness training shows a similar benefit, and there are hints in the research that these changes are trait-like: they appear not simply during the explicit instruction to perceive the stressful stimuli mindfully but even in the 'baseline' state, with reductions in amygdala activation as great as 50 percent.

- More daily practice seems associated with lessened distress activity.

- Experienced Zen practitioners can withstand higher levels of pain.

- A three-month meditation retreat brought indicators of better emotional regulation.

- Long-term practice was associated with greater functional connectivity between the prefrontal areas that manage emotion and the areas of the amygdala that react to stress, resulting in less reactivity.

- An improved ability to regulate attention accompanies some of the beneficial impact of meditation on stress reactivity.

- The quickness with which long-term meditators recover from stress underlines how trait effects emerge with continued practice.

— The Science of Meditation (2017) by Daniel Goleman & Richard J. Davidson

Benefit #2 | Acting Where You Have Power: In the Present

We'll be unpacking this in more detail later, but for now, notice that everything you're trying to effect is either in the future, or in the past. For example, you have goals, or broad intentions, things you want to have happen. Those are in the future. Then you have the things, for example, that you wish hadn't happened. Those are in the past. You, like all people, probably spend a fair bit of time, energy and attention trying to make things happen or wishing that things had not happened.

You can't act in the future. It hasn't happened yet. You also can't change the past, it's gone. There is only the moment you are in right now. Of course, you say, that's obvious, I know that, I've read this before. I'm sure you have. Yet practising it is something completely different.

Do you accept everything about your world as it is right now, or are there things that you're resisting, that you wish were different?

It's most likely there are things you're trying to force, or that you're resisting. If you check in with yourself again in ten minutes time you'll most likely still be forcing, or resisting, those same things, in addition to some other things. And again, if you check in with yourself ten days from now, you'll still be at it.

Presence is like the atom: the smallest element of ordinary matter that contains an enormous amount of power.

What this shows is that you're always treating life in the same way, with the same level of, say, impatience and dissatisfaction. And since life is only available to you in the present moment, your entire relationship with life is, by definition, exactly that: impatience and dissatisfaction. (This notion has been beautifully taught by Eckhart Tolle, author of *The Power Of Now* and *A New Earth*.) This naturally affects the kinds of decisions you make. No wonder you keep getting the same results. Your personal version may be slightly different, but the pattern is likely to be the same.

Until you can completely be *with* and *in* the present moment, no matter what's going on, how good or bad it seems, your experience of life will not change, because the decisions you make will not change. Conversely, when you truly accept the present moment, new possibilities will open up. It will transform the decisions you make and the way you behave. You will recognise what awesome power is available to you from living in that way. Your entire experience of life will change.

A good analogy for this is nuclear energy. Within the tiniest particle of ordinary matter, scientists discovered the strongest force in nature—the force which holds the atom together and which gets released in a nuclear explosion. Similarly, within the present moment, which is the tiniest particle of ordinary experience, all the beauty and power of life opens up.

You make the best decisions when you are present because you are dealing with what's real. You can only experience ecstatic states of flow and awe when you are utterly present. That's when things start to go your way. You probably had moments like that in childhood. They most likely became less common as you got older. However, they are accessible, and mindfulness provides the key. This doesn't mean you have to become all "shoo-wow" and hippy-like, but more on that point later.

REAL-LIFE EXAMPLE

Where You Look, You Will Go

MOTORCYCLES ARE exciting to ride—and dangerous. I learned to ride as a teenager and kept bikes through most of my adult life. At one point I signed up for a superbike track school.

The first thing I learned at this track school was the phrase, "Where you look, you will go." In other words, if somebody overtakes you, for example, it's easy to get distracted and look at him and what he's doing. But if he's going too fast, and he runs wide, or slides off, at the next corner, guess what? If you're looking at him, if your attention is on what he's doing, you'll follow him.

I proved this statement true more than once.

I learned that I had to keep my wits about me—I had to stay present—and be aware of where I was putting my attention. I had to look into the gaps, to where I wanted to go, no matter what was going on around me.

I also learned that if I started to think about what could go wrong—those future thoughts—or about what went wrong the last time—past thoughts—I would tense up and make a mistake, probably the very one I was hoping to avoid.

I learned to be very awake and present. I saw that the more present I was, the more relaxed I was—there were no thoughts of what could go wrong, I was just one with the bike. The more relaxed I was—up to a point—the better I performed and the more fun I had.

In this example, being present was the difference between having an enjoyable and productive day and a very expensive and painful one.

I never made it into the fastest class—those guys were scary. But I did watch them closely and I saw that, for them too, presence was key. One lapse of presence could mean losing a few hundred metres in terms of position. One slip of presence could mean the difference between life and death.

Benefit #3 | Maintaining the Balance of Your Mind

It's interesting how one day you can be cruising along quite fine, happy and confident in yourself, and then the next day you meet someone who represents a romantic or work possibility, and suddenly your whole sense of self is dependent on whether they reply to your next text message or email.

Or you hear that someone has said something about you, and suddenly your mind is busy, trying to figure out a way to counter that statement, either with them or with everyone who might have heard it. You find yourself having to defend your reputation at all costs.

Or you're in traffic and someone cuts in front of you. Or you don't get the promotion. Or you read something in the news that causes you to panic. Or you're not able to read the news because it does that to you. Or your sports team loses. Or your political party gets criticised and you go automatically into defence mode, without considering the facts.

Does this sound like a good part of your day? Of course, that doesn't mean you, it means everyone around you! Ha ha. Some of this is true for all of us. We very quickly and easily lose the balance of our minds.

Day in and day out, we humans are constantly chasing things and running away from things. Attack and defend. Show off and cry inside when things don't go our way. Or deny and pretend everything is fine.

Instead of always *losing* the balance of your mind, how about being able to *maintain* the balance of your mind? This would mean, for example, being unaffected by whether the love prospect replies to your text or not. (It doesn't mean feeling no emotion, it means being able to ride the wave of the emotion instead of being tumbled by it.) It would mean being able to hear yourself being talked about in a negative way and not lose sleep over it but manage what you need to in an effective way. It would mean being able to watch your sports team lose and not make it mean something that it doesn't. It would mean being able to see through party political arguments and address issues in a direct and honest way.

As you've read, we believe that people can learn to manage themselves to have a different, better experience of life, and this is precisely what we mean: being able to ride the waves and tides of life and not get tumbled by them. To have more clarity, and be more effective, with less drama.

Mindfulness provides the key to having a balanced mind.

Some people fear that if they are not reacting, they will have no emotions and life will lose all its dramatic flavour. Some are hooked on drama and negative emotions. Typically, those people might say that mindfulness is not for them. Ironically, they need it as much as the next person.

At some point, every person grows tired of the drama and seeks sanity and a healthy range of positive emotions. If that's the case, then it's time for mindfulness.

PRACTICAL EXERCISE – DO THIS NOW

Reflecting on Your Own Reactions

SCAN YOUR life for some of the more unpleasant dramas or conflicts you've had, based on the following scenarios:

- A time when somebody misinterpreted something you said and wouldn't give you a chance to explain or wouldn't accept your attempts to explain.

- A time when you got upset about something that was said to or about you and you spent a lot of time and energy trying to fix it, either in your own head or "out there" in the world.

- A time when it turned out you had been overly optimistic—or pessimistic—about something; it didn't go the way you'd predicted, but it turned out OK in the end.

- A time when some bad news—not a personal tragedy, but political or economic news, or something to do with the weather, or to do with your favourite sports team or celebrity—had a devastating effect on you.

Can you see in all the above instances how much time and energy you wasted? What if you could still have the feeling (i.e. remain human and having a human experience) *and* be able to let it go and move on more quickly and with greater ease?

Benefit #4 | *It Provides the "Salt in the Mix"*

One thing you've probably noticed is how people look for—and readily believe in—absolutes that can provide a quick and easy answer to everything. Whether it's a religion, a political ideology, or a health regimen, it's as if everybody, at some level, hopes to find that silver bullet, that process or system that will answer all their questions and make their lives perfect.

When they find it, they are liable to want to use it to replace everything they know about the world. In this way, the meat eater turns into the vicious vegan, and the smoker into a triathlete who can't stop posting their victories on Facebook. Then they want to write a book about their conversion, and tell the world how wrong they are, and how you could—or should—be doing the same as them.

Carl Jung introduced the principle of enantiodromia, which is when things turn into their opposite—when the sinner turns into the saint. Very often, they haven't dealt with the underlying issue, they've just flipped it into another form, or given it another face. The meat eater is still a bully at a personal level, trying to force everyone to agree with them and do what they do. They're just doing the same thing with different, perhaps more "enlightened", content. The smoker is still addicted, but now it's to endorphins instead of to nicotine.

You've already been introduced to the idea of maintaining the balance of your mind. You can see that in the above examples, the person has not managed to do that. Instead they have completely lost the balance of their respective minds.

Although there are genuine exceptions, authentic transformation is generally more subtle than what has been described above. It happens slowly, unannounced. The changes are lived quietly. The person changes gradually from the inside. You notice things about them over time.

To the extent that people want to find a system against which they can judge everything as black or white, right or wrong, good or bad, you can say that they don't want to think for themselves. They want to remain like children and be told what to think, what to believe, what to do. They are liable to lose the balance of their minds whenever they are challenged.

The alternative would be to step up and become a fully-fledged adult. To add what you learn to what you already know, to figure things out for yourself and to use discernment at every step. Discernment means maintaining the balance of the mind and choosing how to apply what you've learned.

Our stance on this is clear: mindfulness is not a system. It is not a silver bullet. It does not replace counselling, coaching, religion, or whatever other belief, process or practice you are engaged in. Rather, it is like the salt that brings up the flavour of every other spice in the dish. In the same way, mindfulness will enhance and enrich your life. It will not remove or replace the challenges you are forced to face in your life.

CHAPTER SUMMARY

THIS CHAPTER presents the key benefits of mindfulness.

- The most common benefits associated with mindfulness are the improved ability to deal with stress and improved attention.
- Science is starting to show that long-term, consistent practice of a mindfulness meditation physically changes brain patterns and structure in favour of an improved ability to manage fight-or-flight reactivity—and hence anger and anxiety.
- Long-term meditators also showed a greater presence of stable personality traits that are more desirable for—and representative of—psychological wellbeing. These include traits such as equanimity and compassion.
- Four key practical lifestyle benefits are presented:
  o Getting less hung up about stuff that doesn't matter. This means coming to terms with what you can't control and therefore dealing with life more intelligently, based on what you can control.
  o Acting where you have the power, which is in the present. You can't reach into the future, nor change the past, but only act in the present.
  o Being able to maintain the balance of your mind. Having a balanced mind means being able to ride the waves of life and emotion without being tumbled by them.
  o Mindfulness enhances your experience of life the way salt brings up the flavours in a dish—you can add it to whatever religion or modality you practice.

2 | Thoughts and Attention

HAVE YOU ever wondered about the surge in popularity (in the West) of Eastern mysticism and religions like Buddhism over the past half-century or so? This trend was highlighted when The Beatles went to study Transcendental Meditation (TM) with Maharishi Mahesh Yogi at his ashram in India in 1968. They were no doubt influenced by the hippie movement of the day, and no doubt many more hippies followed.

But it wasn't just the rock stars and hippies who went. Some serious MIT and Harvard psychology students went as well. We've already mentioned Jon Kabat-Zinn. Another was Daniel Goleman, Ph.D., who later coined the term Emotional Intelligence (EQ) and authored the book of the same name. He visited Burma in 1970 and learned Vipassana meditation with SN Goenka, the current global figurehead for this method. Even before all of this, in 1961, the quantum physicist David Bohm found his way to Indian-born mystic Jiddu Krishnamurti.

None of those mentioned were trifling fools. They were all highly intelligent, talented and, in the case of the latter few, scientifically-oriented men. Each was on a mission and all of them have had a major impact on Western thought and culture. What were they after, and what did they find there?

What follows is a possible explanation.

KEY CONCEPT – TAKE NOTE

You Are Not Your Thoughts

YOU'LL FIND out by reading this book, and when you try to meditate, that you struggle to hold your attention still for even a few seconds, let alone decide what thoughts to have and to focus on. You'll also learn that you can observe this phenomenon. Yes, you can watch your own thoughts, even while you're thinking them; you can notice your wandering attention, even while it is wandering (and wondering).

Eastern mysticism and Buddhism have addressed this fact as being of primary importance and relevance, whereas Western religion, philosophy and science have tended to push it into the background, as though it's irrelevant.

This has led to some critically different outcomes. One of these is the Western practice of psychotherapy, which is based on the notion that all your problems stem from childhood conditioning or experiences and that you are an "I" that is locked inside the troublesome thoughts that arose as a result of your conditioning.

Eastern mysticism, on the other hand, places primary importance on the notion that you can observe your thinking. It says that, once you become aware of this and learn to practice it, the "I" can find its true position, which is outside of thinking. Therefore, the "I" that is so troubled can manage itself by managing its thoughts. It just needs to know where and how to look, and what to do, then it can learn to watch and manage that thinking as it's occurring right here and now.

In other words, you can access your thinking directly and change it directly. You don't need years of therapy to do that. Therapy can be useful to uncover some of your thought patterns, and for releasing some of the stored energy related to their origins (which can be traumatic and are usually related to your family of origin). However, it's not always productive in terms of giving you a path forward or knowing what to do with the information. You can get lost inside the content and go over the same old material for years without getting anywhere. Coaching, CBT and mindfulness—as it's being presented here, in particular—are much more useful in terms of moving you forward.

So, the interest in Eastern mysticism—and therefore mindfulness—has arisen because it has addressed the nature of thought and the mind in a more insightful way than has Western philosophy, religion and science. As a result, it has provided an important missing piece of the puzzle in terms of understanding the mind, and its implications for your sense of self, and for human behaviour in general.

THE SOURCE

Vipassana Meditation

VIPASSANA MEDITATION has proved to be an important and common thread in the development of mindfulness. It was an important early source of both Jon Kabat-Zinn's and Daniel Goleman's work. I myself learned and practised it too, and that led me to the creation of my own mindfulness program before I knew about this common thread. Therefore, let's take a quick look at it.

The modern teachers of Vipassana claim that this is the meditation developed and practised by Gautama the Buddha when he sat under the Bodhi tree to achieve enlightenment. At the very least, it has an ancient history and comes from the Buddhist Theravadan tradition. A lineage of masters in Burma have passed it on over centuries, claiming to have maintained its pure form as practised and taught by the Buddha. The current global leader is SN Goenka, a businessman who claims that it solved his migraines when he was younger and who has set up centres around the world which are attended on a donation-only basis.

The basic course is a ten-day silent retreat where you meditate for twelve hours a day, sitting for two hours at a time. You start by observing your breath and related sensations, and then move to observing sensations throughout your body as you sit for long periods. Your job is to keep bringing your mind back to observing those sensations with no judgement, no reaction. By day four you have to sit through an hour without moving or fidgeting, while scanning your whole body with no judgement, no reaction. Thereafter, sitting without moving or fidgeting throughout the sessions becomes the standard requirement and an essential part of the training.

When you complete the course, it is recommended that you sit twice a day, morning and evening, for an hour each time. The long sits are required to push you into and through the discomfort zone where you would normally fidget, rearrange yourself and ultimately give up out of pain or irritation. This is essential to developing the non-reactivity and equanimity that the meditation is designed to achieve, and which science is now confirming that it does.

As you can tell, Vipassana is not for sissies. It's tough. It's hard work. It's the military boot camp of meditation practices. You can be sure that very few people in the modern era are going to give up ten days to learn the practice or sit for two hours a day to become established in it—even though the true benefits come from longer sits, practised daily.

Most mindfulness meditations involve the observation of the breath and/or a full-body scan to observe the physical sensations throughout the body. The latter are generally variations or light versions of Vipassana.

To hear the global head of the Vipassana movement, SN Goenka, speak, one will learn that its application is not merely as a tool to relieve stress. It is a tool to "purify the mind at the root level". This means to reduce and ultimately remove the reactivity that leads to things like anger, hatred, ill-will, jealousy, even depression and addiction.

As we have said, mindfulness is about so much more than just learning to chill, be present while eating, or get off your phone while walking. It has applications in every sphere of life and in the most severe circumstances.

REAL-LIFE EXAMPLE

Mindfulness Is Not for Sissies

I WILL confidently say that 2013 was the hardest year of my life. My mother died, my relationship fell apart, my ex-wife emigrated with my son and my business failed. I had to sell everything and eventually found myself sleeping on a friend's couch. On the last day of that year, I got hit in the face by a cricket ball and ended up in the emergency ward.

I had no way of knowing if I would ever recover from that year. I certainly couldn't see how. Still, amidst those circumstances, I was able to apply my mindfulness training and be present. I was able to surrender any control over what should happen next. In that space I found the most incredible peace and clarity.

I am convinced today that being relaxed and open to the present moment, not caught up in anxiety and fear, not trying to control outcomes, enabled me to be open to take the lessons I needed to. It enabled me to make good decisions where other people may have fallen apart. It led me onto a much better path where, today, I have a different, better experience of life—which includes greater and more meaningful success.

This is perhaps the most important point to be made, and the reason for writing this book and developing the associated program. Many of the people who've attended the live program have signed up as a result of having experienced extremely high levels of stress, anxiety and even depression. In our feedback surveys to date, every single person has scored full marks in response to the question, "What degree of improvement (if any) have you made in the area [of] general mood and attitude towards life?" In addition, people have given an average rating of 94% for the course having a positive impact on their "general level of motivation and enthusiasm and experience that life is not all struggle." In response to the question, "Did the program make a material difference to your personal effectiveness?" there was an 88% average rating.

Now let's move on to the real practical application, so you can see for yourself what we've been talking about.

PRACTICAL EXERCISE – DO THIS NOW

Reflecting on Thoughts and Attention

TAKE SOME time to answer and/or reflect on the following questions:

Reflect on your journey *en route* to wherever you are right now (or the last car journey you took) and answer these questions:

- Can you remember what cars you saw along the way?
- Can you recall what songs played on the stereo?
- Which traffic lights were red or green?
- What can you *not* remember?
- What were you paying attention to?

Chances are you were thinking about other things for a good portion of the journey, right?

- Reflect on the thoughts you had on that journey while you were not paying attention to your environment.
- Did you decide what to think, or did they arise quite randomly?
- Did they contain many judgements and preferences about things, places, people?
- What else did you notice about them?

Having done the previous exercise, what do you notice <u>*about*</u> the content and nature of your thoughts? Here are some pointers to look for:

- They churn, they come and go.
- For the most part, you don't really decide what to think. Instead, thoughts just happen. They arise of their own volition and are replaced by other thoughts. It's very seldom that you sit down and say, OK, I'm going to think about this now, and then keep your attention on that subject until you're complete.
- As much as individual thoughts arise of their own volition, thinking itself arises out of its own volition. You don't have the "on" and "off" switch for thinking. It's always there, even at night in the form of dreams. Just as your heart goes on beating, your mind goes on thinking. When you wake up, thinking is already turned on. You don't turn it on. It's the same for everybody.

If you have any questions about the above, then spend some time observing your own thoughts. This is not something you need to go and get a scientific study and read up on. It's *practical* mindfulness. You can do it as you sit, right where you are. Get out a clipboard, don your white coat and observe your own mind as a scientist would. It will become obvious that the above statements are true.

PRACTICE - SAVE FOR LATER

Follow the Music

TO IMPROVE your ability to hold your attention steady and not be distracted by your own thinking, play a song and see if you can pay attention to the song all the way through without losing focus.

When you find yourself having become distracted by other thoughts, bring your attention back to the music.

Over time, you will get better at this—meaning, you will be able to hold your attention on the music for longer periods, and you will also notice more quickly when you have been distracted.

As you improve, you may want to choose a single instrument within the song and see if you can hold your attention on the chosen instrument for ever longer periods.

Later on, when we deal with equanimity, you'll see another opportunity for using music to train your mind: put your music library onto random play, and don't resist what comes up. Just listen through each song and let go of your preferences—whether you feel like it or not. Also, don't repeat the songs you like, just keep going.

KEY CONCEPT – TAKE NOTE

The Nature and Content of Thinking

NOW LET'S look a little deeper and notice that thoughts are mostly about future and past, and that they mostly contain judgments, particularly the judgement of liking and not liking.

Think about something that happened in the past that you liked. A beautiful sunset with a lover, an incredible business deal. You will find that you tend to spend a good part of your life trying to recreate that experience, or, at the very least, longing for it.

Then let's say something happened that you didn't like. That lover or business partner betrayed you and the relationship or deal went sour. To what extent do you spend your life trying to avoid that ever happening again?

The correlation may not always be that direct and obvious, but the pattern described above repeats itself again and again, endlessly all day, day after day, until you no longer relate to the world, but to your own movie that plays on an endless reel against the screen of your mind. Once again, it's the same for everybody.

To the degree that this is true, you can say that you don't see things as they are, but as you are, through this lens of fear and desire. You are not present.

When my son was four years old, he walked into my office and saw something written on the whiteboard. He asked what it said, and I read the sentence to him. The sentence

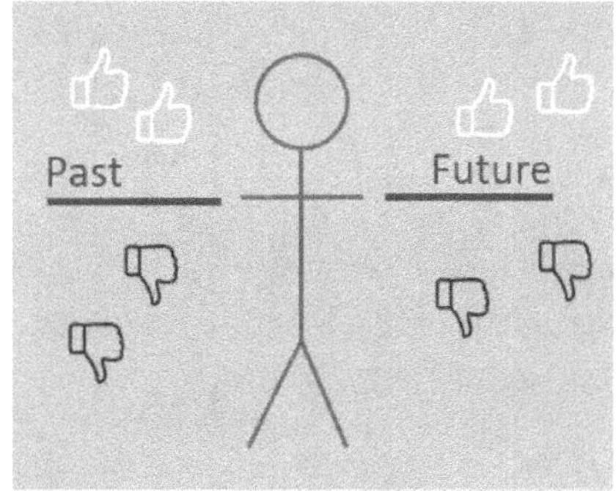

contained the word "future" and he responded with, "I know what the future is." I said, "What?" He said, "It's just thoughts." I was flabbergasted. I said, jokingly, "Don't forget that because you'll pay a lot of money to find it out again when you're older."

You can see that the future is thoughts, and the past is thoughts. Conversely, you can say that future and past only exist in the mind. If you wanted to get more philosophical, you could say that time and mind (and ego) are all one and the same thing. Presence is the absence of time, and mind, and ego. It is pure being. But that's a big subject.

For now, the task is to recognise that this flick-flacking between past and future, and between liking and not liking, is, at the structural level, the habituated nature of the mind. Based on this observation, you can say that the mind is always running away from and towards things. The mind is never still, never with *what is*.

Notice how the earlier image has only two likes and two dislikes in each quadrant. If you think about it, this would probably represent your own mind about two minutes after you've woken up. By the time you get to work, it's probably more like the image to the right. And by the end of the day, who knows how many strong preferences have occurred, how many visitations to the past and the future have been made?

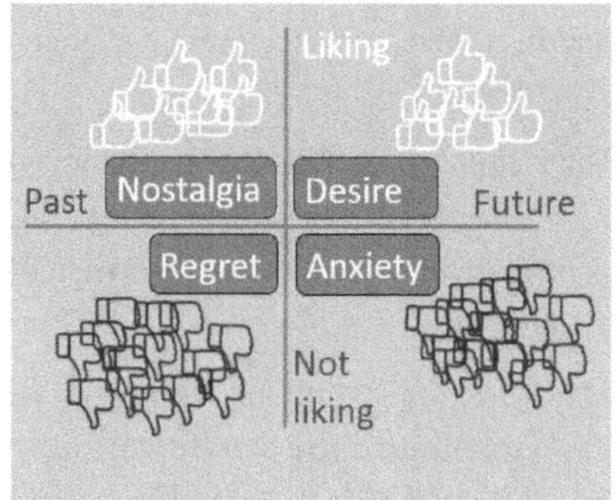

You can see as well that, to the extent that this is true, your thoughts fall largely into one of four categories:

- Nostalgia – Past, liking
- Regret – Past, not liking
- Anxiety – Future, not liking (which implies fear, aversion)
- Desire – Future, liking (which implies wanting, craving)

Gautama, the Buddha, identified this pattern of the mind 2,500 years ago, and he declared that all human suffering is a result of "craving" and "aversion". He arrived at this conclusion through careful observation of his own experience, and you can verify it quite simply and accurately by observing your own mind.

The solution? Well, read on.

WHAT DIFFERENCE DOES IT MAKE?

IF YOU look at it carefully, you will see how insane this is. You chase after something because you think it will make you happy. Why are you not happy right now? Because, you tell yourself, you need that thing to make you happy. When you have that thing? You want the next thing.

Happiness is all around you. It's in the present moment and it's available to you regardless of whether your preferences get met or not. You don't see it because you are an unwitting victim of this habit of the mind.

Importantly, this is not to say that you should not have plans, or goals. The problem is not the goal, it's the relationship to the goal. It's the degree to which you hold on to your preferences and tell yourself that you can't be happy until they are met. It's the degree to which you're all about the destination and not about the journey.

You'll learn about this theme in more detail as we go.

As you progress in mindfulness, you will become better and better at recognising this habit of the mind and resolving it instantly, on the fly, in any situation. You will be able to stay focused on a goal, or on avoiding a problem, and hold it lightly at the same time. You will be able to recognise, and switch easily into, the state of mind that realises that, no matter how it looks, things are unfolding exactly as they should—which is to say, in the only way that they can.

PRACTICAL EXERCISE – DO THIS NOW

Reflecting on Attachment to Preferences

REFLECT ON your current goals. Are there any that you're not acting on? Could it be that you're too worried about the outcome, too afraid of the consequences of failure?

What if you made the outcome less important and turned "at least trying" into the goal?

Now reflect on your current circumstances and your degree of happiness with life. To what extent are you dissatisfied?

Are you waiting for something to happen or be in place before you can be happy? Can you work towards that goal and be happy even while you don't have that thing in your life?

Welcome to the goal of mindfulness, which, as you can see, brings to life the notion that life is also about the journey, not just the destination.

> ## Chapter Summary
>
> THIS CHAPTER looks at the nature of thought and attention.
>
> - There has been a rise in popularity in the West of Eastern mysticism and Buddhism over the past half-century. One possible reason is the way these traditions have taken a more insightful approach to the mind and the nature of thought.
> - You can learn to manage your thinking—and therefore yourself—directly in the moment, and mindfulness provides the key to being able to do this.
> - Vipassana meditation, and mindfulness in general, is not for sissies, and not just for easing stress. It's a tough journey that, taken wholeheartedly, can be applied in every context to manage yourself better and transform your entire experience of life.
> - A review of your own thoughts during your last travel journey can help you to see how much your attention wanders.
> - Thought has its own volition and does not have an "on" or an "off" switch.
> - Thoughts are always in the past or the future, and always engaged with evaluations—liking or not liking what is found there—which is termed judgements or preferences. As a result, the mind is always running away from and towards things. The mind is never still, never with *what is*.
> - Thoughts can be said to fall into four categories: nostalgia, regret, anxiety, desire. Your ongoing attempts to shift from one to the other, while they may look like the answer, are in fact the source of your suffering.
> - This does not mean you should have no goals, but rather that you can hold your preferences less tightly.
> - Being able to have preferences and yet hold them lightly is the necessary paradox that you need to be able to resolve to achieve your goals and to enjoy the journey of life, instead of just obsessing about the destination.

SECTION B | The 3 Key Elements

F YOU do some research into mindfulness you'll come across a great many definitions, phrases, terms and explanations. My own efforts to produce a summary from the book *Mindfulness for Dummies* produced the following list:

- Paying attention on purpose;
- Being in the present moment;
- Infusing your being with qualities:
    - kindness (compassion, warmth, friendliness),
    - curiosity,
    - acceptance;
- Translation from Indian (Sanskrit) word *Sati*, which means:
    - Awareness (being conscious, and being conscious of being conscious; also of inner and outer experiences),
    - Attention (focused awareness; consciously directing your attention),
    - Remembering (becoming aware of the need to be aware once your attention has drifted);
- Japanese character combines the words for "mind" and "heart", implying "awareness from the heart";
- Dr Jon Kabat-Zinn: "Mindfulness can be cultivated in a specific way, that is, in the present moment, and as non-reactively, non-judgementally and openheartedly as possible." This introduces the following aspects:
    - Non-reactive (to react is automatic, which implies no choice, and may not necessarily be the best for you or for others, eg. defensiveness, criticism of self/others versus responding, which means consciously considering and choosing a response that is "better" for all involved),
    - Non-judgemental (not seeing things as good or bad, or through the filter of personal judgements based on past conditioning, but "as they are"),
    - Openhearted (not having to change who you are, but still being able to bring qualities of kindness, compassion, warmth, friendliness to your experience);

- Dr Shauna Shapiro of Santa Clara University:
    - Intention (intention sets the scene for what unfolds in the practice itself—it may begin as stress reduction, then evolve into "greater understanding of thoughts and emotions" and eventually to "being kind and compassionate"),
    - Attention (paying attention),
    - Attitude (in a particular way);
- A process and a set of practices (the journey, not the destination).

As you can see, it can take quite some mental gymnastics to get your head around all of that, let alone apply it in daily life.

In an effort to simplify this into a set of simple, recognisable and memorable steps that could be easily applied, Colinda and I identified the three key elements that you will learn about and which provide the guiding framework for this book and for the live and online program.

These key elements are:

1. Having deliberate **awareness** (paying attention on purpose);
2. Being **nonjudgemental** (not seeing things as good or bad, nor through the filter of personal judgements based on past conditioning, but rather seeing things "as they are");
3. Being **nonreactive** (to react is automatic, which implies no choice, and may not necessarily be the best for you or for others).

This section of the book will define and explain these three key elements in their general sense. In Section C, these elements will continue to provide the framework for the application of mindfulness into various contexts, like emotion regulation, handling stress and building resilience, complexity and decision-making, creating and sustaining the state of flow, and authentic being and relating.

Just in case the question arises for you, we have not specified "being openhearted", "being compassionate", or "lovingkindness" as a key element, as we say that those states arise out of practising the other three—in particular, being nonjudgemental—which are more gettable and practical. There is always the risk, too, of overidentifying with one of those aspects of mindfulness, and developing an ego state around it. For example, you might see someone go around preaching how everyone should just chill and be openhearted, the way they are, and that's not what we're after.

We say that the ability to autogenerate those states develops naturally and authentically after one has practiced and become familiar with being nonjudgemental and nonreactive at a practical level. Those states are also mentioned specifically in the chapter on authentic being and relating.

> **KEY CONCEPT – TAKE NOTE**

Information Versus Practice

IF YOU needed to learn to ride a bicycle and you sat down and read a book about it, you might have the information, but you would not necessarily be able to ride the bicycle. Why?

What is the core competence required for riding a bicycle?

The answer is: balance.

Balance cannot be acquired through reading, learning, or information. It can only be acquired by doing. And once acquired, it is always available.

Similarly, you can say that the core competence for swimming is flotation—being able to float. This, too, can only be acquired by doing.

What is the competence required for practising mindfulness? Come on, see if you can get this for yourself.

The answer is: presence (which for our purposes is synonymous with deliberate awareness).

As with balance, presence cannot be learned about or studied if it is to have practical value. It needs to be gained experientially.

PRACTICAL EXERCISE – DO THIS NOW

Experiencing Presence (Deliberate Awareness)

RIGHT NOW, while you are reading, what are you aware of? Are you present to your environment, to your own thoughts and feelings, even while you are reading? If someone walked in, would you get a fright, or would you have heard or felt them coming from a mile away? And we're not talking about the kind of vigilance that arises out of anxiety or paranoia, but an open, calm awareness where there are no surprises, no frights, no anxiety or sudden panic. Just continuous presence.

Once you have ridden a bicycle, you will naturally discover that balance is easier when you are moving, which comes about by pedalling. And the thing that makes you most comfortable with moving is knowing how to stop!

You could say, therefore, that these are the three key elements of bicycle riding: balance, movement, and knowing how to stop. Everything else fits in and around that. Similarly, when it comes to mindfulness, everything can be said to fit in and around the three key elements.

Below is a short introduction to each key element. The chapters that follow will expand on each of them in more detail.

Key Element #1 | Being Aware

You've already read about presence, for which you can also use the word awareness. You can say that, at a practical level, awareness means paying deliberate attention, not only to your external environment, but also to your own thoughts. However, as you have seen, the mind has a mind of its own, and so this is a challenge. Therefore, awareness is a step in itself.

As you will see later, to be aware of your thoughts, you have to be aware of your own awareness so that you can stay tuned in to the whole process. This is called meta-awareness—being aware of being aware. For example, in the earlier illustration of motorcycle riding, I had to be aware of what I was paying attention to—and aware that I was remaining aware—in order to stay on the track.

Later on, you'll see that being aware also applies to each of the fields of application we have chosen. For example, you need to be aware that you're experiencing an emotion, and what that emotion is. This enables you to do something about it, instead of just acting it out.

Being aware gives you power. It is the critical first step to personal power and personal mastery.

Key Element #2 | Being Nonjudgemental

The great Indian teacher, Jiddu Krishnamurti, who was regarded as the "guru's guru" once stopped the mental traffic of his audience when he announced that he was about to share his secret. What he shared was this simple statement: "I don't mind what happens." This is what it means to be nonjudgemental.

Being non-judgemental means giving up your attachment to your preferences, to having to have things go your way. This makes no sense to the Western mind, which is so goal- and achievement-oriented. This is precisely why we need mindfulness—and this book. So read on and you'll discover how this is possible and why it's so valuable.

Key Element #3 | Being Nonreactive

As soon as you collapse into your preferences—your strong attachments to what must and must not happen—you lose presence, and you lose the balance of your mind. You become reactive—jealous, possessive, defensive, aggressive, anxious—and either act in ways that are unnecessary or do things you're likely to regret.

Analagous to knowing how to stop on a bicycle is being nonreactive. Taking that awareness and nonjudgemental attitude and applying it to the situation so that you don't just react based on your own conditioned fears but respond based on what the situation needs.

Once again, this may seem counterintuitive. If so, then that's why you're here.

You will see that you are able to apply these three elements into any context, whether it be emotion regulation, handling stress, decision-making, activating and maintaining a state of flow, and even relating authentically to others. They can also act as a kind of checklist of stages: Am I aware? Am I being nonjudgemental? Am I being nonreactive?

The chapters that follow will define and explain these three elements and take you through a set of practices so that you can experience and practice them.

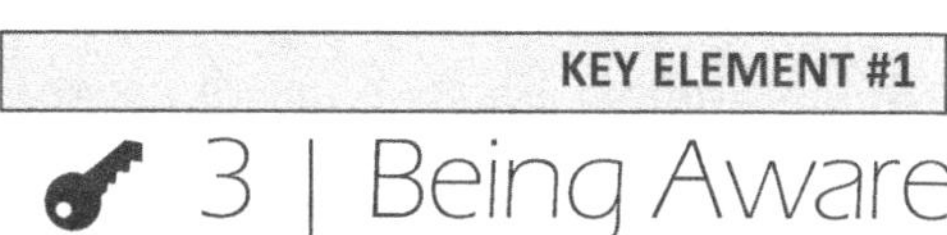

3 | Being Aware

THERE IS a humorous quote that goes like this: "I was watching the frisbee, wondering why it was getting bigger and bigger, and then it hit me." Get it? Things are happening, and your attention is on your thoughts—those may be thoughts about what's happening, or about something else entirely—rather than taking in the reality and the totality of the picture. You only become present when something drastic happens, and reality "hits you in the face".

Another example would be when you're driving. You stop at a traffic light and a person walks up and knocks on your driver's window. If you were aware, you would have noticed that person long before. If not, because you're lost in your thinking, you jump, and perhaps shriek, with fright. Likewise, in a business meeting, you get caught out by something someone says because you're not paying attention. Perhaps you're too busy queueing up your own arguments instead of listening and paying attention.

To take in the reality, the totality, as it is, you must be paying attention to the situation in its totality. That means not getting lost in one tiny aspect of the reality, and not getting lost in your thinking. Remember the earlier exercise when you had to review where your attention had been in the last hour or when you travelled to where you are now?

To the extent that you could not remember, to the extent that you were lost in your thinking, you lacked presence, and therefore awareness. Even the parts you could remember might have been coincidental: you were forced to pay attention because of something out of the ordinary, or potentially dangerous, that happened: a car pulled in front of you; a bird flew in through your window.

The state of awareness can be likened to being vigilant, awake, alert, the way a soldier would be while on guard duty, or an inspector arriving at a fresh crime scene: noticing everything and being able to report on it later. This may sound a little obsessive or paranoid, but it's not meant to be like that. It's about being present in a relaxed, rather than a tense or nervous, manner. We're talking more Agatha Christie's Hercule Poirot than Johnny Lee Miller's portrayal of Sherlock Holmes in the series *Elementary*.

THE SCIENCE

You Can Improve Your Attention

IN THE book *The Science of Meditation* by Goleman & Davidson, the subject of attention is given plenty of, well, attention. In our age of distraction, there were some interesting findings.

An EEG measure of advanced Zen monks showed that their attention had not tuned out of a task (listening to a series of monotonous sounds) after more than 20 beeps, whereas most people tuned out before 10. This suggested a link between long-term meditation and sustained attention, even when the task becomes familiar or boring. This could have practical implications for, eg.. radar operators, soldiers on guard duty, even cricket players who bat or field for long periods.

Another study showed that, after eight weeks of an MBSR (mindfulness) program, subjects showed a far better ability to focus on sensations—in this case a carefully calibrated tapping on the hand or foot—than they had done before starting the training, as well as better than those who were still waiting for the training.

Of even more relevance was a study that showed how short breathing meditations can improve attention that gets diminished by (especially digital) multitasking, and how sustaining these practices can have a lasting effect.

The above studies, among many others, challenge accepted scientific thought that attention is "mostly stimulus-driven, automatic, unconscious, and from the 'bottom up'"—in other words, it challenges the notion that you can't do anything to improve levels of attention.

The authors concluded that "mindfulness (at least in the MBSR form) strengthens the brain's ability to focus on one thing and ignore distractions".

They do caution that "quickie, one-time interventions" are unlikely to make a *lasting* difference. "Our hunch would be that [improving]

> a neural system like attention in a lasting way requires ... continued daily practice [and] intensive booster sessions."

With heightened awareness, you can become like the martial arts guru who senses when trouble is coming and is able to move to anticipate it. Reality seems to slow down for that person. He or she can operate in that zone that most of us only get into when we are caught up in, say, a motor accident and we report that "time seemed to slow down". He or she is not taken by surprise.

Mostly you only get to see this in movies, and yet it's possible in real life. Having this capacity has obvious benefits. If you're in a business meeting for example, you are better able to "read the room". You become the person who "doesn't miss a thing". In sports, you can remain calm and make better decisions under pressure.

Conversely, one indicator of a lack of awareness is that sudden, unexpected events take you by surprise. Like when that person walks up and knocks on your driver's window. Like in that business meeting, when you get caught out by something someone says because you're not paying attention. In sports, this is when the play breaks down. The person was not concentrating. There is even a term for it: "brain fade". You know how easy this is. You've seen how thinking happens autonomously and of its own volition. Our mind tends to drift off. Our attention follows that thinking, rather than staying with the totality of the situation, rather than staying with the present reality.

There are two levels of awareness. The first is awareness of your environment: being aware of everything that is going on outside of and around you. This can be extended to being aware of your own internal state, including your emotions, and your physical state. The second level of awareness, known as meta-awareness, is being aware, in particular, of your thoughts and your focus of attention: *What am I thinking right now? Are these useful thoughts? What should my attention be on?*

As you progress through this program, you will see the theme of awareness being extended into other contexts: being aware of your cognitions, emotions, and physical state; being aware of your decision-making modality; being aware of your motivational state relative to the state of flow; and so on.

In the background, and always on, should be that meta-awareness, the awareness of your level of awareness. To be consistently aware, you must be in the habit of noticing when you have become carried away by your thinking and bring your attention back again and again to the present reality. Developing this ability is one of the main objectives of mindfulness. Training to habituate this ability is one of the primary purposes of mindfulness meditation.

PRACTICAL EXERCISE – DO THIS NOW

Placing Yourself in Space and Time

HERE IS an exercise that will introduce you to the first key element mentioned above, which is awareness.

It's important that you actually *do* this exercise, in order to have experienced it for yourself before you read the discourse that follows. Remember, you can't gain balance on a bicycle by reading about it. You have to actually *ride* the bicycle.

This exercise will only take a few minutes. In addition, it will put you into a more mindful state.

Instructions

With your eyes open, remember the journey you took to get to where you are now—the physical journey, today, or the things you have done leading up to sitting down to read as you are doing right now.

Now become aware of the boundaries of the room you are in—the walls, windows, door, ceiling, floor.

Now become aware of the air inside the room—the light, temperature, movement.

Now become aware of any sounds outside or inside the room. Don't wish them away, or do anything about them, just notice them.

Now become aware of the clothes on your body and the feel of those clothes on your skin.

Now become aware of the weight of your body on the chair—or cushion or bed—that you are sitting on.

Now become aware of the sensations inside your body. Be careful not to imagine stuff, just notice if there are any sensations: an itch, perhaps, or a toothache, a feeling of hunger in your stomach, your clothing that is tight. Don't react to it or try to fix it, just notice it.

Now become aware of your breath. Don't try to change your breathing, just notice it: is it fast or slow, is it easy or difficult, is your one nostril blocked, is there a sound? Feel the movement of the air in your nostrils or perhaps just at the outer rim; notice the temperature of the air as it comes in and goes out.

Now close your eyes and try to keep your attention on your breath for as long as possible. Keep trying for, say, two minutes. Set a timer if you need to.

Are you done?

Once again, it's important that you actually *did* that exercise.

If not, please go back and do it.

Once you have done it, then consider the question, *What did you notice?*

Most people report that they struggled to keep their attention on the subject at hand, i.e. their breath. They were distracted by their own thoughts, which kept coming in. Or they say they were not able to stop their thinking.

Those who do not report either of the above were either asleep or wholly unaware of their thinking. If you are reading this and believe that you could stop your thinking, then the thought, "I'm not thinking," or, "I have stopped thinking," is still a thought, it's thinking—and, you'll notice, that erroneous thought happens by itself, you do not decide to think it!

KEY CONCEPT – TAKE NOTE

Can You Stop Your Thinking?

MANY PEOPLE have tried meditation and given up because they have not been able to stop their thinking. Others try very hard to do that and get more stressed out from the effort than they were before they tried to meditate.

Let's take a closer look at the phenomenon of thinking.

When you wake up in the morning, you don't have a switch that you turn on, or a timer that you can use to activate your thinking. You don't, for example, say, "At eight-fifteen, when I arrive at work, I'll start thinking. Until then, I'll just maintain pure mental silence." No, that doesn't happen. From the moment you wake up, you are thinking. You might be very bleary-eyed and groggy, but you're thinking. What day is it? What's the time? What's on the news? Do I have any emails? Where's my phone? Where's my wife? Yes, it's usually in that order.

You can say that you wake up into thinking. In fact, if you take a step back you can see that you were dreaming, so in fact it was going on all night. And then, all day, it goes on and on. It never stops. This is an interesting phenomenon and an important one. It's the one fact that psychology and most religions don't look at long enough or hard enough. Because if you can't stop your thinking, and you don't start it, then thinking is just there. It's autonomous. In fact, if you think about the earlier breathing exercise, you can't even hold your attention on something for more than a few seconds. Nothing wrong, it's the same for everyone, that's why you're learning mindfulness.

And yet, this process that you have almost no control over, you use to run your life. Well, you believe you are using it, but if you use the term correctly, thinking uses you. You are a vehicle for thinking to happen. Thinking is generalised, like a cell phone signal, and you are the cell phone. Yet within that you use the word, "I". You say, "I think that…". Yet you did not originate that thought process. The more accurate phrase would be, "I *find* myself thinking that…"

This may seem like trivial semantics, but it's at the core of everything you do in life. It's a big subject too, and one that is studied in the field of ontology, the study of the nature of being.

> *The bad news is, you can't stop your thinking. You don't have that power. The good news is, you don't have to.*

The important point, for our purposes, is that *you can't stop your thinking*.

So, if you're trying to stop your thinking, give it up, you can't. Human beings don't have that power. That's the bad news. The good news is, you don't have to.

You can become *aware* of your thinking, and of your reaction to your thinking, and you can direct your thinking by inserting new thoughts into the stream of thinking. These are all outcomes of mindfulness.

However, you can't *stop* your thinking any more than you can stop your heart from beating. It happens by itself.

You can view the process of awareness as being like an aircraft on autopilot. It recognises when it has drifted off and brings itself back on course. The quicker it does this, the smoother the flight.

The more you practice (note, not the *harder* you practice, but the *more* you practice—the more minutes and hours you put in), the easier and more natural it becomes.

The practice of awareness through meditation very quickly has an impact in your normal waking and working life, where your attention can stay focused for longer, despite the many mental distractions created by technology and open workspaces.

PRACTICAL EXERCISE – DO THIS NOW

The Clouds Are Not the Sky

IF IT'S daytime, go outside and look at the sky. Hopefully there are clouds in that sky. If that's not possible right now, then here is the YouTube link to a short 30-second video that shows clouds drifting across the sky: https://youtu.be/0_jNjpVxUt0. Take a quick look at that video so that you have an active image in your mind for the questions that follow.

Q: What do you perceive when you see sky?

A: A vast, clear, empty space.

Q: What do you perceive when you see the clouds?

A: Objects, or things, in space (and whether you like them or not, they are there!)

Q: What else do you notice about those things (clouds) in the sky?

A: They are:

- Transient (they change while they are there);

- Impermanent (they eventually disappear altogether);

- They arise from and dissolve back into the clear empty space which is the sky.

KEY CONCEPT – TAKE NOTE

The Clouds Are Not the Sky

YOU HAVE seen that you can't stop your thinking. Similarly, you can't stop the clouds in the sky. There are many other similarities between the clouds in the sky and your thoughts.

You can say the same about the mind and the thoughts that occur within the mind. The mind is potentially a vast, clear empty space in which awareness can occur. Thoughts, like those clouds, are things within the mind. In other words, just as sky and clouds are not one and the same thing, but rather clouds are things that occur *within* the empty space which is the sky, so thoughts are not the mind, but rather things which occur *within* the space provided by the mind.

In addition to the above, and once again, just like clouds, thoughts are transient, they change even while they are there. If you're not sure about this, try it. See if you can hold a single thought about a subject and hold that thought steady in your mind without that thought changing. It's impossible. The thought has a life of its own.

Eventually, every thought disappears, and another one takes its place. Therefore, you can say that thoughts are impermanent.

You can also see that thoughts arise from and dissolve back into the mind.

So, you can say that the mind is a space in which thinking occurs. That mind can sometimes be quiet, with few thoughts, like a clear, blue sky. Other times it can be crowded with many thoughts, like a cloudy or stormy sky.

The good news implied by all of this is that you don't have to be controlled by your mind and its thoughts (and feelings). Instead, you can learn to control and direct your mind and decide which of its thoughts (and feelings) to pay attention to.

You can see each thought happen and, instead of becoming that thought, you can watch it go by just as you would watch a cloud go by in the sky. You can watch the weather, without becoming the weather. You can watch your thoughts without getting lost in the *content* of your thoughts.

WHAT DIFFERENCE DOES IT MAKE?

A REAL-LIFE application of watching the weather (or thoughts) without becoming the weather (or thoughts), would be when you are angry, anxious or depressed. If you can see that a thought is occurring in your mind—a thought that is not you—then you can decouple your sense of self from that thought.

You can choose to put your attention on, say, your work instead. You would most likely feel better once you've completed a task, and over time you'll learn to trust that the angry, anxious or depressed thoughts will eventually dissolve or disappear without you having to engage them.

Note that this does not mean that you should not seek help at a broader level, nor that you should just ignore what those thoughts are saying. It means that once you have understood the thought, or feeling, and put it in context, then you can manage its energy in this way.

You'll discover more about how mindfulness can be applied to emotion regulation in Chapter 6.

If you buy into any thoughts and feelings, which are temporary, you are liable to become affected by those thoughts. You "become the weather". If you have learned to observe your thoughts, you will see that they are just thoughts occurring in your mind and that you are independent of them. You will be able to "watch the weather, without becoming the weather".

Hence, you can say that the purpose of mindfulness is to be able to *watch* the weather without *becoming* the weather.

REAL-LIFE EXAMPLE

The Endless Search for Meaning

I WENT through a time in my life when I became obsessed with finding meaning. I wanted a conclusive, definitive statement, something I could put on a plaque on the wall and say, "That's it!" Perhaps I thought it would solve all the world's problems—and make me rich and famous at the same time if I could write it up into a book!

I spent a lot of time ruminating and thinking and found it hard to focus on work. My attention kept getting pulled to this problem. Yet, the more I thought about it, the more meaningless everything seemed, and the things I wanted to do in the world seemed ever more enormous, ever further away.

Naturally, I became quite unproductive and this set up a cycle of negative reinforcement. My response was to search deeper still. It was as if I believed I could think my way out of the problem and, by thinking about it, land up at a perfect solution.

I reached a point of crisis before I learned that I was not my thoughts, but my actions. I saw that I could choose to put my attention on work and productive outputs, even though they seemed mundane and even though holding my attention there—

and not drifting off into the search for meaning—was probably the most difficult challenge I had ever encountered.

I generally felt better once I'd completed a task, and over time I learned to trust that, if I remained productive, the thoughts that called me like a siren's voice towards the search for meaning would eventually dissolve and disappear without me having to engage them.

I learned that I could watch the weather without becoming the weather. (A bit of journaling each morning, to get those thoughts out of the way, also helped.)

In the introduction to this section, you saw that you can't just "know" about presence and think you are being mindful, just as you can't just "know" about balance and think you can ride a bicycle. You have to gain it experientially. If you wish to gain value out of this book and program, then you need to gain presence—which starts with awareness—experientially.

The meditation that follows is your entry point into mindfulness. Do it to gain the competence of awareness—and presence—at an experiential level.

PRACTICAL EXERCISE – DO THIS NOW

Breathing Meditation

HERE IS a shortened set of instructions for the Breathing Meditation, also known as the Clouds-Are-Not-The-Sky meditation. For the full guided version, purchase the download on our website at www.practicalmindfulness.co.za.

NOTE

The times given below are a guide. You may spend longer if you wish. Resist the urge to rush through any faster.

Keep your eyes open until you see the instruction to close them.

Instructions

Find a position where you back is straight, but not tense.

Place yourself in space and time. <15 secs>

Now become aware of the boundaries of the room you are in—the walls, windows, door, ceiling, floor. <30 secs>

Now become aware of the air inside the room—the light, temperature, movement. *<30 secs>*

Now become aware of any sounds outside or inside the room. Don't wish them away, or do anything about them, just notice them. *<30 secs>*

Now become aware of the clothes on your body and the feel of those clothes on your skin. *<30 secs>*

Now become aware of the weight of your body on the chair—or cushion or bed—that you are sitting on. *<30 secs>*

Now become aware of any sensation inside your body. Don't react or try to fix it, just notice it. *<1 min>*

Now become aware of your breath. Don't try to change your breathing, just notice it. *<1 min>*

Now close your eyes and try to keep your attention on your breath for as long as possible.

When you have noticed your attention wandering, notice the fact of your mental activity and how that distracted you from the awareness of the breath, and return your attention to your breath.

Each time you do that, notice how your thoughts are like those clouds in the sky...

Keep repeating this process for as long as you can, for up to 15 minutes. *<5-15 mins>*

Once you have completed the Breathing Meditation practical exercise, consider these questions:

- How long was it before your attention wandered for the first time? Less than two minutes? Less than one minute? After only a few seconds? (A few seconds is normal when you're starting out.)
- Did a few minutes of practice seem like a very long time? (That's also normal when you're starting out.)
- Did the time seem to speed up as you relaxed? (You should find that as you sit for longer, as long as you don't try too hard, you will relax. When that happens, you will find that a minute feels like a lot less time than it did at the beginning of each sitting.)
- Did you manage to hold your attention on your breath for longer as you went on? (Once again, you should find that as you relax, your ability to hold your

attention on your breath may increase, though it won't necessarily be significant. The real benefits come after you have done the meditation many, many times. Even then, you'll have good days and bad days.)

PRACTICE - SAVE FOR LATER

Breathing Meditation — Guided Audio

RESEARCH HAS shown that 10 minutes of breath awareness can significantly improve your attention and focus immediately following that practice. If you do this regularly for 20-minutes—even three or four times a week, if you can't manage every day—it can help to create a lasting and stable improvement (our scientists' trait effect) in your ability to focus.

If you need assistance, a guided version of the Breathing (Clouds-Are-Not-The-Sky) Meditation is available on our website at www.practicalmindfulness.co.za. There is a 10-minute and a 20-minute version.

In case you need further incentive to practice the above meditation regularly, consider this.

The psychologist William James, in his *Principles of Psychology*, published in 1890, unwittingly pointed to this fact. He said: "The faculty of bringing back a wondering attention over and over again is the very root of judgement, character and will. An education which should improve this faculty would be *the* education *par excellence*." He added a caveat, however: "But it is easier to define this ideal than to give practical directions for bringing it about."

Richard Davidson, co-author of *The Science of Meditation* with Daniel Goleman, had his own insight into a possible solution to James's caveat after attending a Vipassana retreat: *meditation* was his answer. After all, they write, "Whatever specific form it takes, most every kind of meditation entails retraining attention."

It's important to recognise that the regular practice of meditation is critical to strengthening the "muscle" of attention. Just as sportspeople know they have to practice off the field in order to get something right on the field of play, just as you need to actually practice yoga in order to get strong and supple, so you actually need to sit and meditate in order to develop your faculty of attention.

THIS CHAPTER expands on the first of the three key elements of mindfulness, that of awareness / being aware. Key content includes:

- Awareness can be likened to being vigilant, awake, alert, the way a soldier would be while on guard duty, or an inspector arriving at a fresh crime scene: noticing everything and being able to report on it.
- One indicator of a lack of awareness is that sudden, unexpected events take you by surprise.
- There are two levels of awareness: awareness of your environment, and awareness of your thoughts and your focus of attention, also known as meta-awareness.
- Practical exercise of placing yourself in space and time, becoming present to your environment—outer, then inner—then placing your attention on your breath.
- The problem of thinking and the verifiable fact that you can't stop your thinking, plus the good news that you don't need to: the capacity you have is awareness of thinking and that is the main objective of most mindfulness meditations.
- Practical exercise of observing the clouds in the sky and the nature of those phenomena, followed by the analogy that "the clouds are not the sky" and how this can be applied to the nature of your mind and thought.
- The postulate that you can learn to *watch* the weather without *becoming* the weather and how this can be applied to anger, anxiety and melancholia.
- The Breathing Meditation, which is an awareness-training meditation, including some supporting arguments as to why it's beneficial to practice this regularly.

KEY ELEMENT #2

 4 | Being Nonjudgemental

R EMEMBER THE observation in Chapter 2 that your mind is always in past and future and is always liking and not liking what it finds there?

This liking and not liking was termed "having preferences" and the point was made that it's not your preferences that are the problem, but how tightly you hold onto them—how insistent you are about how things should turn out.

Once again, Gautama, the Buddha, pointed out this irony 2,500 years ago: you think that having your preferences met is the source of happiness; yet, in fact, this very need to have them met is the source of all suffering.

In this chapter, you'll learn more about the counterpoint to this, which is being nonjudgemental.

You saw earlier how your mind is always in the future or the past, and that most of your life is spent liking and not liking what you find there. This is as natural to you as breathing, and to do otherwise may seem as pointless—and as dangerous—as not breathing. If you give up liking and not liking things, or give up going after what you like and don't like, surely everyone else would just take over and invade your space? Besides, what would you live for?

Precisely. Nobody's advocating that you should become a "shoo-wow" hippy, where everything is just "Groovy, man!" We're not saying you should not be able to stand for anything, or fight for anything, or hold people accountable. Nor are we saying that you cannot have goals and work hard towards them.

It's not the thing itself, but your relationship to the thing, that causes all the trouble. We all tend to have strong preferences for things happening or not happening, and you're quite entitled to those preferences. The operative word is "strong", and the question is, how tightly do you hold onto those preferences? It's like you *must* have things happen the way you want them to, or else! Or else what? Or else you'll die. At least, that's the conclusion you—along with everyone else—

seem to carry around in your head. You'll discover more about this later in the section about the defensive emotional state we've called the "red zone".

For now, take the simple outcome of a traffic mix-up. It can quickly turn into an altercation, simply because of how tightly you're holding onto your preference for going first, or whatever it happens to be. Then consider bigger issues, like the shape and outcome of a job interview or business deal, or your child's career and romantic partner choices. How tightly wound up you can get about what you want in those situations!

THE SCIENCE (& THE SOURCE)

Equanimity: An Extremely Positive Altered Trait

ALL THE great spiritual and philosophical traditions of East and West place this one virtue among the most desirable: equanimity—being unaffected by what happens.

In verse 2.48 of the ancient Hindu text the Bhagavad Gita, Krishna says, "Perform your duty equipoised, O Arjuna, abandoning all attachment to success or failure. Such equanimity is called yoga."

We all know that the Eastern mystics—both ancient and modern—who follow the "deep path" of the contemplative tradition emerge from their years of solitude with a heightened ability to remain peaceful no matter what's going on around them—the state of equanimity.

The Greco-Roman philosophical school the Stoics held that "our feelings about life's events, not those events themselves, determine our happiness"—a statement of equanimity.

Equanimity (*hishtavut*) is a stage on the development of the Jewish Kabbalistic path—measured by treating others equally whether they have honoured or insulted you.

Before his crucifixion, Jesus is credited with saying to God: "Not my will, but Yours be done,"—a demonstration of equanimity.

When Muslims speak about the future they append the word *Inshallah*, meaning *if Allah wills*—again, equanimity.

Vipassana, the meditation practice taught by Gautama the Buddha, has equanimity as its primary outcome.

The modern German philosopher Eckhart Tolle has said that, "The only true spiritual practice is to renounce the next moment." He means to give up your preference for how the next moment should turn out—equanimity, in other words.

Interestingly, a search for the word equanimity in the modern corporate leadership lexicon does not turn up too many results. The closest is in one of Peter Senge's suggestions for the characteristics associated with his idea of personal mastery: "[People high in personal mastery] see current reality as an ally, not an enemy." Author and speaker Debashis Chatterjee mentions it in his book *Leading Consciously*, for which Senge wrote the foreword. Chatterjee says: "Equanimity gives the mind purity of perception, clarity of vision and effective decision-making capacity."

Scientists and authors of *The Science of Meditation*, Daniel Goleman & Richard Davidson, identified equanimity and compassion as two of the key "extremely positive altered traits" that can arise as enduring qualities out of the "deep path" of meditation—they took those ancient yogis and their texts as their reference points.

They've both long held that these have "value in lessening human suffering, a goal shared by science and meditative paths alike" and their research has shown that we can all develop equanimity—just like those yogis. Naturally, the hope is that we will act on it and thereby save ourselves and the planet from destruction.

You've been introduced to this before, but it deserves another mention, now that you have witnessed first-hand what a struggle it is to hold your attention on your breath, or any single thought, for more than a few seconds. By extension, if you were to beat your own heart and work any one of your organs by paying attention to it, you'd be dead in a minute. Fortunately, your autonomic nervous system takes care of that.

So then do you still think that you can control events outside of yourself and have them unfold according to your preferences—what you want or don't want to have happen—simply by holding your attention on them, and figuring out ways to force your agenda onto the world? You may succeed for a time, but, even if you're Robert Mugabe, sooner or later the party must end!

If you're even remotely rational and scientific in your approach to life, you would see that you seldom get your way with everything. Yet, how much do you still try and remain attached to the outcome?

Perhaps Hollywood is to blame for always presenting a happy ending. If so, then *Game of Thrones*, which spares very few of its protagonists, provides a necessary counterpoint and everybody should watch it for that reason. You would be better placed to align yourself with this fact, that things don't always go your way, and learn to flow with what life offers up instead. You'll probably get the same—maybe even better—results (see Chapter 9: Creating And Sustaining A State of Flow) and enjoy the journey more.

REAL-LIFE EXAMPLE

The Surrender Experiment

BACK IN the 1970s, a young man named Michael Singer noticed the "voice in his head"—that endless stream of thinking that was constantly telling him what to do—and he went on a journey to find out more about that voice. He discovered meditation and, through that, noticed how this voice is constantly expressing "preferences", based on which we then live our lives.

Singer made a commitment to respond positively to whatever came into his life—whatever he got invited to do—rather than to make decisions based on his preferences.

The first invitation led him to becoming a university lecturer, despite his having attempted to drop out of academic life.

He had built himself a cabin in the woods that he used for meditation, and requests to build similar cabins, and then whole wooden houses, for other people led to him developing a successful construction business on the side.

One day, he bought one of the early computers and wrote a program to manage the accounting for his construction business. Someone asked him if he would write a similar program for their medical practice, one that enabled them to automate the submission of medical insurance claims.

He did this, and it went on to become one of the biggest software programs of its kind in America and his shares became worth hundreds of millions of dollars.

Singer has written two books: *The Surrender Experiment*, a memoir that tells his story; and *The Untethered Soul*, a brilliant exposition of his philosophy of living without holding onto personal preferences. They are both well worth reading.

If you look at life, you see that there is an irresistible force of growth always happening. Plant life is totally surrendered to this force. It grows without judgement. If the sun is to the left, it grows to the left. If there is a rock or a building foundation in the way, it grows around it and allows itself to be shaped by the experience. But not us humans. If you were a tree you would probably try to drill through the rock in order to grow the way you want to. You would try to move the sun so that you could grow to the right instead of to the left.

In Jungian dream symbolism, the tree is often seen as a symbol of the Self, that unique person that life wants you to become. It is considered to be so, precisely for this reason, that a tree grows into its unique form because of its circumstances. You do the same—or life does the same to you, it shapes you—only you don't like it, and you spend a lot of time focused on what you like and don't like, what you want and don't want to have happen.

Once again, this is not to say that you should not have goals, or intentions. That's one of the other cognitive mistakes we humans make: that everything is *either-or*. Instead, look at a *both-and* solution. You have a preference; you try for making it happen and, at the same time, you allow that it might not happen. Or that it might not happen *the way* you want it to happen. Sometimes you get stuck on what you think is the only possible path to the goal. It *has* to happen in this way. The deal *has* to be delivered by *this* person saying yes to *this* proposal by *this* time. It is possible to stay focused on the goal itself and accept that some deviation in your path to that goal may help you in the long run.

Another YouTube video that points to this is Steve Jobs' famous *2005 Stanford Commencement Address*. In this address, Jobs talks about how his different "failures" came together to provide the key elements of Apple. When you're not getting your way, life may be pointing you to an even better goal, or bringing things together in a way that you could neither imagine nor predict. It might also be delivering a lesson that you need in order to get to the main goal. However, you would have to let go of your preferences to be able to see any of this. Being nonjudgemental—and, consequently, non-attached—opens you up to this force of life.

> **PRACTICAL EXERCISE – DO THIS NOW**
>
> *Taking A Mindful Walk*
>
> TAKE TEN minutes to walk around in a comfortable, safe environment (your garden or a courtyard that is familiar to you) and remain present.
>
> Pay attention to what you like and don't like about what you see and experience. Perhaps the place is untidy, perhaps too neat. Perhaps there is something broken that needs to be fixed, or things that need to be put in their place. Perhaps there are people and you wish there weren't, or vice versa.
>
> This is not so you can do anything about your likes and dislikes, but precisely the opposite, so you can notice them and let them go. Let the situation be as it is. Be alert, to the situation and to your preferences, as though you were a detective at a crime scene—noting them and letting them go.
>
> When you find your mind has wandered, bring your attention back to the present and notice the details and your likes and dislikes.
>
> At the same time, remain mindful of the bigger scene. Notice who and what is around you. Notice the movements, the weather. In addition, remain mindful of the time and end the exercise after 15 minutes.

What are the benefits of being nonjudgemental and non-attached? Why would one develop equanimity towards things that really matter? Well, that's the subject of this whole book. For now, let's say it's a lot like the story of Abraham, whom God asked to sacrifice his own son, Isaac. When Abraham proved that he was authentically willing to do what he'd been asked, an angel appeared, and he no longer had to go through with it. Instead, he received a blessing and a promise that his offspring would number as many as the stars in the sky, and that they would "be blessed". The moral of that story is that when you are truly willing to surrender your preference for something, and your attachment to that preference, that's often when life will grant it to you. Until then, as Carl Jung said, "What you resist, persists." Until then, you keep getting the lesson instead of the thing.

> **KEY CONCEPT – TAKE NOTE**

The Label Is Not the Thing

YOU ARE now going to get a view through another lens at being nonjudgemental, with a view to becoming nonreactive.

Consider the thing you are sitting on right now. What would you name it? Most likely it's a chair, a couch, perhaps a bed or a cushion or a carpet. Whichever, just name it in your mind the way it is normally named.

Now, what if someone came along and named that thing a "dog"? (Because, hopefully, you are not sitting on a dog.)

Chances are, you would correct them, right? And what if they continued naming it a "dog" and insisted that it's name is, indeed, "dog"? You would probably think they're mad, and ignore them, or you would argue with them. Let's say you did the latter. While you were arguing, what would happen to that thing you are sitting on? Would it change? Clearly not. And even if the other person managed to convince you to go with their version of things, and you both decided to name it a "dog", what then? Would that thing change? Once again, no, it would not.

This probably seems like a silly example, and you may well ask, where is this going? The point has been made: things don't change for the names or labels that you give to things, and yet you are probably willing to fight pretty hard for those labels. And while you're fighting about your labels, you're not present to the fact of the situation, which is that the thing remains unchanged, unaffected, and really exists independently of your label for it.

As an aside, consider this: if enough people agree on a label, we call it the "truth". Whether it's actually true or not is another matter. Similarly, the rule of thumb of propaganda is that "a lie repeated often enough becomes the truth".

A chair may seem like a simple example, and deliberately so. Let's consider a more complex example, like a parenting issue. For example, the child is "not doing well at school". There's a label. You could argue about whether that's the case or not. You could argue about whether it matters or not. You could argue about the cause of the "problem". You could argue about the solution.

Now let's say you start to do something about it. Special lessons. Change their routine. Ban friends. Ban phones. Still, the results remain unchanged. They may even get worse. You argue some more. You feel that you must do something else. You find a therapist. More arguing about the label.

Let's say you're right and your actions fix a genuine problem. All well and good. However, very often, despite your efforts, the child continues, unaffected, unchanged. You make more and more noise about it, until the label becomes the thing. What the child learns, instead, is that they have a "problem". Or that they *are* a problem.

They might respond and "fix" the problem, in the process becoming something they are not, but which at least removes the "problem" label. They'll have a problem they'll have to "unfix" later on in life, but it's their life, not yours, so you won't have to worry about it. In fact, when it does happen, if you're still around, you'll see it as more evidence of their being the "problem". Or they might acquire and become the label—they identify as the problem child and the problem becomes a real thing.

Let's say that one day the child starts to study and get A's. The truth might be that they found their own reason from within their world and they didn't need all your efforts. You, however, will give yourself all the credit. Or perhaps they never study hard and "do well". Yet they find a happy and fulfilling path in life, and it's you who gets the lesson, but only when it's too late to do anything about it.

> *Learning to be nonjudgemental means learning to see things as they are, without labels, without judgements.*

Learning to be nonjudgemental means learning to see things as they are, without labels, without judgements. When you do that, you start to align with what's real, with what can and can't be influenced. In some cases, you were right to act. The problem was real and needed a solution; you made the right call, and it went away. Other times, the problem doesn't exist except in your mind, and it goes away. Or a solution presents itself—despite you, not because of you. In other situations, *you're* the one with the problem, and *you're* the one who needs, and hopefully gets, the lesson.

As you can see, this is not to say that you should not try to recognise and address problems or stand for things or get behind a cause. The question is, what is real? Is there really a problem, or does the problem exist only because you say so? Does it exist only because you've named, or labelled, it as a problem? For example, you were brought up in a certain way, with particular values, and you're going to insist that your children live out those values, even if it breaks them in the process.

In the latter instance, you are most likely reacting to the situation defensively, based on your own conditioned fears and desires. You're not responding according to what's really going on, according to what the situation presents, or what wants to happen. Perhaps the child is destined to be great artist. Perhaps they're destined to just be an ordinary person. Is your wanting the best for them really about you, or about them? Are you responding based on what's real, and what matters? Can you go along with what wants to happen or is going to happen anyway, and align yourself with it, instead of trying to force reality to align with you and your labels of things?

Sometimes, it's very hard to see that your values might just be labels and that you could ease up on them. So hard, in fact, that people will rather die, or destroy relationships, than let go of holding their values so tightly.

The above example applies to parents with teenage children. The principle that "the label is not the thing" could equally be applied to your own career and work life, your relationship partner, your political beliefs and actions. For example, how often do you try to make something happen in your work or business life that is all about the label of reputation, instead of what matters? How often do you try to bend your relationship partner to be a certain way, instead of accepting them as they are? In the political arena, all political parties ultimately want the same outcome. What they quibble about—and sometimes go to war over—is the path to that goal; their respective labels of how it will best be achieved. What if they could drop their labels and work together?

The Most Common Labels

So, what are the most common labels that we use? Consider these:

- Good / bad
- Right / wrong
- Like / don't like

And what gives the above labels real power is their proximity to the most powerful label of all:

- Me / my / mine

Let's look at these in more detail and examine their impact.

Good / bad

Have you ever gone to a movie that you chose, and it turned out to be not so good, then, on another day, gone with someone else's suggestion and it turned out great? Or perhaps you've heard someone say, about an incident from their past, "I wouldn't wish that on my worst enemy, yet it was so good for me, I learned so much from the experience."

We humans are awfully poor predictors of what's good or bad in any situation, and yet we continue to deny the evidence and strive to control outcomes.

Author Eckhart Tolle tells the story in his book *A New Earth* about the man who wins the lottery and buys a sports car. People say, "How lucky you are." He replies, "Maybe." He drives the sports car and has an accident and ends up in hospital. People say, "How unlucky you are." He replies, "Maybe." While he is in hospital, there is an earthquake that destroys his home. By not being there, he survived. Of course, you can see where this story goes.

You—like everyone—are probably quick to evaluate whether a situation is, or is going to be, good or bad, desirable or undesirable. You do this all day, with everything that happens, or doesn't happen. Often, it doesn't turn out that way, but it turns out OK. Or, however it turns out, you deal with it. A lot of energy gets wasted on the good / bad label. As you'll learn in Chapter 9, dropping this label is one of the key factors for creating and sustaining a state of flow.

Once again, this does not mean you should not have preferences. It's about how tightly you hold onto them, and how wrong you can be about how things turn out. Can you learn to listen more, pay attention more, trust more? Can you learn to hold onto your ideas of what constitutes good and bad more lightly? Can you see that every situation is ultimately neutral, and that your power lies in your ability to respond?

Right / wrong

This label is probably only one degree less ubiquitous than the previous one, however, it holds a lot more energy. After all, how hard do you fight to defend your point of view on things? How reactive do you become when someone else tries to make you wrong about something?

How is this a problem, you say. Take a look at it: whenever you argue your point of view, you can find all the evidence you need to support that argument. Yet, right in front of you, there's someone equally convinced, finding just as much evidence to support an apparently opposing point of view. Of course, your view is right, never theirs. If everyone just listened to you, then the world would be fine. It would be a perfect place. Seriously, most people do behave as if this was the case.

You can quite confidently say that to give up being right, and to give up making another person wrong, is the hardest thing for a human being to do. It seems to defy reason. And, precisely for that reason, it's also the most powerful thing that a human being can do. After all, it was for having demonstrated this power that Nelson Mandela was so revered.

Quantum physics (search "wave-particle duality" on Wikipedia) has shown that reality will match whatever lens you observe it through, or whatever evidence or outcome you are seeking. Similarly, when you give up having to be right, you become present to what is; you see the bigger picture, and new possibilities open up. Chances are, when you give up making the other person wrong, they will give up having to defend themselves by being right (and therefore making you wrong) as well.

If you can't give up being right, you can take the first step, which is to stop making the other person wrong. Try it and see what happens. At the very least, you won't die!

Like / don't like

This label is a variation on the good / bad theme. Where good / bad applies to events outside of yourself that have happened or are happening, the like / don't like axis is more about what you want to have happen in the future. Most people are very determined to steer their lives using this compass, despite the evidence. For example, how many marriages don't work out, despite all that frenzied attraction that occurs up front? In fact, there is evidence to suggest that arranged marriages can be as successful as ones based on romantic love.

Or, how often have you set yourself some career or business goal, only to get there and find that it was not at all what you expected? I was once called in to coach a man who felt suicidal. Why? He had achieved everything he ever wanted to by the age of forty. He had hundreds of millions in the bank, and no purpose.

The emphasis on chasing your dreams has become epidemic in the modern age, and yet we do not see more fulfilment. As Carl Jung pointed out, meaning is more important than happiness and Victor Frankl made it abundantly clear that meaning can be found in any context.

Perhaps we all need to heed the fate of Sisyphus, the Greek mythological king who was punished for the sin of hubris by having to push a rock up a hill every day for the rest of his life. At the end of the day, it would roll back down again. His victory came when he accepted his fate and performed the task with a smile on his face.

Me / my / mine

Imagine that you walk into a room and see people staring at a box. Then suddenly they all jump up and start shouting at the box. Yet nothing appears to have happened. Then imagine you move around and you see that there are moving images on the box. It's a television, and the people are watching sport. You find out what sport, which teams. It's Italian Serie A and two teams you've barely heard of. You go over to the bar and have a drink, nonplussed.

Imagine, instead, it was *your* team playing. Suddenly you would be engaged, leaping up at the screen just like those people!

Once again, imagine you're at the bar, having a drink. There's a story on another television, a different channel, about an earthquake in some town you've never heard of. People have lost family members, children. Now imagine it was *your* family members, *your* children.

You can see from these examples, the power of the labels "me", "my" and "mine". You probably spend a lot of time and energy defending against what happens to your own version of "me".

Another way that this shows up is when people won't act to fix a situation, because it shouldn't be happening and the all-important "I" is not going to be the one to do it. There are many situations where, if you were to treat the situation as it is, you would just get stuck in and do the thing. When you see stories of celebrities rolling up their sleeves to do something ordinary, you may well admire them for their humility and willing to be human and ordinary. But when it's *me*? Never!

To conclude then, when you get stuck arguing about labels, you get lost in the content. You lose presence and become reactive. You become the weather.

Your labels are your interpretations, your preferences, your ideas of what ought or ought not to happen. When you become aware of this, you can still present your case, but be equally open to other possibilities. You may be surprised by what opens up in that space.

When you become present, and aware of your thinking, which consists of so many labels, you begin to get more in touch with reality, with "what is". You pay attention to what matters and respond appropriately. You become creative. On that point, did you notice that *creative* is an anagram of *reactive*?! Perhaps that can act as a clue.

PRACTICE - SAVE FOR LATER

Sensation Meditation

REMEMBER THE mindful walk you took earlier and how you paid attention to all your preferences for the place you found yourself in? Another way to pay attention to your preferences is to try to sit still for a few minutes and pay attention to the information coming in through your five senses.

Instructions

Make sure you are sitting comfortably.

Place yourself in space and time.

Now become aware of the room that you are in: the walls, ceiling, furniture, floor.

Notice the light inside the room—its colour and brightness. No need to change anything, just notice.

Now close your eyes and, once closed, pay attention to what you can see: the back of your eyelids, the darkness, the afterimages. Rest your attention there for a while. Notice how the afterimages fade or change. Rest your attention there for a while, then open them again and return to these instructions.

Now, with eyes open or closed, your choice, shift your attention to what you can hear. The sounds that may come from inside or outside the room. Rest your attention on those sounds.

Notice when your mind starts to imagine and then label the sources of those sounds. Gently let go of that imagined source—and of the label—and bring your attention back to the sound itself. Rest your attention on the sounds as they occur. Just the sound itself.

Notice when you start to judge the sound. *It's good. It's bad. I want it to last. I want it to go.* Gently let go of the judgement and embrace the sound, allow it to become part of your meditation environment.

Now repeat the above step for any fragrances in the room.

Now repeat the above step for any tastes lingering in your mouth.

Now repeat the above step for any sensations on or within your body. Do this by actively scanning your body with your attention, from head to toe and back again.

Notice when you start to judge the sensation. *It's good. It's bad. I want it to last. I want it to go.* Gently let go of the judgement and embrace the sensation, allow it to become part of your meditation environment. Then move your attention past it and continue scanning your body.

Notice if you have the urge to move your body in some way to react to the sensation. Perhaps you want to scratch an itch or move to relieve some pressure. Do that if you must, and if you can, notice the urge to react and, instead of doing anything, just move your attention past it and continue scanning.

Keep scanning your body and moving your attention past the sensations, just noticing, not reacting.

Do this for as long as you can. Start at 10 minutes and work your way up to 20, 40 or even 60 minutes. When you are done, put yourself back in time and space and, when you are ready, continue with your day.

NOTE There is a guided audio version of the Sensation Meditation available for you to purchase and download at the website www.practicalmindfulness.co.za.

By doing the Sensation Meditation practice regularly, you will train your mind to let go of its automatic reactivity and to develop equanimity.

Think about it. If you're not able to resist a little itch, or a little pressure on your skin without having to scratch yourself, or change your position, how can you expect yourself to be less reactive on the bigger things, like when people irritate you in the traffic, or when things don't go your way at work? The principle in sport is that you have to practice it "off the field" in order to be able to do it "on the field". The Sensation Meditation is your "off the field" practice for developing equanimity.

Notice how the Sensation Meditation draws on the sensory elements within your environment as points of focus and so does not require a silent or structured setting. This also means that you can take any element of this meditation and practice it wherever you are, whenever you can, or need to. Simply choose any one of the five senses and do the meditation right where you are, using your environment to provide the stimulus and training yourself to become non-judgemental.

As you use it more and more, you will become more skilled and easily able to do this on your own for a few minutes anywhere, anytime. Naturally, the long-term benefits will be enhanced by following the full guided meditation daily or as close to that as possible.

THIS CHAPTER expands on the second of the three key elements of mindfulness, that of being nonjudgemental. Key content includes:

- The mind's habit of liking and not liking everything that it encounters and how this plays out as "preferences".
- The problem is not the preferences themselves, but how tightly you hold onto them.
- The term equanimity, which can be translated as "being with what is", and how important it has been to the spiritual and philosophical traditions.
- The delusion that people have about their ability to control external events.
- A real-life example about the life of American entrepreneur and spiritual teacher Michael Singer, who has authored two books on the subject of surrendering to what is.
- Equanimity does not mean you should not have goals, but that you can have them and remain open to what might happen instead.
- The exercise of doing a mindful walk to practice awareness, including awareness of one's own preferences.
- The distinction between labels and reality and the fact that the label is not the thing. Yet you're likely to get stuck more often than not arguing about your labels.
- The most common labels that human beings use to express their preferences—good / bad, right / wrong, like / don't like—and their identity with those preferences, in the form of me / my /mine.
- The Sensation Meditation as a means to training the mind to develop equanimity.

 5 | Being Nonreactive

WHEN YOU get angry in the traffic and start moaning—or shouting—about what idiots people are; when someone talks about you or challenges you at work and you feel that your reputation is in danger; when your lover or spouse doesn't pay attention to you in the way that you would want and you feel jealous or insecure: these are all examples of being reactive.

Being reactive is something that just happens. You don't sit back, think about it, and choose, or decide, to be reactive. It's your natural, most basic response, which is why it's often termed a "knee-jerk" reaction. Often, you'll defend it by saying, "That's just how I am," or, "That's just what I need to do in order to deal with the world the way it is." You experience yourself in that moment as having no choice but to react in that way.

However, it doesn't have to be that way. When you are mindful, or conscious, you create some space between the trigger (the event) and your reaction. Instead of just that knee-jerk reaction, it's possible to have a moment of awareness and, in that space, mindfully or consciously *choose* a response. That response is likely to be one that is more appropriate to the situation—in particular, one that involves some understanding of the bigger picture, one that does not create anger or hurt in yourself or the other person.

As you can see, the words used above are *react* and *respond*. We'll use the word react and its variants to describe the problem state mentioned above, and the word *respond* to describe the alternative state, the state of being *non*reactive, which is indicated by the exercise of a mindful, conscious choice.

Responding, or being nonreactive, is not the same as suppressing the reaction. It also doesn't mean that you can't *act* in any situation. The difference is that you act with *choice*. You take *considered* action. You act based on what is appropriate for the situation, so as to not cause harm to yourself or others.

The bottom line is that reacting is automatic. It's what follows when things don't go the way you want them to, and you don't stop to think about it, to understand or reframe, nor to check whether your own reaction is appropriate. You just lash out. You say what you say. You do what you do. It feels wholly appropriate in the situation and, if asked about it, you add another layer, the layer of justification. You say something like, "Yes, of course I reacted like that, because that's how I am and that's how the world is." There's not a lot of thought behind it. And whatever thought there is just adds fuel to the fire.

On the other hand, when you know what reactivity looks like, and you've set yourself the goal of being nonreactive, you create the possibility for awareness to occur. When awareness gets activated, you'll experience it as that moment in which you notice your reaction arising. Instead of just acting out the reaction, you can take a step back. In that space, you become aware of your judgements and preferences and do an evaluation. What matters? What doesn't? What assumptions am I making? What else do I need to consider? You look at the situation, you look at yourself, and you make a choice. Shall I continue with this verbal outburst, or physical action, or shall I count to ten and take a different, more considered action?

> *Reactivity implies no choice, and no presence, and may not necessarily be the best for you or for others.*

Being nonreactive is like having an earth leakage in an electrical circuit. When the charge gets too high for the circuit, instead of exploding the circuit, it finds its way out of the system and back to earth. Another analogy might be a pressure release valve, or an overflow pipe in a geyser. It's there when you need it. (Note: you always need it.)

This is where the possibility arises for you to have a different, better experience of life—a life of responding instead of reacting; a life of sanity instead of insanity; a life of harmony instead of drama.

Remember, the key point is that being nonreactive is all about having awareness, followed by being nonjudgemental, and then exercising *choice*.

Everyone Else Can See

Think about that annoying boss archetype, the one who will not listen to input from others, but who insists that things be done their way, simply "because I said so". They carry on like that even when things are not working—they just shout louder, as though that will make a difference. Then when they finally make the change that was suggested to them, they make like it's their own idea. You and everyone else can see what they are doing, but they refuse to.

Or think about a work colleague who never admits to a mistake, but always blames someone else, or makes excuses. Once again, everyone else can see what they are doing, but they think not.

Then there are those who are nauseatingly dependent on others for approval. They can't see it, but others can. There could be many more examples, but hopefully you get the point. We all have blind spots. Usually other people can see your blind spots, but when they point them out to you, you go into defence mode. You deny them and offer all kinds of explanations as to why they might think that of you and what's really going on.

When you're being reactive, you generally don't see it as that. For all the world, you feel justified in your reaction. When someone has made you angry and you're spewing out all your arguments, you can find all the evidence in the world to prove you right. Recognising that you're being reactive is one of the hardest thing in the world to do. Very often, especially in the beginning, you need someone to point it out to you.

The Zulu word *ubuntu* translates as, "I am what I am because of others." In African culture this is generally understood as having a sense of community. It often gets used as a moral imperative for belonging to and supporting your community.

Here is an alternative, ontological interpretation of that word: first, consider that you can't see your own eyes without a mirror; similarly, you can't know yourself without having that self reflected back at you by others, especially when you're being reactive. In Chapter 7, which is about mindfulness applied to emotion regulation, you'll be advised to find a partner who can tell you when you're in the "red zone" (that amygdala hijack space).

THE SCIENCE

The Amygdala Hijack

THE AMYGDALA acts as the brain's radar for threat. It constantly scans the input it's receiving from the senses for signs of danger. If it perceives a threat, the amygdala circuitry triggers the flight-or-flight response: hormones like cortisol and adrenaline that spur us into action.

In modern life there are relatively few physical threats, but plenty of verbal ones. At work and on social media, we see and hear things constantly that threaten our idea of ourselves or how the world should be.

"The amygdala connects strongly to brain circuitry for both focusing our attention [in the case of real physical danger] and for intense emotional reactions," say Goleman & Davidson in *The Science of Meditation*. "The amygdala rivets our attention on what it finds troubling so when something worries or upset us, our mind wanders over and over to that thing, even to the point of fixation."

No wonder we become so defensive and immovable when we believe we've been offended!

Conversely, the prefrontal cortex, the most recently evolved section of the brain, manages the reactivity of the amygdala. It's the guard at the gate. It does a check, evaluates, and decides whether to let the reaction through or not.

However, that guard can have a difficult time when there are angry or anxious hordes at the gate. "When anger or anxiety is triggered the amygdala hijack paralyses executive function," say Goleman & Davidson. In other words, you find yourself reacting without thinking.

Neuroscientists know that the stronger the link (i.e. the greater the number of physical connections) between these two parts of the brain, "the less a person will be hijacked by emotional downs and ups of all sorts".

Studies performed and/or evaluated by Goleman & Davidson, and reported in their book, have shown that seasoned meditators' brains "had stronger operative connectivity between the prefrontal cortex, which manages reactivity, and the amygdala". Other combinations of studies showed that [mindfulness] training "did reduce the reactivity of the amygdala", although this was likely to be more of a state effect in the beginning, without long-term practice of meditation.

Long-term meditators showed "both this reduced reactivity in the amygdala plus strengthening of the connection between the prefrontal cortex and amygdala".

These results imply that "when the going gets tough—for example, in response to a major life challenge such as losing a job—the ability to manage distress (which depends upon the connectivity between the prefrontal cortex and amygdala) will be greater in long-term meditators compared to those who have only done [a mindfulness] training.

"The good news is that this resilience can be learned. What we don't know is how long this effect might last. We suspect that it would be short-lived unless participants continued to practice, a key to transforming a state into a trait."

Let's get real.

Think about your average daily stress levels. What if you could dramatically reduce your experience of being stressed? What if you could handle both the big life events as well as the many small ones with a degree of calmness?

Think about your own friendships and/or intimate relationship. What if you could tell each other what you really thought, and what you really want and need, without the other person reacting, taking it personally, or shooting each other down?

Or think about social media, which so dominates our lives. What if you could read other people's posts without feeling inadequate, or jealous? What if you could read opposing political views without having to start—and attempt to win—an argument that you have no chance of winning?

Or think of the type of leader who is willing to listen, to admit to not knowing something or having made a mistake, who asks for opinions and really takes what other people say into account. How much more inspiring is it to work for a person like that? Do you think you'd perform better? Don't you think they'd get better results from people in the long-term?

The possibility of people being nonreactive exists, even though it's not easy to achieve. When you learn to be nonreactive yourself, you will develop your ability to surf the reactivity of others. You will also naturally start to influence others to be nonreactive. You may also start to choose to be with people who are nonreactive. You can have a different, better experience of life.

REAL-LIFE EXAMPLE

Seeing Things for What They Are

ABOUT A year after I got divorced, my young son let slip that he had missed a day of school the week before. The reason? His mother had decided to extend their weekend away.

I was livid. Our divorce had been amicable, but this I could not accept. I contemplated finding a lawyer and fighting a custody battle.

Then I stopped and evaluated. In that space, I remembered that my ex-wife's own father had often placed a priority on travel and other experiences over attendance at school. In addition, she had been allowed to spend some of her high school days and weeks travelling to work as an international model.

Therefore, I saw that such behaviour was not out of alignment with her upbringing and values, not nearly as much as it was out of alignment with mine.

When I spoke to her again I didn't come flying out of the blocks the way I would normally have done. In fact, I let her bring it up. "Luke didn't go to school on Monday," she said. "We were out at Kommetjie with [his godmother, who was visiting]. She hasn't seen him for so long; it was such a beautiful day, and we decided to spend it out there."

"I know," I said, "and as much as I don't agree with it and would never do that myself, I understand it, coming from you."

Silence. It was not the response she had expected. If I'd been reactive and attacked her, she would naturally have defended herself and fought back. Instead she said, "Of course, it won't happen all the time."

"If it does I'll have more to say about it," I said.

That was it. Nothing more said, and it never happened again. In fact, from that day on, our relationship improved as mutual respect returned, and we became friendly towards each other once again.

Non-reactivity can be developed. In fact, to put that correctly, it can *only* be developed; it cannot happen by itself. To quote one of the fathers of the modern consciousness movement, G.I. Gurdjieff, "Consciousness can only develop consciously."

When you are consistently nonreactive, you can say you have developed a degree of *personal mastery*.

Personal mastery has been defined in various ways by various people and schools of thought. It's an ancient idea, one that has been around at least since the time of Aristotle, who "posited the goal of life as a virtue-based *eudaimonia*—a quality of flourishing" (Goleman & Davidson, p.54). "And, he added, we are not by nature virtuous, but all have the potential to become so through the right effort. The effort includes what today we would call self-monitoring, the ongoing practice of noting our thoughts and acts."

One of the leading modern academic proponents of personal mastery is the leadership guru Peter Senge, who has talked about the need for people to be able to learn about themselves and apply that learning to their choices and behaviours in order to be more effective in their particular context.

We are going to offer a definition of personal mastery as "a state of being mindful (of one's own conditioned thoughts, habits, reactions) and responsive (being able to make attitudinal and behavioural choices, i.e. nonreactive)".

So, you can say that mindfulness leads to personal mastery, and personal mastery is necessary for you to have a different, better experience of life. We're also saying that personal mastery has to be developed and is done by *learning* to *manage* yourself better.

PRACTICAL EXERCISE – DO THIS NOW

Training Non-Reactivity

NOTICE HOW you began the awareness and meditation practices in Chapter 3 by first observing the physical room and then drawing in closer and closer—at which point you may have closed your eyes—until you became aware of your internal sensations and eventually your breath and, finally, your thoughts.

You are now going to add an element to this practice. (This is not something you will do all the time, it's an exercise to demonstrate a particular concept which you will read about afterwards.)

Do this now.

Step 1 Sitting comfortably, and with your eyes open, become aware of the room you are in: start with the walls, ceiling, floor (just notice them and how still they are); then move to the light (brightness and colour) and air (temperature, movement). Then move your attention to the furniture in the room (just notice it; also notice how still it is). Hold your attention there for about 30 seconds. Then move your attention to your breath. You may keep your eyes open or close them at this stage—your choice. Keep your attention on your breath for two minutes. Then come back and read the next instruction.

Step 2 Find a position that is just a little less comfortable for you. Perhaps you could remove a cushion, or sit cross-legged on the cold, hard floor. Or you might choose to sit on the carpet with your legs straight out in front of you and touch your toes—be careful, you're going to stay in this position. Do whatever you can that leaves you just less than comfortable.

Don't do anything that will cause injury or that puts strain on an existing injury. Just create a mild level of discomfort for yourself.

When you are ready, repeat step 1 and see if you can complete it without adjusting your position to achieve less discomfort. In other words, move through the steps and hold your attention on the room, and then on your breath (eyes open or closed—your choice) for the same amount of time as before without moving or attempting to get more comfortable.

If that's too easy, then sit for longer until you've experienced enough discomfort to make you want to move at least a few times (but not having moved).

When you have completed the exercise—or collapsed—move to Step 3.

Step 3 Review the exercise using the following questions:

- Did you notice how strong and repeated the impulse was to fix what was wrong? (This is your brain being reactive: you can liken it to an amygdala hijack, which would be more severe or intense.)
- Did you notice that you had the capacity—however great or small—to make a *choice* to consciously control that impulse? (This is your executive function: the prefrontal cortex being activated. If you had given in to the urge to move, you would have surrendered that power to choose.)
- Do you see the possibility for strengthening that capacity, and the potential benefits of doing so?
- Can you think what scenarios you could apply this ability to in your life?

Note that Vipassana involves an hour of sitting—not in a contorted position, but in a normal meditation position—where this level of discomfort builds up, purely as a consequence of the length of time spent sitting in one position without moving.

Science has shown that long-term Vipassana meditators showed a strengthened connection between the amygdala and the prefrontal cortex, thereby reducing emotional reactivity. You don't have to do two hours of Vipassana every day, but you can certainly sit through discomfort for longer. In fact, even just making the time in your day to meditate and sticking to it is a good start.

You can create your own discomfort by extending your meditation time and creating the agreement with yourself that you won't move to manage discomfort. You can also do it when you're sitting in a waiting room, in traffic, or at your child's prize-giving ceremony. Sit still, be mindful, and don't react to small discomforts, like an itch, a drop of sweat, or too much pressure from your clothes or the chair. Let them be there, without judgement. You'll notice that as your attention moves onto something else, they'll disappear from your awareness. Sometimes, they literally disappear altogether.

This is a way of training your brain "off the field" so that it automatically recognises and does the same thing "on the field"—i.e. when you're having that next big reaction—that amygdala hijack.

The Monstrous Ego

When you are reactive, who is it that is being reactive? Is it you? Certainly, you experience it that way: you see—and feel—yourself to be the product of your thoughts. However, as you've already seen, your thoughts arise of their own volition. You don't create them. They're like those clouds in the sky, arising, changing and dissolving.

You've also seen that the problem state of reactivity arises when you just act on those thoughts without awareness. Conversely, awareness is possible and activates a part of yourself that can exercise choice. When people become aware of this, they seldom choose to continue acting out every reactive thought or feeling. They usually start to operate from that place of awareness. They usually start to exercise choice over their responses, instead of just reacting.

For example, when you become aware that your outbursts with your partner are because you feel insecure, you start to manage your internal response and consequently your external one—your behaviour—too. This is not easy, and you may struggle to always get it right, however, the distinction between these two parts of yourself—the reactive part of yourself and the more mindful, considered part of yourself—should be clear to you.

If you look at this carefully you'll see that the difference lies in *choice*. If you don't have a choice when you're being reactive, then you're being a slave to whatever thoughts and feelings come up—to your reactive self. Conversely, if you exercise choice over that part of yourself, then you're stepping out from under its spell and taking charge—you're putting your more mindful self in charge.

That reactive part of you likes to be in charge. Note how hard it is to let go of a jealous or angry reaction. When it's active, it grabs your attention and doesn't let go easily. This is why it feels so much like the real you.

There is an advertisement in South Africa for a fast food franchise called Chicken Licken. You can find it on YouTube. It starts out with a young man who has a miniature orangutan on his back, and which starts trying to get attention.

When the orangutan doesn't get attention, it gets bigger, and bigger, until it's bigger than him—and it's still on his back. He knows what to do: he has to take it to the Chicken Licken to get some chicken wings. Once he does that, and begins to eat them, it disappears. However, before he even gets back to work, it returns, at its original size.

It's useful to see the reactive self—more commonly known as the ego—as being a monster exactly like that orangutan. It exists as an autonomous set of thoughts—which, as you now know, are mostly preferences—and which must be attended to. If you look carefully, no matter who you are, you'll see that you live to appease them, for fear that they will take you over completely.

If you look carefully, you'll see that the reactive self, that monstrous ego, is not you. At least, it doesn't have to be you. You do have a choice, and that choice is activated by being aware that the monster is about to take over, then letting go of its labels and judgements (its preferences, which are expressed as some form of *good / bad, right / wrong, like / don't like* and also *want / don't want* in relation to *me / my / mine*).

Let's look at a practical example. Say you'd like to get fit, but your intention is weak. That monster is on your back, whispering negative thoughts like, "It's no use, you're too fat. Feed me burgers instead."

You didn't create that monster—you didn't create those thoughts, you just find yourself having them.

Then you read an inspirational story and latch onto the idea that you can get fit. In that moment, you say, "I *will* go to gym." You have just created an intention.

This intention is small. You jump on your bike and head to the gym. You still get tossed about by that giant monster on your back, telling you that it's no good, but you manage to hold on and get there.

By acting on your intention, you've proved to yourself—and your monster—that you have at least some strength in your ability to hold to your intention, even while it climbs all over you. You develop some belief in yourself. You develop the strength to wrestle the monster.

Each time you hold yourself to an intention, that part of you becomes bigger, stronger—you become more capable of wrestling that monster—and capable of wrestling it in more and more situations. (By the same process by which you manage your intention to go to gym, you can manage your anger, or any other reaction you choose to conquer.)

Each time you do this, you feed yourself—your new, mindfully created self— instead of the monster. In this way, you begin to mindfully create the "I" that you call yourself.

Recognising and exercising this power is the key to becoming nonreactive in all areas of your life. This is the full implication of being mindful and being nonreactive. It is the ego that is reactive. Being nonreactive means rising above and taking charge of the ego. The task is not to destroy or get rid of your ego, but to be in charge of your ego. After all, you'll probably want to keep—and even strengthen—most parts of yourself, that's expected. However, there are likely to be parts that you may choose to work on, and transform. The difference is exactly that: *choice*.

To reiterate, we do not advocate destroying or getting get rid of ego, just as we do not advocate getting rid of your thoughts. We advocate *learning* to *manage* (become mindful of) and direct your thoughts and your ego so that you can have a different, better experience of life.

In Section C of this book you'll learn how to apply this principle to manage your emotions, stress, make better decisions, create and sustain a state of flow and develop a more authentic way of being and relating.

An important note: Anyone who says they do not have an ego is stating an impossibility. They probably have the ego of non-ego. You can test them by challenging them on it and see how they react. Reaction, for example defensiveness, is a sure sign of the presence of ego.

A word of caution: you can never assume you've beaten the monster of reactive thinking into submission. You can only become very alert and very quick to spot its activities. If you ever think you've conquered it, then you've become the monster yourself!

To support this point, here's a quote by Peter Senge which pulls together a number of threads introduced so far in this book: "People with a high level of personal mastery live in continual learning mode. They never 'arrive'. Sometimes, language, such as the term 'personal mastery', creates a misleading sense of definiteness, of black and white. But personal mastery is not something you possess. It is a process. It is a lifelong discipline. People with a high level of personal mastery are acutely aware of their ignorance, their incompetence, their growth areas. And they are deeply self-confident. Paradoxical? Only for those who do not see [that] the 'journey is the reward'."

PRACTICAL EXERCISE – DO THIS NOW

Imagination Versus Visual Perception

NOTICE HOW we've introduced the awareness and meditation practices by asking you to observe the physical room and then drawing in closer and closer, until you became aware of your internal sensations and, eventually, your breath and, finally, your thoughts, at which point you may have closed your eyes.

You are going to discover another distinction to add to this process.

Do this now.

Step 1 With your eyes *open*, become aware of the room you are in. Hold your attention there for about 30 seconds. Then move to the next instruction.

Step 2 Now *close* your eyes and, once again, become aware of the room that you are in. Hold your attention there for about 30 seconds, then open your eyes and move to the next instruction.

Step 3 Now *close* your eyes again, and, this time, pay attention to what you can *see*: the back of your eyelids, the darkness, the afterimages. Notice how they change and fade. Do this now for about 30 seconds and then open them again.

Have you done that? Good. Then you'll get more value from what follows.

KEY CONCEPT – TAKE NOTE

The Imagination is Not the Sensation

WHEN YOU closed your eyes for the first time in the above exercise (Step 2), notice that you couldn't see the room, yet you were aware of it. You probably had images in your mind. Those images existed, in that moment, as memory, and possibly imagination. Nothing wrong, you need those. Just notice.

When you closed your eyes for the second time, you paid attention to what you could actually *see*: the backs of your eyelids, the darkness, the afterimages. You may have noticed that this required a deliberate instruction and a conscious decision and effort.

What this demonstrates is how your attention more naturally goes to what you remember and what you imagine about a situation, rather than paying attention to the objective reality, the facts that are available to you (which in this case was the darkness and the afterimages at the back of your eyelids).

To pay attention to the sensory information, you needed particular instructions—and it was probably an effort; your attention didn't stay there for long. Left alone, your mind would keep going back to its memories and imaginings.

This awareness is beneficial at two levels.

The first is the outer, or macro, level. You saw earlier that we humans are quite poor at determining what is good or not good in a situation. We're more attached to our labels than to reality. For example, you've probably seen how people would rather defend their original opinion than admit they were wrong when confronted with the facts. Later on, for example, you'll read that people actually experience the flow state more often when they're at work than at home, and yet they're always wanting to get to Friday, when work is over.

These examples point to the fact that humans are poor at looking at the facts of their experience, as it is in the present moment, and rather get lost in their thoughts, which are memories, imaginings and interpretations. This practice of paying attention to what you can see when you close your eyes provides an instant short-circuit to that mental process and is a good off-the-field practice for remembering and working with what's real rather than what's imagined.

The second benefit of this awareness is at the inner, or micro, level. The main problem you may have when meditating is being able to still your mind quickly enough to get into the beneficial state. If you're like most people, you might find that your thinking is very "loud".

The problem is that thoughts are generally experienced behind the eyes and as visual. They're also experienced as real. (Just think how a mere thought can make you anxious.) So it's no wonder that your attention stays with those thoughts instead of moving into the meditation. The above practice provides a shortcut that uses the visual sense to shift your mind instantly from dealing with what's not real to dealing with what's real.

By shifting your attention to what you can see you very quickly send a message to the brain to notice the distinction between that imagined imagery and the information coming in through the visual cortex—the latter being very little information and certainly very distinct from the imagery of thought. This break in the flow of imagery does not happen when you put your attention directly on the breath, for example, and so it takes longer to reach the same point of interrupting thinking.

You only need to do it for a few seconds, then you can move your attention to your breath or whatever the next focal point is for your meditation. You'll find you have a much deeper experience, much sooner, than you would have otherwise.

PRACTICE - SAVE FOR LATER

Micro Meditations

AS OFTEN as you can during the day, and certainly at times when you have become aware that you're being or about to become reactive, presence yourself by doing a micro-meditation.

Start this by going through the steps you have used to begin every meditation so far.

Place yourself in space and time. <10 secs>

Become aware of, and pay attention to, the room you're in: the walls, windows, ceiling, floor and the furniture. Notice how still they are. Notice that they are not paying attention to you, or your problems. Notice that, whatever happens, they'll probably still be there tomorrow. <10 secs>

Become aware of, and pay attention to, the light inside and outside the room. Let go of judgements, just notice. <10 secs>

Become aware of, and pay attention to, the temperature and any movement of the air. Let go of judgements, just notice. <10 secs>

Become aware of, and pay attention to, any sounds outside or inside the room. Let go of judgements, just notice. <10 secs>

If your mind is still very busy, then close your eyes and shift your attention to the visual sensory information—what you can actually see, which is the backs of your eyelids. Focus on the darkness and the afterimages that you see there. <10 secs>

Then move your attention to your breath and hold it there for a few seconds, or a minute or two. <10 secs-2 mins>

You may choose to scan your body for sensations for a few seconds, or a minute or two. <10 secs-2 mins>

At any point, you may choose to return through the previous stages in reverse order—paying attention to the sounds, the air, the light, the physical furniture and boundaries of the room—and place yourself back in space and time.

This whole sequence should take you less than three minutes, and you can stretch it out for as long as you need to and are able to. You can choose to stop at any one of the stages and make that the element of focus for a longer time, then move on again.

There is evidence to suggest that smokers are more productive immediately after they've taken a smoke break. Work places have traditionally provided a smoking area and a play area for extroverted activities like pool or foosball. More often now they're providing a lawn or a walking track—and chill rooms and meditation spaces.

You can use these areas during the day—or find and create your own space—to practice your micro-meditations. It's better than doing it at your desk—the change of physical environment enhances the experience, and you're less likely to be interrupted.

You can add another dimension to your mindful awareness practice by setting times, or time ranges, in which to practice micro-meditations. For example, you might set yourself the target to do one micro-meditation before breakfast, one before midday, one between midday and three o'clock, one between three o'clock and sunset, and one before bed. Clearly if you do this, you're getting the benefits of the micro-meditations. In addition, there's a second level to the exercise, and that is practising ongoing mindful awareness by being aware of the time and when you need to perform your next micro-meditation.

Of course, it makes no sense to use an alarm clock or a watch or phone app to remind you. The whole point is to remain mindful throughout the day. Being aware of the time so that you don't miss your micro-meditation deadlines is the perfect way to accomplish that. You remain mindfully aware throughout the day, rather than becoming unaware and relying on technology to bring you back to awareness.

CHAPTER SUMMARY

THIS CHAPTER expands on the third of the three key elements of mindfulness, that of being nonjudgemental. Key content includes:

- A description of reactivity as being that automatic, unconsidered, knee-jerk reaction you have to situations, including some examples of what reactivity looks like when it happens.
- The alternative to reacting is to respond.
- The distinction between reacting and responding—reacting is automatic, there is no choice; responding, by definition involves making a mindful, conscious choice.
- When you're being reactive, you're usually the last person to know. Other people can see, and will point it out. However, you're most likely to deny it and defend yourself instead.
- The science of reactivity through the lens of the "amygdala hijack".
- The idea of personal mastery as "a state of being mindful and responsive", how practising mindfulness leads to personal mastery, which equates to *learning* to *manage* yourself better.
- A meditation exercise with a twist—using physical discomfort during meditation to demonstrate reactivity.
- A description of the ego as an autonomous monster on your back; how that monster needs to be fed regularly.
- Mindful self-creation as the ultimate goal of mindfulness. What it is, what it looks like and how you can build this muscle and apply it to ever more situations.
- The distinction between sensation and imagination, and an exercise to recognise the difference. The benefits that this distinction provides for daily life.

SECTION C | Practical Applications

BEFORE I met Colinda, I had a book and program like this in mind and my title was Applied Mindfulness and Personal Mastery—AMPᵐ was to be the acronym. I felt this was appropriate because applying mindfulness properly can really power up your life. Colinda suggested that we link it to the simple practicality of CBT—and pointed to the fact that, as an eldest daughter, she likes practical—and suggested the name Practical Mindfulness.

I agreed, because I could see the point: most people associate mindfulness with helping you to destress, which is often perceived as the opposite of performance. The unfortunate consequence of this is that mindfulness has been watered down to a narrow set of activities, like paying attention while eating and using your smartphone less often—and, ironically, using a smartphone app to remind you to do all of that!

While there's some benefit to be gained from doing those things, what's the point? You could just as easily do Pilates. One of the attendees on our public course highlighted this dilemma. He had just come back from a business trip where they'd been introduced to mindfulness. He told the story how one delegate had stood up and protested that if he did all that stuff he'd lose his competitive edge.

Precisely, and that's not what we're after. We're about understanding and getting the full benefit of being mindful. We're about making it relevant to all aspects of your life by showing how it can be learned and applied practically to be the best version of yourself that you can be. To perform at your peak, whatever you're doing. To transform your experience of life. To develop personal mastery.

How is that possible? Let's look at two key features of the world we currently live in.

Firstly, there's the frantic chasing after future goals—very often, it's to be the next corporate giant or Internet gazillionaire—while desperately trying to shorten timelines. More and more, people are starting to see that goals like those are elusive, and therefore, if you don't enjoy the journey, you're not going to enjoy much at all.

Secondly, human beings are experiencing a fragmentation of established reference points. You can no longer rely on broad social conventions, beliefs or stereotypes to define yourself or to guide you. It's become a world of infinite individualised options—career options, gender identity options, etc. It's also become a world where there is a high degree of complexity and little certainty. Think of fake news, cryptocurrencies, and the speed at which companies can take over the world, or disappear—literally—overnight.

In this world, you need to be able to define yourself independently as an individual. Then you need to be able to self-reference in any situation. For that, you need the key feature of mindfulness, which is being able to maintain the balance of your mind, i.e. being able to bring yourself back to centre, to reference who you are and what matters most, right here, right now.

To that end, Colinda and I identified five areas of practical application that mindfulness can have a major impact on, and which are most relevant to people's lives in the modern context. Those areas of practical application are:

- **Emotion regulation** Mindfully applying a CBT-based practice that will enable you to manage and direct your emotions in a way that is purposeful and constructive;
- **Handling stress and building resilience** Learning to combine mindfulness with coaching tools to manage your stress effectively, in a way that you can recover more quickly and build resilience.
- **Complexity and decision-making** Using mindfulness to read situations accurately and make clear decisions based on what matters, rather than on reactive emotions, or the expectations of others.
- **Creating and sustaining the state of flow** Applying mindfulness-based practices to develop presence in a way that can activate and sustain the flow state, which leads to high performance and optimal experience.
- **Authentic being and relating** Learning to integrate your mindfulness-based practices in a way that can lead to a more authentic way of being and relating to others.

For each of the above areas of practical application, we'll introduce some key concepts, then show you how to apply mindfulness to that area using the three key elements: being aware (what to be aware of within that area); then being nonjudgemental (letting go of labels and preferences and developing equanimity within that area); then being nonreactive (what nonreactivity would look like within that area and what it takes to remain nonreactive).

For each area of application, we'll also introduce some relevant coaching tools and/or CBT-based practices to further support you in applying the three key elements.

6 | Emotion Regulation

D O YOUR emotions sometimes overwhelm you, or get you into trouble? Or do you have them so well under control that you barely notice them? If the latter, then how alive do you feel? And what kind of feedback do you get from people and life in general?

As you can see, having too much emotion can often be as much of a problem as having too little. And even that statement is relative. What's too much for some is way too little for others.

At the end of the day, emotions are not necessarily "good" or "bad". They are in fact messengers that tell you important things about your world!

With this in mind, perhaps a better set of questions would be: Do you direct your emotions, or do your emotions direct you? Do you let your emotions serve the purpose that they are meant to serve?

Don't worry if you don't quite get that—it's the whole point of this chapter! You're about to learn a CBT-based practice that will enable you to manage and direct your emotions in a way that is purposeful and constructive.

With this chapter you will:

- Gain an understanding of your own emotions and how they work;
- Learn to identify your triggers and know when you are in the "red zone";
- Know what to do when are you are experiencing high levels of emotion;
- Be better able to regulate your responses to emotion.

The "What Is" Of Emotions

HAVE YOU ever noticed that the word *emotion* contains the word *motion*? This may be more than coincidence. Consider how a thought doesn't necessarily lead you to act, but an emotion does. For example, you think about helping someone, but you don't; then someone "makes you feel guilty" and you do it. Or you write that angry email that you know you should not send; you do your best not to, but the anger rises in you and "makes you" press send.

Whoever's job it was to come up with words hundreds of years ago might have been onto something. In fact, according to Dictionary.com, the origin of the word *emotion* is "apparently Middle French … from *esmovoir*, to set in motion".

We know that energy is needed for action, so let's separate the word *emotion* into its components of *e + motion* and posit that the *e* stands for energy, and that emotion is "energy in motion". In other words, emotion is energy attached to the thoughts that you have, and it causes you to go into motion—to *act*—on those thoughts.

What causes that energy, where does it come from? Consider the possibility that the energy arises out of your judgements (preferences) of *good / bad, right / wrong, liking / not liking*.

In that first example, you weren't going to help the other person, however, chances are, something that someone said, or a second thought that popped into your mind, told you that *not* acting was *bad*—or, at least, *not good*. This *judgement* provided the energy that tipped the scales.

Judgements in this context don't have to be moral or critical, they can also just be preferences, i.e. liking / not liking something.

Let's say your friend gets all excited about a new iPhone release. If you don't pay any attention to new technology releases—for you, it's just a phone—then there's an absence of judgement (preference) on your part and so you don't feel anything at all. If you like them—positive judgement (preference)—just as much as she does, you're likely to get equally excited. If you're an iPhone junkie—extremely strong positive preference—you might experience an overwhelming thrill, and perhaps dread at the prospect of having to pay for it!

So you can see that, in the absence of a judgement (preference), little or no energy attaches itself to a thought, and little or no emotion is experienced. Conversely, the presence of a judgement (preference) results in the presence of energy attached to a thought, and the presence of emotion. By extension, the *strength* of that judgement determines the *level* of energy that attaches itself, and the strength or intensity of emotion.

Crucially, any given level of energy will be upped by the degree of *proximity* to the label *me / my / mine*. For instance, if you hear that your friend's new iPhone was stolen, you might experience some mild emotion, like sympathy, around that. Now let's say the phone was stolen during an event at *your* house. In that case, you might suddenly become very concerned, perhaps you might feel insulted, even angry. And if it was *your* phone that got stolen, you'd probably experience even more intense emotion.

The next thing to note is that the higher the level of energy—and therefore emotion—the more it distorts and exaggerates the *motion*—or *action*—in response to a given set of circumstances. For instance, with regards to the iPhone theft, one person might investigate and confront the suspect privately. The next might lay a charge against the suspect. Another might take revenge, like shaming them on Facebook.

Such exaggerated action is linked to the degree of *identification* with—or *importance* attached to—the label *me / my / mine*. In the iPhone theft example, your sense of self could be identified with the notion that "nobody makes *me* look bad", or "nobody takes advantage of *my* hospitality". Any overidentification with such ideas would cause a quantum shift in the level of energy, and therefore emotion, experienced. This would in turn impact the level of action taken.

> *The higher the level of energy, the more it distorts and exaggerates the action in response to a given event.*

It's important to note that, just as thoughts lead to emotions, so emotions also feed back to and influence your thoughts, adding fuel to the fire. It can become a self-reinforcing closed loop. In mindfulness terms we'd call this a reactivity spiral. It's often this second layer, where you have a judgement about the emotion itself, that drives emotional disorders like depression and anxiety. More on this later.

One more element that is important to consider when it comes to emotions is that the body doesn't know the difference between an actual situation and a thought. It can react to both as if they were real. Consider how an actor in a movie is able to conjure up tears—and how you can be moved to tears by watching them. Or how you can have an adrenaline rush—or be moved to tears—just watching sport.

This last point is relevant for emotional disorders, like panic. Often a person who has suffered a panic attack, let's say in a crowded mall, starts to feel afraid when they return to any mall, and that thought can set off the symptoms again. This is why mindfulness is used in treatments for this and other disorders, of which more later.

The fact that the body doesn't know the difference between thought and reality, also relates back to the amygdala hijack that has been mentioned in previous chapters. For example, your mind recognises a current situation as being similar to one from the past (boss, angry and shouting equals father, angry and shouting).

The situation in the past seemed rather life-threatening (you were five years old), and now your mind treats this one as though it's also life-threatening, even though it's not. Still, you experience that same freeze-fight-or-flight response, because the amygdala doesn't distinguish between what's real and what's not. This points forward to when you will read about the "red zone" later in this chapter.

Now let's discover what you can do about emotion through the lenses of the three key elements of mindfulness.

 ## Applying the Three Key Elements

YOU WERE previously introduced to the concept that thoughts cannot be started or stopped at will. You've seen that emotions are linked to thoughts and are therefore just as unstoppable. Often, as a therapist, clients want Colinda to "take away" or "stop" their negative emotions. She reminds them, however, that just as you can't stop thinking, you can't stop feeling either. In just the same way that thoughts are like those clouds in the sky—transient, impermanent, arising from and dissolving back into their source—emotions also change, and come and go.

You've already learned that it's not the thing itself, but the relationship to the thing, that matters. In the case of emotions, it's often the fear of the feeling, or your judgement that the emotional experience is bad, that causes distress and plays a role in developing and maintaining the symptoms of emotional disorders.

For example, someone feels anxious or depressed, and then has a judgement that they should not feel that way. In the failed attempt to get rid of the feeling, they become more anxious, or more depressed. Or something makes you angry. Your attempt to get rid of the anger, for example by shouting, only makes it worse. This secondary reaction arises from people not knowing how to tolerate and deal with uncomfortable emotions.

In the *Science* section of this chapter, you can read about cognitive behaviour therapy (CBT), which is an advanced, "evidence-based" modality of psychology that also incorporates mindfulness. One of the global thought leaders in the field of CBT, David Barlow, says this about emotions: "Getting rid of … uncomfortable emotions would not be very helpful or adaptive and in fact would actually work against you. The truth is that all emotions, even the uncomfortable ones, play very important roles in our lives and provide us with a lot of important information.

"The goal … is not to eliminate uncomfortable emotions like fear, anxiety, sadness, or anger, et cetera. Instead, [you need to] learn how to better understand and tolerate ... and manage uncomfortable or distressing emotional experiences, and begin to ... lead the life you want."

As the saying goes, if you can't beat 'em, join 'em. In the case of emotions, this means learning to work with them, which means learning to harness their underlying energy constructively and using that energy mindfully to take you in a new direction.

You can achieve this by applying the three key elements of mindfulness to your experience of emotion. Let's take that journey now.

Being Aware | Observing Emotions

If you've been doing mindfulness meditations, you've hopefully become accustomed to observing your thoughts. Learning to observe your emotions is the next layer. To some people that may be anathema—they want to *feel* and *express* their emotions. Awareness doesn't preclude that. You can be mindfully aware of an emotion while feeling and expressing it.

Barlow describes emotion awareness as "the skill of stepping out of the cycle of interacting thoughts, feelings, and behaviours, in order to view your experience objectively". This enables you to distinguish what's real from what's not real, so that you only deal with "what is" and don't add more fuel to the fire.

Awareness is the key that gives you access to the underlying energy of an emotion. With awareness, followed by being nonjudgemental, you're able to direct that energy purposefully, instead of letting it direct you. In more practical terms, it means you're able to make behavioural choices instead of being driven to act out the emotion—joy, anger, jealousy—in the same way every time.

What that means and how to do that is what we'll cover with the next key: being nonjudgemental. For now, let's continue to unpack what awareness of emotions looks—and feels—like.

In the early stages of this journey, you'll probably only become aware of your emotions once they've already become a behaviour—when you've already acted them out. You've helped somebody you felt sorry for, you've maxed your credit card on the new iPhone, or you've sent that angry email. It may even require somebody pointing it out to you: "Hey, that was very kind," or, "Hey, you're being a bit emotional."

In this phase, and especially for strong emotions, it may take you some time to recognise—or admit—that you're being emotional or experiencing an emotion. We're talking as long as a few hours, even a day or two. With time and practice, you may start to catch yourself without anyone having to tell you. This may still take a few hours or even a day after you've acted out.

In the above scenarios, even though the emotion has passed, and the action has happened, it's still useful to rerun the process in your mind in the way that you'll learn to do with the next key element (being nonjudgemental). This will prepare you for the next time you experience that emotion and, having practised the scenario in your mind, you'll be more likely to catch yourself earlier in the cycle, hopefully even before you've acted.

With time and practice, you'll start to be aware of your emotion, as an emotion, even while you're doing it. At this point you can stop yourself from taking those harmful or destructive actions. You may decide that compulsively helping every person you see is not the right thing, but to be more selective. You may decide to put away your credit card rather than blow the balance on the new iPhone. You may let yourself type the angry email, but you don't press send. As you'll see with the next key element, this is not about suppressing the energy, but redirecting it.

As Barlow, says, "[This] does not mean *resignation*—it is not the same thing as saying you must 'just live with your anxiety' or uncomfortable emotions and 'just deal with it,' or 'grin and bear it'. Instead, [it] allows us to begin to respond to our experiences in a more thoughtful, realistic way, rather than through knee-jerk reactions." When you do this, Barlow adds, your emotions "begin to lose a little of the power they may have over [you]".

At an advanced level, you'll know before you even go into a situation that this is how you normally react, and so you'll have already chosen how you will respond when that thing happens that normally triggers you. You'll be ready to say no to helping the other person when it's appropriate. You'll view the iPhone without even entertaining the temptation to buy. You'll engage the criticism without having to defend yourself.

At a super-advanced level, you'll be able to notice and watch emotions—the energy attached to thoughts—while you're meditating, but that's black belt stuff. To begin with, you're probably going to do this more in your daily life than in your meditations. For now, let's stay on the ground. Let's get to the point where you can notice when you're experiencing an emotion, even if you're already acting it out—just as you've learned to do with your thoughts.

At the risk of overstating it, when you can do this, you'll discover that getting rid of uncomfortable emotions is neither possible nor useful. In fact, it works against you. This is because all emotions—even the uncomfortable ones—play an important role in your life: they provide you with important information. When you learn to read that information, you can take the same energy and use it mindfully, directing it into a constructive purpose. Read on and you'll see what this means.

THE SCIENCE

When Psychology Met Mindfulness

THE FIELD of psychology has developed along two broad, but distinct, paths: one that speculated on the inner workings—or ramblings—of the mind, and one that looked primarily at external behaviours that could be measured. We can put Freud and Jung, both of whom talked about dreams and the subconscious, in the former category and Pavlov, who famously trained dogs to salivate at the sound of a bell, Watson and Skinner, who experimented with rats, in the latter.

While both approaches are valid, the one that focused on external behaviours—known, unsurprisingly, as behaviourism—lent itself more easily to scientific study. Changes in behaviour as a result of a particular intervention, for example, giving a food pellet to a rat, or a sweet to a child, can be objectively measured and peer-reviewed.

It's much more difficult—if not impossible—to scientifically verify the progress of a person as they go through psychoanalysis. The outcomes are too nebulous and, in any case, any study would rely on the person reporting on their own progress. That's like relying on an unsupervised worker to be honest about how they've spent their day: highly unreliable from a scientific point of view.

The problem with behaviourism, however, is that human beings do have a linguistic framework—and therefore a more complex inner life—than animals. The thoughts and feelings that make up this inner life do influence outcomes and so a way was needed to access that black box—a way that could be measured.

The field of cognitive therapy emerged as an answer to this problem. It was developed primarily by American psychiatrist Aaron Beck, who noticed what he termed "automatic thoughts" in his clients' and in his own mind. These are the thoughts that arise constantly in your mind—the same thoughts you learned to observe in Section A—and which you can recognise and act upon.

For example, if somebody tells you that your anxiety—and consequent inability to go out at night—is being caused by your fear of sunsets, you can look and see that, in fact, it's being caused by your fear of meeting new people. With the right guidance, you can then make the necessary adjustments and change the behaviour.

Freud, on the other hand, would have insisted that the anxiety was being driven entirely by an "unconscious" urge, like guilt over your secret desire to have sex, and that you as the client simply can't see or have access to those urges. You would have needed to listen to your therapist and accept what you were told about your own "unconscious" urges. Anything you said otherwise would simply have been brushed off as denial or resistance.

Beck's approach—and he was supported by others, like Albert Ellis, Arnold Lazarus and David Barlow—gave people some credit for being able to look into and know their own minds, at least to a degree, and to be able to work effectively with what they found there. You can liken this to being able to see to the horizon from wherever you are on earth right now—you can't see the whole earth, but you can see a fair bit; enough to function and make good decisions, which is all you need.

This evolution of the psychological model meant that, instead of just applying external stimuli to see what happens to the external behaviour, scientists could now work more objectively at a subtler level, at the level of ideas (beliefs, thoughts, cognitions) within the mind. They could apply an idea to a belief and see what behavioural outcome happened as a result. And they could standardise the treatment and measure it across multiple clients in a way that stood up to scientific standards.

Cognitive behaviour therapy (CBT) is the branch of psychology that has evolved out of the work of Beck, and those who followed him.

It's referred to as an "evidence-based" approach and can be applied with great effectiveness to managing extreme clinical states of emotion which have become disorders—such as Generalised Anxiety Disorder, Major Depression and others.

In practice, this means that CBT can be used to diagnose and treat an emotional disorder like anxiety, social phobia, OCD, addiction and even depression, within a finite number of sessions. It makes a noticeable difference to actual, observable behaviours, and it can get a person back on their feet without having to go through an interminable process of endless self-reflection.

Until recently, the emphasis in CBT treatments was on cognitions (your thoughts and beliefs) and behaviours (habits, habitual responses). It was not until the last few years that the role and function of emotion in the development and maintenance of these disorders became emphasised.

This followed the introduction of the Unified Protocol (UP) by David Barlow, who is widely recognised as one of CBT's modern flagbearers and thought leaders. The UP introduces the concept of emotion-driven behaviours (EDB's) as key to understanding and managing all of the mood, anxiety and addiction disorders. Insight into the nature and function of emotion, the value in grounding yourself during periods of intense emotion, as well as how to regulate your emotions across a range of contexts, is now central to CBT treatment programmes.

In addition, these same behaviourists have come to recognise the importance of mindfulness in supporting people to accelerate their treatment even further. Awareness of thoughts, or cognitions, is naturally key to being able to work with them. Being present in the moment and nonjudgemental enables you to focus your attention on what's real, instead of what's not, and thereby gather better evidence about your reality. Naturally that can make a big difference to conditions like depression, anxiety, phobias, OCD. For example, mindful awareness helps to reduce the ruminating that comes with depression and being nonjudgemental, or objective, helps to reduce the catastrophising that accompanies anxiety. These mindfulness key elements all contribute to—and accelerate—the CBT process, which similarly results in being nonreactive.

Colinda is a practising clinical psychologist who has specialised in CBT for the past 25 years. To hear it from her: "I've experienced first-hand the value of CBT in getting to grips with dysfunctional thought patterns and behaviours. Having added the UP to my repertoire over the past three years, I've been pleasantly surprised—and, at times, astonished—at what a difference it makes when emotion (and its regulation) is directly addressed. The effect is exponential when you add mindfulness."

KEY CONCEPT – TAKE NOTE

The Function of Emotions

EMOTIONS ARE not necessarily bad or dangerous, although they can sometimes feel that way. As Barlow points out, "You need the full range of emotions—'good' and 'bad'—to be able to function in the world."

Imagine if you had no emotions, you would be like a robot, without any emotional ups and downs. You may say you'd like that, but if you had it, you might soon change your mind. Life would be a monotonous hum. In addition, you'd struggle to make decisions and the ones you did make would be without context or meaning. Later on, in Chapter 8, which deals with complexity & decision-making, we'll go into this in more detail.

Or what if you only had the "good" emotions? Without the physical pain of a toothache, you wouldn't know you had a problem and you'd end up without teeth much sooner than you'd like. Similarly, without fear, you wouldn't know if your life was in danger. Without anger, you wouldn't know that you need to stand up for yourself.

You sometimes see this in people who are overly positive in their outlook: they remain far too long in situations that are not good for them because they keep rationalising the situation. "Everything will be OK," they say, "I just need to do X, Y or Z." Or they make excuses for the other person in the relationship who is not pulling their weight. Often, what's really going on is that the person is trying to hold onto the "good" and avoid the "bad" emotions. (Their underlying judgement may be that they don't want to be seen as a negative person—that, for them, would be *bad*.)

You can see that your emotions tell you important things about the world. To paraphrase Barlow, they help you to navigate it and motivate you to act in ways that are adaptive—and, in some cases, necessary—for your wellbeing, even your survival. In the case of the overly positive person mentioned above, that person might benefit from recognising their frustration or anger and allowing it into their life. With mindfulness, they'd hopefully be able to channel it in a constructive, purposeful way, for example by making some requests or setting some boundaries.

The problem arises when you're not able to separate out what the emotion is trying to tell you—its message—from the experience of the emotion. You're not taught this in school and there are no formal training programs, except perhaps some leadership programs. Without this awareness, you have no choice but to *become* the emotion, to *become* the weather.

A good analogy is your email inbox. What do you do when you receive a message with an attachment? You could save the attachment in a folder for easy access later and delete or archive the message to save disk space. Most people just leave it. If you do leave it, your computer will slow down because of all the unnecessary data and you'll have to do long, clumsy searches for information when you need it. When you hold onto your emotions instead of dealing with their messages, your consciousness becomes cluttered and slowed up in the same way. It becomes harder to make decisions. We'll talk about this some more in the next chapter, which is about dealing with stress and building resilience.

Of course, there are those people who identify strongly with their emotions, and with being emotional. They like to feel their feelings intensely and to express them overtly. If you're that person, you might be ready to stop reading right now. Or, perhaps you know someone like that who you hope will read this, but you know they won't want to give up their rich emotional life.

The simple response to this dilemma is this: although you may believe that you're choosing your emotions, you're not. Your emotions are choosing you. Your proof is that as much as you try to hold onto the good ones, you can't; you also get swamped by the bad ones. Therefore, your emotions, and not you, are running your life. How long do you want that to go on for? Getting ahead of your emotions doesn't mean you won't feel anything ever again. It means you'll have some choice and freedom around what you feel and for how long, and how you act in response to them.

Interested? Let's move on and find out: what are the messages in the different emotions and how do you read them?

Being Nonjudgemental | Reading the Message in the Emotion

What can you do about an emotion, once you've become aware of it? Once you've recognised that you're experiencing an emotion, the next step is to be cognisant of the judgements that you have about the emotion itself.

Consider for a moment the type of relationship you usually have with emotion. Usually, you unconsciously label each emotion as *good / bad, right / wrong, like / don't like*, and you want to experience the good ones, while avoiding the bad. What this means in practice is that you spend your efforts either trying to stretch out the good emotions or turn the bad ones into good ones by resolving them.

For example, you try to stretch the party out for as long as possible. Or you nurse the anger or sadness in the hope that you can make it better—you can spend days having that argument in your head, looking for someone to blame, making sure somebody pays, or plotting revenge. Usually, this doesn't get rid of the emotion, it only makes it worse, as your own reactions lead to further reactions from the outside, and you enter a vicious cycle.

The upshot is that either way—whether you see the emotions as good or bad— you tend to hold onto them and even get lost in them. Remember the clouds in the sky? You can become distracted by thoughts within your mind, but when it comes to emotion you get carried away—you *become* the emotion, you *become* the weather.

So, what new type of relationship can you have with emotion? Since emotions are driven and sustained by judgement, it would make sense to establish a relationship with emotion that is nonjudgemental. As Barlow points out, "By learning to observe how our emotional experiences are unfolding, accepting *without judgement* that our initial emotional reactions are sending us a signal that something is occurring that may or may not be important to us, we become able to stop the vicious cycle of interacting thoughts feelings and behaviour before it has a chance to run away with us."

A starting point would be to see that emotions are just energy in motion. Without a label or judgement attached, they are neutral, neither good nor bad. There is no need for them to lead to a reaction. Think about it like this: if somebody shouts a warning at you that a car is about to run you over, do you go tell them they've been rude, or do you thank them? There's your clue about how you could treat emotions. You could take the message, say thanks, and move on!

If you're struggling to accept that emotions are neutral, neither good nor bad, then read on. The examples below might illustrate this for you in a way that works.

Example #1 | Anxiety

Anxiety is an uncomfortable emotion that you probably don't want to experience. Yet, feeling anxious is useful. It puts your body and mind into a vigilant state so you can assess whatever threat may exist out there—and prepare to deal with it.

For example, if you have an important presentation coming up, you would start to think about it and may even become anxious as the date approaches. The anxious feeling tells you that it's time to prepare. If you take the message, instead of wasting energy trying to distract yourself or get rid of the emotion, you will do just that. You might even rehearse with a friend to make sure you're ready.

On the day of the presentation, that anxiety may get you up earlier, lead you to dress with care and go over your presentation once more. That, in turn, reminds you to check certain facts, which might turn out to be crucial.

Here you can use awareness after the fact to see that the uncomfortable feeling of anxiety served a clear purpose—it motivated you to think about a future event in a functional way; it got you to focus your attention on the relevant tasks, and to prepare adequately and with enough time to fill in the gaps that you found.

If, instead, you had tried to drive away the anxiety by distracting yourself, then preparing at the last minute, you would probably have caused yourself—and others—even more, unnecessary, stress. Your quality may have suffered, too. When challenged by your boss, as to why you hadn't prepared, you may then have tried to defend yourself. Reactivity drives further reactivity. You move further away from being authentic or effective.

It's also important to note that anxiety is a response to a future threat, and at times such threats can be more perceived than real. Whether the threat is real, perceived or a combination, anxiety does bring attention onto what you perceive as the threat. When you take the message, it enables you to decide which elements, if any, you need to focus on in order to prepare for it.

Example #2 | Anger

Let's take another uncomfortable emotion—anger. This emotion is a natural response to when you feel you've been harmed, mistreated or victimised in some way. The call to action (which arises out of the message in the emotion) is to defend yourself, a loved one, or a boundary that has been violated.

Imagine you discover that you have been overcharged for your internet subscription/ rent / a monthly expense, and that it has been going on for a long time. When you attempt to get your money refunded, you get told by the call centre agent that it's too late to query it now, you just need to accept that you were overcharged.

Anger can be used to give you energy to become assertive, and even demand to speak to a manager in order to be refunded and for the mistake to be rectified. It doesn't mean you have to shout or be rude. In the same way that a fire can be contained, instead of getting out of control, you can use your anger to fuel your determination to be heard, to have the issue addressed, to not give up—and sometimes you do need to know when to give up, especially if not doing so means you will explode!

So, anger can be useful in that it alerts you to when someone has treated you unfairly or unjustly and helps you to channel your energy into expressing this as well as getting it resolved.

PRACTICAL EXERCISE – DO THIS NOW

Find the Message in the Emotion

MAKE A list of the emotions you are currently experiencing (or the last few times you experienced a strong emotion).

Use the list in the Practice – Save For Later *section later in this chapter if you need some ideas or direction.*

Name the emotion.

Ask yourself what the message is inside that emotion.

Once you've identified the message, see if you can find the related question that implies an action. Don't complicate the matter. Use the ones in the table below as a guide.

Now answer that question by making a decision to take the necessary action.

As you can see from the previous examples, as well as from having done the above exercise, the message in the emotion can always be expressed as a *call to action*. Remember, emotions are energy in motion. They put things in motion. They cause you to act. By being mindfully aware and then nonjudgemental, you are not suppressing the emotion in a way that means not taking action. You are mindfully, consciously *redirecting* the energy to fuel a *different* action. Hence, the promise of this book and program that you can have a *different*, better experience of life.

PRACTICE - SAVE FOR LATER

Key Emotions and their Messages

Here are six key emotions and their related messages and calls to action, which you can use as a checklist:

Emotion	Message	Call to Action
Anger	A boundary has been violated.	*What boundaries do I need to set?* *How can I act assertively and not aggressively?* *How can I channel this anger into a constructive action?*
Anxiety	There's a future threat, real or imagined.	*Is this threat real? If so, do I fight or flight?* *Is this threat imagined (perceived)? If so, how can I ground myself in reality? What plan do I need to make?*
Frustration	Things are not going my way.	*What do I need in this situation and who do I need to ask?* *What reality am I not accepting about the situation?*
Sadness	I've been hurt / wounded / disappointed.	*Do I need support?* *Do I need to withdraw for a while and regroup?*
Guilt	Have I wronged someone?	*Is there any part of what happened that I need to correct or atone for?*
Joy	Things are going my way.	*Who can I share this with?* *What good can I do with this energy?*

Hopefully you're convinced that emotions have an important function, that they are neutral, that they are messengers that tell you important things about your world. Hopefully, too, you've managed to read a few of those messages and convert them into new, different actions. If not, it may be wise to take some more time at this stage to explore this. Try it on with some "easy" emotions and see what you can identify. Start to build a case with real evidence that you can take the same energy and use it constructively, rather than being used by it—that you can respond instead of react.

To summarise, the important thing to know about emotions is:

- Emotions are neither good nor bad, they are neutral;
- Emotions have a function: they are messengers, they tell you important things about your world;
- The message always contains or implies a *call to action*. You need to decipher the message, and the call to action, then act mindfully in the chosen direction.

REAL-LIFE EXAMPLE

Turning Anger into Passion

ANGER IS an emotion that has generally received a bad rap. We teach children from an early age to not be angry, and rightfully so. However, we also throw the baby out with the bathwater, in that we end up not learning how to manage and direct our anger, which is very closely aligned to our life force energy.

If you think of fire, or nuclear energy, it can be used destructively, or constructively. The energy that underlies anger is also neutral, until it gets applied to a constructive or destructive purpose.

The energy that gets released with anger is very powerful. Consider how charged you feel when you're angry. If you can take that same energy and put it to good use, like motivating yourself to go to gym, or finish writing that report, or that book, wouldn't that be useful?

During my coach training, we learned to consciously generate and moderate our anger. At first, the exercise we used was a fictional setting and the anger we generated was the typical reactive anger that we all know.

As we progressed through the program, we learned to generate that same anger consciously, by means of a simple decision, and to use it, for example, to power up your enthusiasm for making a presentation. Like an actor, we learned to turn it on and turn it off, at will. We called this process "turning anger into passion".

This experience showed me that the energy underlying emotions is: (a) real; (b) powerful; (c) neutral; (d) abundant; and (e) available to be used for conscious purposes, if applied mindfully.

Of course, I made all sorts of mistakes when I started out on the journey. I sometimes raised my anger at inappropriate times and scared people. I quickly learned not to do that.

I also noticed that I was very good at turning anger on myself in the form of self-criticism. When I realised this and started to use anger to defend myself instead of attack myself, it initially felt quite wrong, even dangerous. I realised that I had developed some bad habits with regards to my emotions.

As I progressed, I learned to recognise that anger was a useful indicator that a boundary had been crossed and that I needed to defend myself, rather than just agreeing to stupid stuff or turning it on myself. I also learned that it provided fuel for me to honour my commitments, for example, when I said I was going to gym, or that I'd get back to somebody, I could call on that same neutral energy that underlies anger, and get it done.

This became a self-generating cycle and raised my overall level of energy and performance. At times I surprised myself by what I was capable of doing, just by mindfully using this energy.

If you're still here, perhaps you're ready to deal with those stronger emotions, the ones that have you in their grip, that keep recurring and which you seem unable to master.

Please note, if the recurrence of an emotion interferes with your ability to function effectively in your daily life, it could be classified as an emotional disorder. If you're experiencing extreme anxiety, phobias, panic attacks, sleep dysfunction or OCD then you should seek help, probably with a CBT therapist. You can continue to use this book and program in parallel, and it will provide the "salt in the mix" for that treatment.

If, on the other hand, you don't have an emotional disorder that interferes with your daily life, but you do often act in ways that are not in the best interests of yourself or others—and those behaviours are driven by strong emotions, or by the absence of emotions, then it may be time to look deeper. The trigger is likely to be in the judgement (preference) that underlies the feeling, and whether there's a strong *me / my / mine* element to the situation.

These recurring patterns usually point to strongly held values and beliefs, or defence mechanisms. When that's the case, then for all the world, you can't see how you could possibly shift those. For example, if you're consistently beating people up for poor performance, and hence losing staff, or losing your connection with your staff, you're probably going to ask, "Why should I lower my standards?" To do that, it seems, would be like death—the end of your career, the end of your business. Yet, there is a way of finding an integrated solution that does not mean dying, or even giving up your standards.

Later in this chapter we'll deal with one aspect of this problem—defence mechanisms—when you read about the "red zone". In Chapter 8: Complexity & Decision-Making, we'll deal with values and beliefs. Engage with those sections and then return to applying the practice of being nonjudgemental to those stronger, recurring emotions. You'll find you have a better chance of dealing with them once you've accessed those deeper layers.

 ## Being Nonreactive | Being with "What Is" & Focusing on What Matters

As you know by now, the primary indicator of being nonreactive (i.e. responding) is that you have choice. In other words, you know that you are being nonreactive when, even though you've been emotionally triggered, you can see more than one option for how to act, and you choose the one that is most realistic, relevant and/or productive instead of destructive.

For example, you hear that someone has said something negative about you. Instead of jumping in to defend yourself, you choose to find out the truth from them first. Your action is based on a deliberate, mindful choice, the options for which became available to you as a result of the gap you created by being aware, and the objectivity you activated by being nonjudgemental.

When you're nonreactive, says Barlow, you "respond to [your] experiences in a more thoughtful, realistic way, rather than through knee-jerk reactions". There are two key words in that sentence: thoughtful, and realistic. Let's unpack them.

First let's look at thoughtfulness. It's clear that being aware creates space for thoughtfulness to occur: that moment when you are considering your options.

Some people are afraid of silences, or those still, quiet moments, and some believe that to not act immediately—*read: reactively*—is a sign of weakness. If this is you, then you may need to reframe that. Consider the possibility that being temperate is a sign of wisdom, not weakness. In the old days, this was expressed more simply, as, "Count to ten," and, "If you're not sure, rather walk away." There is no weakness in that, and most situations are better dealt with when one is calm and has had time to think. Most situations, as we've seen and will see some more, take care of themselves when you do that.

All that said, this thoughtful moment also doesn't have to take a long time. To someone on the outside, you may hesitate for only a few seconds, and then you decide, and act. When you've developed a level of personal mastery it can be instant.

As with any learning process, it may start slowly and clumsily. This is not a reason to give up. A baby has to fall many times before it can walk, and it doesn't give up. The response time from reactivity to becoming aware becomes exponentially shorter the more you do it—and, says science, the more you practice certain meditations. Similarly, your ability to move through a nonjudgemental assessment of the situation, to read the message in the emotion, and then choose your response, becomes shorter with practice.

When you're well ahead of yourself, your mindful response can flow as naturally as your primary reaction might have done. That's called transformation, when you've become a wholly more mindful, more conscious, person.

Now let's look at Barlow's use of the term realistic, and how that applies. Remember in the introduction, one of the benefits of mindfulness was given as being able to make decisions based on what matters. According to Barlow, it's only when you're being mindful that you can begin to "distinguish between … an accurate reflection of what is going on in [your] world … and what is a false alarm".

For example, if you've had a bad experience on a train in the past, it doesn't mean it's going to happen every time you go on a train. It's not a reason to fear trains, and being mindfully aware and nonjudgemental enables you to assess the situation objectively and see that.

Or, let's say that you as a manager picked up a problem with the stock register instead of one of your employees picking it up. That doesn't necessarily mean that there's a problem or that they're incompetent. It might just mean that you were present enough in your business—so well done to you—that you were in the right place at the right time, and thank goodness you picked it up. The only way you could reach this conclusion—presuming it's the right one in this instance—would be if you were able to look at the situation as it is, instead of through the lens of something that happened in the past, or something you fear might happen in the future. Once you've assessed the situation objectively, you might decide that there's nothing that needs to be said, or done.

"The fact is that our moment-to-moment judgements about, and responses to, our emotions often have very little to do with what is actually going on right now," says Barlow. "Instead, our reactions to our emotions are oftentimes rooted in what has happened in the past, or what we think might happen in the future." Does that sound familiar? That's the state of reactivity, and reactivity fuels more reactivity. You become less authentic, less present, less effective. It's a downward spiral. Barlow calls it "a vicious cycle of interacting negative thoughts, behaviours, and feelings that are serving to intensify, heighten, or even worsen your experience".

Conversely, he says, "The only way [you] can determine whether ongoing emotional responses are an accurate reflection of current situational demands or needs, is to anchor [your] awareness within the present context." You can see that the opposite—let's call it an upward—spiral is that of being aware, being nonjudgemental, and being nonreactive.

Barlow refers to this as a skill, which is good news. That means it can be learned, practiced and improved. He likens the process of being mindfully aware and nonjudgemental to "using a time-lapse camera to better understand how your emotional responses unfold ... stepping out of your experience and observing your responses as they are happening moment by moment [to] get a much better sense of where you might be leading yourself astray ... [and] to determine how you should respond given the current circumstances".

He also points out that "this focus on the present moment also allows you to take new information in, and learn new associations with your emotions (e.g., feeling fear does not always mean you are in danger), ... [to] become fully rooted in present reality, and the choices that are available to you right now. Only then can you allow new learning and new reactions [responses] ... to occur."

One of the risks with any skill is that you can become complacent. Usually, when that happens, you take your foot off the gas, you slack off a bit. In the case of being nonreactive, that would mean believing, even insisting, that you're being nonreactive, when in fact you've gone back to old ways, and you're using the language of mindfulness to justify and explain your reactions. Don't laugh, this happens, a lot!

The first indicator that you're exercising this capacity to be nonreactive with regards to your emotions is, firstly, that your reactions have become considered responses. They're more likely to take into account—and benefit—the greater good, rather than being designed to defend yourself or get what you want at all costs. The second indicator, and perhaps the better test for complacency, is that you're not reacting in the same way every time. Your responses have become more nuanced, more relevant to the situation, and less about you, your fears, your concerns.

Perhaps the best indicator that you're being consistently and authentically nonreactive with regards to your emotional responses, is that you'll be having a very different, much better, experience of life. Instead of the energy of emotions taking you over and using you for destructive means, you'll be converting and using that same energy for constructive purposes. In other words, you'll feel consistently more positive and motivated.

In the next section, called The Red Zone, you'll be introduced to an important concept that is bound to come up for you as a potential obstacle to your application of the three key elements of mindfulness that you've learned above. So, read on—and pay attention!

KEY CONCEPT – TAKE NOTE

The Red Zone

WHEN YOU have people working or living together, sooner or later you're going to get somebody treating something like it's the end of the world. When this happens, you literally say that to them: "It's not the end of the world." Often, to calm your children down, you might say: "You won't die."

This language is quite apt. It addresses what's literally going on in the body, and then in the mind. If the fear is one of life-or-death, even if only in the mind, then treating it quite literally as a life-or-death matter may be the most direct and effective method to break the reactive spiral. Let's see how this works.

Firstly, you've seen, based on Barlow's comments, that you can have a maladaptive emotional reaction based on things that are not real. For example, you fear that you're going to have another panic attack in the mall, just because the first one you had was also in a mall.

You know that emotions are messengers and so you can say that the emotion that protected you, and was useful when you first experienced it, is no longer useful.

It's not relevant to the situation, but you're not seeing that because you're not being present, aware and nonjudgemental. You're hooked in to your mental and emotional activity. You've *become* the weather. You're in a reactivity spiral.

Secondly, as you've seen, your body doesn't distinguish between thought and reality. You can have a very visceral expression of emotion, even when you're just watching a movie.

Thirdly, if you refer back to the information about the amygdala hijack, you can see that there are indeed situations where your body literally tells your mind that you might be in danger of death—or, put differently, that it may be the end of (your) world.

If you combine these three notions, you can see that an external event can trigger, not just your emotions, but your deepest survival instinct, even if only psychologically, and this puts you into fight-or-flight mode. For example, you fear that making a mistake will get you into such trouble—because that's how it was when you were a kid—that you'll lose your job and your life will be over. Specifically, your mind goes directly, all the way, to "life-or-death", without passing begin, without collecting any cash—without any possibility of awareness.

We can explain how the mind develops these life-or-death (fight-or-flight) scenarios through a number of lenses—neuroscience, behaviourism and ontology (the philosophical study of the nature of being):

1. **Neuroscience** Anything that you do often enough, the brain recognises and decides, "This must be necessary for survival." It sets up stable neural pathways that support that behaviour as an automated function, so that you can do it in an emergency. For example, learning to drive a car. It becomes so automatic that you can text and drive. Only joking, we hope you don't do that, but you get the point.

2. **Behaviourism** When you're a young child, there is usually some balance between reward and punishment. For some the punishment is mild; for others, it's severe. Either way, there's a threat that lies beyond awareness: you're totally dependent on your family for your survival. If you break the rules of that family, you surmise, it could have dangerous consequences, because if you get kicked out, you're not able to look after yourself. Fitting in becomes a life-or-death matter. That's the equation that happens in your juvenile brain, without you even realising it.

3. **Ontology** You saw in Chapter 5 that you did not create an ego for yourself. Yet, you find yourself with one. You experience your ego as though it's yours, as though you created it and as though you're choosing it from

> moment to moment, and yet an ontological enquiry (an enquiry into the nature of being) will show you that it's more like a monster on your back. It took residence like some kind of squatter or parasitic entity; it grew by feeding you its ideas, and now it uses you for its survival. For one good reference on this, read *The Voice of Knowledge* by Don Miguel Ruiz.
>
> The important point here is that your ego would rather have you die, than die itself. The ultimate proof of this is suicide: your ego would rather tell you to kill yourself than live with life not being the way your ego tells you it should be. It doesn't have to be that extreme either. Your ego would rather have you work yourself to death, or drink yourself to death, or give up your life for a religious belief, than throw off its yoke by changing what you believe about yourself and life. It's that powerful.

The nett effect is that when your ego becomes identified with something, it usually shows up as something you're willing to give your life for. For example, a man who becomes strongly identified with his career—or the money and/or status that he derives from it—will literally work himself to death for the sake of that career/money/status. If he loses it, say in a stock market crash, he may commit suicide. He'd rather be dead than not be that guy. A woman who becomes strongly identified with being a good mother may give up her life—in the form of never doing anything for herself—to serve her children. A person who is strongly identified with their country or religion may demonstrate that by being willing to die for that cause.

In all of the above, you can see this theme of life and death, which gets established at a psychological level. This life-or-death scenario exists because your brain treats something like it's a life-or-death matter and stores it for future reference. When that button gets pushed by a situation that has similar attributes, you start treating that situation like it's the end of the world—even when, in fact, it's not. It might be important, but it's not life-or-death. It's not the end of the world.

It's easy to see this when a small child doesn't get what they want: they cry like it's the end of the world. It also happens, for example, when an adult sees, or gets asked to do, something that challenges their identity to the core. They treat it, quite literally, like it's the end of (their) world.

Let's look at some examples.

Let's say that *not* breaking the rules was important in your family system when you were a child. You'd have learned very quickly to not cross that line—you'd have learned it as though your life depended on it, because that's how it would have seemed at that age.

Now let's say that for someone else, representing the family in the right way, looking the part, performing well, always coming first, was the important thing in their family system. They'd have learned very quickly to behave in that way—once again, they'd have learned it believing that their life depended on always winning, succeeding and looking the part.

In both scenarios, when you followed the rules, or when that other kid came first, you might each have gained recognition and reward—no guarantees. But certainly, at the very least, it would have kept you both out of trouble—and that, you would have calculated, kept you alive.

You'd probably have put a positive spin on that behaviour when you took it out into the world. So, you went to school, and you followed the rules, and that got you recognition and reward. Alternatively, that other kid shone the way their family system liked them to—they won at everything, no matter what it took. Well, that also got them recognition and reward.

> *I've literally heard my clients say this: "I'm afraid that if I give in, I'll lose my job, my children will suffer, and I'll die."*

Now let's say you both became lawyers. You might be the one who's a stickler for being ethical and following the rules. You would sometimes give up winning in order to abide by the law. However, the other one might eschew such details for the sake of winning at all costs.

You can see the types of arguments that these two might have, even—or especially—if they were in the same team, representing the same client.

If you were the person for whom not breaking the rules seemed to be a life-or-death matter as a child, you might freak out at the suggestion that you cut corners or bend the rules in order to win. *No,* you would say, *we must follow the rules! We must do what's right!*

This is where the amygdala hijack happens. For you to go against your conditioning and your inherited values in this way is experienced as a life-threatening situation. I've literally heard clients say this: "I'm afraid that if I give in, I'll lose my job, my children will suffer, and I'll die."

For the other person, the same thing is happening. He or she is also re-experiencing their childhood, where winning—they believed—was what kept them alive because it kept them functioning within the family system.

Both parties get locked in a fight to be right, to win, to get their way. Neither one realises that the only reason why they have that fear—and that particular focus of attention—in the first place is because that's what they developed a radar for when they were five years old.

Neither one wants to give up their position, because that bears the threat of death for them. The amygdala hijack is fully active. Their executive function has shut down. They are in a purely reactive state. Neither one is exercising any choice.

Being unable to choose, or even think rationally, both parties are unable to treat the situation as it is. They're acting—or reacting—based on who they are, through the lens of their own fear, which their mind is experiencing as a fear of death, or the end of the world. They are not acting based on the situation.

Perhaps in one instance, the first party could accept cutting corners and bending a few rules for the sake of making the deadline—we're not advocating that you go as far as being unethical, just that you learn to be flexible where reality allows, that you treat the situation as it is, not as you are. Perhaps in another instance, there are no rules to bend and the other person must accept that they simply cannot win this time around. Each situation is unique and deserves a unique approach.

At the end of the day, they could choose either route, and it may work, or it may not. The bottom line is, they would not die. It would not be the end of the world. In fact, even the worst-case scenario that people fear when they're reacting like this is most unlikely to happen. Even if it did, they would pick themselves up and continue.

Now we're not advocating that you become blasé, or careless. We're not saying you should do anything recklessly, or even less than your best. For the most part, your desire to follow the rules, or the other person's desire to win, helps you both to produce good results in the world. Where it becomes a problem is when either of you gets into the red zone, which is when your mind is treating the situation as though it was something else from the past, and you have that amygdala hijack.

In those moments, you lose touch with reality. You don't make good decisions. You may even do or say things you'll regret.

Now let's look at what you can do about it.

Exiting The Red Zone

We've already presented the idea that when you're being reactive—and especially when you're in the red zone—you're the last one to know. Everyone else can see it, except you. It's like you've gone to sleep on your ability to self-manage. When that happens, you need an alarm clock, one that will activate self-awareness.

Your alarm clock is to (a) know what triggers your red zone reaction and (b) recognise your particular behaviours or cognitions that show up when you're in the red zone.

Being Aware: Red Zone Triggers

Your red zone gets triggered when you feel forced to do something you don't want to do, either because it's against what you see as your core personality, or because it's against your priority of values. Below are two fairly comprehensive lists, one for each category just mentioned—personality and values.

A. Core Personality

Your red zone might get triggered when you're expected to participate in a project or activity that rubs up against your core personality because:

1. Key Factor: Control

    a) It's not under your control;

    b) It's too boring or there are too many rules;

    c) It's likely to fail or damage your reputation.

2. Key Factor: Rules & Standards

    a) It's unethical, noncompliant, or of a poor standard;

    b) It's unkind or inconsiderate of others;

    c) It's too risky and/or there's not enough information.

3. Key Factor: Other People

    a) It's noisy, silly, mundane, meaningless;

    b) It's outside your area of specialisation or you haven't had time to prepare;

    c) It's too noisy, busy, aggressive, or conflictual.

B. Priority of Values

Your red zone might get triggered when someone expects you to participate in or support a project or activity that rubs up against your priority of values because:

1. It's a family or social event and you feel it's time to work or study;

2. It's a work obligation when you believe it's time for family / sport / leisure;

3. It involves spending money on something that you think is not important;

4. It goes against your strong spiritual or ethical beliefs;

5. It's plain dumb, stupid, and doesn't involve learning.

Having read those lists, you've probably recognised some as being more familiar to your personal experience than others. Below is an exercise to support you to discover your personal red zone trigger.

PRACTICAL EXERCISE – DO THIS NOW

Identify Your Red Zone Trigger

REFER TO the two lists above and complete the steps below in order to identify your personal red zone trigger. You may identify more than one.

Step 1 Think of the last time you overreacted by getting angry (asserting yourself) or avoiding something (withdrawing or running away). This is especially easy if someone told you, while you were having that reaction, that it's not the end of the world.

Step 2 Refer to the two lists above and identify what *really* pushed your buttons in that situation. If you're struggling, spend some time with it, perhaps ask a few people who know you well—especially someone who has witnessed you in those situations.

Step 3 When you've identified your red zone trigger, write it down in the box below. If you can't get it exactly then write down what you think it is and look out for it the next time. Or, once again, ask someone who knows you well.

My Red Zone Trigger(s)

Now that you know what your red zone trigger is, let's move on to what behaviours show up when you're in the red zone. We'll call these your *red zone indicators*, because they'll act as indicators that will support you to become aware of when you're in the red zone.

Being Aware: Red Zone Indicators

Your red zone indicators will usually be in three broad categories: being assertive or aggressive; being compliant; and being withdrawn. These are based on the work of psychologist Karen Horney, who defined these in the 1940s. You can read more in her two books on the subject: *Our Inner Conflicts* (1945) and *Neurosis and Human Growth* (1950).

Assertive or aggressive responses may involve making overt attempts to micro-manage and tell other people what to do in order to get things done a certain way—it's *your* way, or the highway. They may also involve trying to escape from a situation that is seen as being too boring or negative, or that you suspect is likely to fail and damage your reputation and so you want no part of it.

Compliant responses are likely to involve attempts to align with what's "right". This would probably involve the word *should*, whether you speak it or just think it. For example, you'll hear yourself thinking—or saying—that people *should* align to some or other rules or standards. Those may be ethical standards, quality standards, compliance standards, standards of care and kindness towards others, or levels of risk.

Withdrawn responses will probably involve less overt action and more retreating into thinking and feeling. This will most likely be triggered when you're asked to participate in something that you think is "beneath" you and which involves the hairy, hoary masses, all those "idiots" out there, all that "noise" and "trivia".

If you're doing any of these things in an extreme way—if you're doing them like it's the end of the world if you don't get your way, that's your red zone indicator. The more precisely you can identify your behaviour, and especially the things you think and say during those moments, the better it will act as an alarm clock so that you can become aware without having to wait for someone else to point it out to you, by which time the damage is already done.

In addition, you can support yourself by telling someone about your red zone trigger and sharing your red zone indicator—those behaviours that indicate when you're in the red zone. This should ideally be the people closest to you at home and at work! Then, give them permission to point it out to you when you're doing that thing—when you're in the red zone. Finally, and most importantly, agree to listen to them. You might also get them to agree that they can't use it against you!

Being Nonjudgemental & Nonreactive

When you recognise that you're in the red zone, your challenge is to let go of the strong preference you have for not giving in. Remember, your preference is so strong that your brain is telling you that you'll die, or that it'll be the end of the world—your world at least—if you're forced to do, or allow, whatever it is you're not wanting to do, or allow.

This is difficult, if not impossible, to do by addressing it directly through logic or understanding, because that's gone out the window. It's like that monster on your back has grown to epic proportions and is threatening you with your very life if you don't feed it.

The solution is to first apply the mindfulness practice of grounding and presencing yourself. The next step is to recognise that, no matter what happens, you won't die. This puts you in a position to let go of those judgements and attachments, and to treat the situation as it is, not as you are.

PRACTICE - SAVE FOR LATER

Exiting the Red Zone

THE STEPS for when you find yourself having a red zone reaction— or amygdala hijack—are as follows:

Step 1 Presence and ground yourself by doing the following:

a) Place yourself in space and time;

b) Look outside (actually look—your brain needs this) and see that the sky, the sun and the clouds are still in the sky and will still be there tomorrow;

c) Look at the room you are in: the floor, ceiling, walls, furniture. Walk over and touch them if you can. Notice how still everything is, and remind yourself that it'll still be there tomorrow;

d) Pay attention to your own body—your heartbeat, your breathing—and recognise that you're not doing any of that, it's just happening by itself. Remind yourself that it will still be happening tomorrow.

If these prove insufficient, you can also use the "crossing the bridge" exercises that will be introduced in the next chapter, i.e. Box Breathing and/or The Flop.

Step 2 Remind yourself that whatever happens in this situation, you won't actually die. It won't be the end of the world. It's just your mind treating it that way, but it's not a real threat. Your identity might suffer, but your body won't. Whatever happens, you'll live to fight another day.

Step 3 Now respond based on what's right and reasonable in the situation, not based on your fears about the situation. Sometimes, you may be right, and you should continue on your course of action; other times, you may need to move in the direction of your fear, relax your stance and take a different approach. For example: you may need to allow people to bend the rules, or lower the standards; you may need to allow people to miss the deadline; you may need to take the risk / speak up / wing it. In either case, you won't die. Unless you will, then don't do it!

When you've managed to successfully exit from the red zone and deal with a situation as it is, instead of as you are, then you'd be well advised to do that thing that human beings are so bad at, which is to gather objective evidence from your actual experience. This is important because the chances are good that you didn't get your way—and so some part of you will be feeling a bit miffed—and yet you survived. If you gather evidence according to that disappointed part of yourself, you'll see the whole exercise as a failure and, the next time, you'll just go into the red zone and do what you always did before.

So, instead of asking the question your identity wants to ask, which is, "Did it work?" or, more precisely, "Did I get my way?", you can ask yourself, "Did I (we) survive?" The answer is usually yes! Then you might ask, "What did I (we) learn?" You might also ask, "How did things turn out for the better, even if I don't like to admit it?"

By gathering the evidence that you survived, and acknowledging what you learned, you're addressing the problem as it exists erroneously in your mind—that it's a life-or-death matter—and you build a case for not falling victim to your red zone trigger in the future.

WHAT DIFFERENCE DOES IT MAKE?

THINK OF a tree. It can stand for hundreds of years. Yet a core part of its strength and durability is the fact that it can flex in the wind. Modern skyscrapers use this principle in that they are built with flexible steel so that the buildings can withstand high winds and earth tremors. Cars have been made safer with the introduction of crumple zones.

You'll notice that the suggested course of action above—for building a case against your red zone trigger—recommends breaking your core rule, or moving in the direction of your greatest fear. You literally fear that you'll die if you do that thing, because that's how it felt when you learned that behaviour—or, because of its sheer repetition, how the brain has stored it.

When you cross that line—when you allow yourself to do that thing that until now you have not allowed yourself to do, or not been able to do, because you thought you might die or the world would end—you enable yourself to become more flexible.

With greater flexibility, you will be able to treat each situation based on its own merits. You'll be a more integrated human being and you'll have more freedom of choice in different situations.

In addition, by identifying your red zone trigger you'll cut to the chase in terms of your primary behavioural driver. This can potentially save you years of therapy and psychological treatment—and, therefore, heaps of your hard-earned cash.

If you found it difficult to identify and work with your emotions and/or red zone trigger and phrase, know that you're not alone. It can be difficult—a bit like trying to catch a view of yourself in the mirror after you've moved. Like most people, you may not want to look at this dark side of yourself. It may feel uncomfortable, even unnatural. It may also be the case that you don't have massive emotional outbursts, that you're the quiet, even-tempered type. It may even be that you're the "kind", "generous" or "fun" person who's always happy and never wants to do harm, so how could you possibly have negative emotions, or a red zone?

If that's the case, take a step back and think again about the things you really don't like doing, or that you're really bad at, and which frustrate you. The things you wish weren't there in the world, whether in yourself or in others. Then think about what happens when you're forced to do, or to deal with, those things. Once you have them, then go back and try the exercise again.

Similarly, you might find that the practice of grounding yourself and telling yourself that it's not the end of the world seems trivial to you. You might tell yourself that this is silly and can't possibly work, that life is much more complicated than that. After all, your problems are more severe, more complex, and they require a psychologist and years of therapy.

That may be true in some instances. However, we're willing to bet that the voice that's telling you that is the voice of that monstrous ego that you read about in Chapter 5. It's the voice of that monster on your back that gets you into the red zone in the first place.

Of course, that monster doesn't want you to find a simple solution to ending its tyranny. It would much rather that you fed it every few days. The better question to ask yourself is, *Will I die if I don't have that monster on my back?* Hint: the answer is no; you might actually find a doorway to happiness, and a different, better experience of life.

CHAPTER SUMMARY

THIS CHAPTER looks at the application of mindfulness to emotion regulation. Key content includes:

- Emotions lead to action and can be broken down into e + motion = energy in motion.
- A phenomenological definition of emotions as energy attached to the thoughts you have.
- Exaggerated levels of energy, driven by overidentification with the label *me / my / mine*, leads to exaggerated actions.
- Like thoughts, emotions are like the clouds in the sky.
- Cognitive behaviour therapy (CBT) advocates that emotions are adaptive and necessary and should be treated as such.
- The CBT-based practice of reading the message in the emotion, with examples for six core emotions—anger, anxiety, sadness, frustration, guilt and joy.
- The primary benefit of being nonreactive with regards to your emotions is that you treat situations and make decisions based on what's real and what matters.
- The indicators of being nonreactive with regards to your emotions.
- How the two broad paths of the field of psychology— psychodynamic therapy and evidence-based behaviourism— converged in the form of cognitive therapy, and how mindfulness came to be incorporated in the latter.

- The defensive emotional state called the "Red Zone": a deeply reactive state when you treat something like it's life-or-death, or the end of the world, when in fact it's not.
- Tools for recognising when you're in the red zone.
- How to build a case against your red zone trigger so that you can become less reactive and more flexible.

7 | Stress & Resilience

THE GENERAL public view of mindfulness is that it's primarily as a tool for stress reduction. As you've seen from this book, it can be applied to a great many more aspects of your life—and it does have particular relevance to the experience of stress.

Notice we say the *experience* of stress. We say this for a number of reasons. Firstly, stress is not a *thing*, but something you *experience*. This is precisely why mindfulness is so relevant to the phenomenon—because a large part of mindfulness is about adapting or improving your relationship to, or with, reality.

The dictionary.com definition of the word *stress* is particularly interesting. As a pure noun, the first meaning is the "importance attached to a thing, eg. *to lay stress upon good manners*". As you'll see, that definition is very apt—those language inventors knew what they were doing!—when you consider the mindful approach to stress that will be proposed in this chapter: greater equanimity, or attaching less importance to the thing, or situation.

Of course, that's not the definition of stress as we usually refer to it. The one that applies to the human experience of stress goes: "physical, mental, or emotional strain or tension, eg. *Worry over his job and his wife's health put him under a great stress*". With this chapter you will:

- Gain an understanding of the key determinant of—and solution to—stress from a mindfulness perspective;
- Identify your own "red flags" for when you are entering the stress zone;
- Develop your ability to instantly reduce your experience of stress in any situation;
- Be able to identify and clear out one of the main causes of stress from your life and keep it clear.

The "What Is" of Stress

AS WITH anything in life, stress is not all bad. In fact, according to a statement from Colinda's doctoral thesis, "Physiologically, the complete absence of stress is equivalent to death." OK, so we're not going there. Instead, as Colinda is always quick to point out, what you're really driving towards is an optimal level of stress.

To quote her thesis—which measured stress and anxiety levels in cancer patients—again, "The aim … is to manage the degree of stress one encounters effectively, thereby functioning at an optimal level of arousal. Such a level would entail the individual being in balance, where stress is a positive resource versus a hindrance and precursor to illness."

That optimal level of functioning has been defined by Hans Selye, the scientist often considered to be the pioneer of stress research. It's defined as that point where stress, health and performance have all increased simultaneously and are at their peak. This may be seen as the positive phase of stress and is represented by the upward-sloping phase and topmost point of the graph in the related image. Finding and sustaining that optimal level, as you'll see in Chapter 9, results in a state of flow.

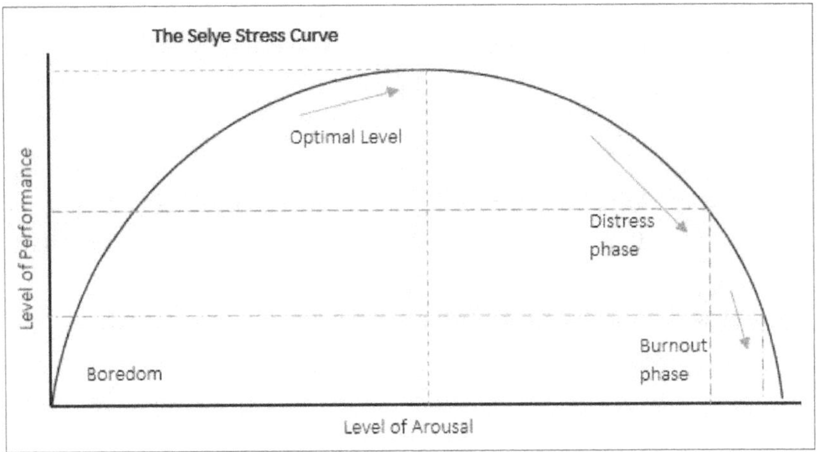

The distress phase occurs when stress continues to increase, but health and performance decrease. This is the negative phase of stress that ultimately leads to burnout.

Your position on the stress curve is dynamic and varies according to the nature of stresses encountered and coping resources you have available to you.

Each person has a unique tolerance for stress which is determined by their unique genetic and social background and related factors. Each person also encounters a unique set of internal and external stressors, and experiences stress in a different way.

KEY CONCEPT – TAKE NOTE

The Stress Equation: Demands v Resources

BEING ONE of the leading experts in her field on stress, Colinda has generously offered to share her Demands v Resources model with us here in this book.

If we refer to the definitions of stress—and if you look a little deeper into some of the other definitions—you find that stress is present when things are out of balance, in favour of an external force that's been exerted. In human terms, this happens when the many *demands* that are coming at us from so many sources exceed the available *resources*.

Demands would include, for example, the volume of tasks at work, multiple demands at home, like financial pressure, young children, a problem relationship, and a family member with a chronic illness, plus your own health and need for leisure and/or study time. If these were to occur all at once, that would equate to a high demand level.

The coping resources you might be able to draw on to deal with these demands would include things like: basic needs such as food and shelter being provided for; a strong support system including some combination of parent, sibling, friend and/or therapist; your own good health; a sense of humour; and so on.

When these two are in balance, the result is *coping*. However, the pace of modern life is intense. Often, the sheer quantity—and sometimes the scale—of external forces exceeds our capacity to deal with them. When demands are too high, or a resource is lost, or a combination of the two, you have the experience of *stress*.

Now let's unpack the balance—and sometimes imbalance—between demands and resources a little further.

THE SCIENCE

Chronic Stress and Mindfulness

THE IDEA that stress is the result, not of external events themselves, but of one's reaction to those events, is not just a fanciful philosophical notion. The leading scientists in the field have come to the same conclusion.

To once again quote from Colinda's thesis: "The stress response can … be understood as a process in which a stressful stimulus triggers a sequence of physiological events. Cognitive interpretations of the event can heighten the degree of response. … Such interpretations can maximise stimuli, misinterpret or mis-attribute meaning to them, and be causal in over-arousal and reactivity."

The human body is equipped to deal with acute (short-term, in-the-moment) stressful situations: it activates the fight-or-flight response. However, the effects of chronic (long-term, ongoing) stress are more dangerous to physical and mental health than are those of most acute stressors.

Chronic stress results in the release of a different range of stress hormones, which trickle out constantly over many months, and are being associated more and more with severe illnesses such as cancer, fibromyalgia, lupus and arthritis. There is also a relationship between chronic stress and depression.

It's important, therefore, to do something about chronic stress, even though it's the one we're most likely to ignore.

This is where the long-term practice of mindfulness comes in, as it develops and enhances your ability to distinguish what's real from what's not, and what matters from what does not. Practicing meditation also develops the ability to do a constant "reset" of your attention, so that you don't get drawn into unnecessary areas of focus that can unconsciously create tension, which is a symptom of stress. Instead, with meditation, you can train your mind to recognise the build-up of tension in your body and to consciously release that tension.

The Stress Equation: Demands

Typically, demands will be related to yourself and to others, and will feature in the following areas:

- Your health (physical, mental, emotional, spiritual);
- Your support system (emotional, practical);
- Your financial status (assets, debts, income, expenses);
- Your relationships (partner, friends, family, work); and

- Your work (formal job, in the home, studies).

Looked at along a different axis, demands can be acute (short-term), chronic (ongoing) and hassles (small individually, but taken together they mount up). Let's look at some examples.

Acute demands

Acute demands are usually short-term, intense, and out of the ordinary. These could be things like an injury, car accident, a sudden deadline, organizing an event or occasion, needing to make a large, especially unexpected, purchase or repair, or being ill.

Acute demands are often quite visible and it is easier to ask for, and find, support (resources) to help meet these demands.

Chronic demands

Chronic demands are ongoing. They will have been present for a longer time. They may even have become familiar and seem like they're just a part of life. Think of chronic health conditions, ongoing financial obligations and pressures, constant work stress such as limited staff but high expectation of delivery, sitting in peak-hour traffic daily.

The familiarity of these stressors means you are less likely to ask for support to deal with them. You may feel reluctant to ask for support, or you may tell yourself that "it's a part of life" and you should "get on with it and not make a fuss".

To illustrate the difference between acute and chronic stressors, let's consider the problem of being retrenched or losing your job.

For the first week or two after a major loss, people will treat it like the acute stressor which it is. Then over time, they will most likely stop calling and bringing meals, or offering to help in practical ways. The loss is still being experienced, and a one- to two-year period of grief is considered normal, yet when the stressor endures and becomes chronic, support is less forthcoming over time. This lack of support compounds the effects and experience of stress.

Hassles

Have you had days where nothing acute has happened, and the chronic stress is the same or maybe even less than usual on that day, yet you feel strung out or exhausted by the evening? If there is no physical cause, you may want to consider how many hassles you had that day.

Hassles are small stressors, which individually are not noticeable in their effect and would not stress you out, but which, taken together, can be very stressful.

For example, you're in a bit of a hurry—not a big hurry, but time is limited—and you can't find parking. Then on your way out, you can't find your parking ticket; you realize you need to refuel your car but there's a long line at the garage; you didn't pack lunch and your blood sugar is crashing; your phone battery is low and you left your charger at home; and, yes, your hair looks bad!

None of these alone would have been insurmountable, yet the accumulation of these small stressors through a day can drain your resources and leave you stressed and vulnerable by evening.

The Stress Equation: Resources

You can see that there are many ways in which you experience demands, and you need to counter them by finding and/or using coping resources.

You will notice that all the areas in which you experienced demands also contain potential resources. Despite your chronically ill family member, for example, you may enjoy very good health. Despite a challenging intimate relationship, you may have extremely supportive friends, or a fulfilling job.

Just as demands can arise from people, tasks, time pressure and events, resources can also arise from various sources. And, like demands, resources can be related to the self (inner resources) and others (outer resources). Resources can include:

- Good health and nutrition;
- Enough help with tasks at work and home;
- Stable finances or reliable fall-back position;
- Comfortable environment;
- Knowledge, ability to think rationally and/or see the gift in adversity;
- Strong spirituality;
- Satisfying career.

It's also possible to separate resources into *current* and *ongoing*.

A medical professional can be a resource for an acute illness or injury, but doesn't have to be present in your life permanently. You may see a coach or therapist when there is an acute need, and you may do so many times over a number of years, but not necessarily on a regular basis throughout.

Similarly, you may study a piece of work or a specific topic for a reason, or practise a skill for a specific demand situation, but not use those resources daily.

These distinctions are less important than being able to access resources when you need them, whether they arise from within or around you.

One more distinction to consider when it comes to resources is real versus false resources. For example, when you're feeling tired, a cup of coffee or a piece of chocolate may give you a temporary lift. However, once the effect has worn off, it may leave you feeling even worse. If your response is to then reach for another false resource, you can see what kind of roller-coaster you can get yourself onto.

It may be appropriate to reach for some temporary relief when you're under pressure, however, any temporary solution that is used as a substitute for a real solution could be termed a false resource.

PRACTICAL EXERCISE – DO THIS NOW

Balance Your Stress Equation

At the end of this book is a table (TABLE A: Stress Equation) which you can use to make a list of your primary demands and resources. Once you have drawn up a list, your next task would be to identify where you need to reduce demands and/or increase resources and then find a way to DO something about it, which usually involves telling or asking somebody. If you find this impossible, then your work is to remove that obstacle.

KEY CONCEPT – TAKE NOTE

Context v Content

THINK ABOUT all the incredible creatures of the earth and how each one has adapted to its environment by growing claws or tentacles, or a covering that enables it to become camouflaged within its environment. That's an example of how content (the features) evolve naturally out of the context (the environment) within which the creature finds itself.

Note that this evolutionary response happens naturally, organically. The creature doesn't have to decide to do it, it grows of its own accord, perhaps as a result of some greater, or deeper, intelligence. We're not getting spooky here, or trying to imply God or anything. That's up to you. We're just pointing to the phenomenon at a practical level.

Now consider that thoughts arise out of a context in the same way that any living organism grows out of, and in response to, its environment.

For example, let's say you and a friend decide over dinner one night that you'll climb Kilimanjaro within the next year. The next morning, you'll have a whole new set of thoughts in your mind, won't you?! Firstly, you might think, *What the hell have I done!* Then, if you're serious about honouring that commitment, you might think, *What the hell do I need?* You'll need to get costs, book flights, buy equipment, get fit. You'll probably notice a hiking store in the mall that you've never seen before, even though you've walked past it a hundred times. Once you've visited that store a few times, you'll start to distinguish between details of products within the store, and so on.

Notice that all those ideas would come to you naturally as a result of your decision, and that it was the decision—and your commitment to that decision—that made the difference to your future thought process. It provided the context out of which new thought content evolved. If you'd just had a random conversation, with no decision or commitment, you'd probably have had no further thoughts on the matter.

Some thought contexts arise out of decisions you make, as in the example above. Others are already there. You find yourself with them. For example, some people's inherited beliefs about race, religion, or politics can be very strong—and very unconsidered. Such people will tend to regurgitate what they learned as children and interpret every new event through that same lens. Their thought content arises naturally out of the context of their inherited beliefs. If they shifted their beliefs, new thoughts would begin to arise instantly.

This is what happens when people experience a religious or political conversion. Their context shifts massively, and suddenly they find peace, or hope. The elation they experience is a consequence of the flood of new thoughts they have. Similarly, the hope and expectation that comes with falling in love.

You can say, then, that your thoughts are like any living organism—their content evolves out of their context. Another metaphor for this phenomenon is a set of Russian dolls: one sits within the next, which sits within the next. The outermost one is your belief about something, and that belief provides the context out of which all other thoughts naturally grow and evolve.

The good thing with thoughts and beliefs is that you can consciously shift them, and thereby create new thoughts, just as you did when you committed to climb Kilimanjaro in the next year. I mean, you did, didn't you?! Just joking.

Read on and you'll discover how this is relevant to the topic of handling stress and building resilience.

Applying the Three Key Elements

IN THE same way that thinking and feeling cannot be started or stopped at will, so you can't stop stuff—events—from happening out there in the world in all kinds of ways that don't suit you. In other words, in the same way that thoughts and emotions are like those clouds in the sky—transient, impermanent, arising from and dissolving back into their source—events also change and come and go. However, you can look at stress as being more like the climate, while thoughts and emotions are like the daily weather.

This phenomenon is perhaps best described by the famous saying, "This too shall pass." You'll probably recognise that saying and think, *Ah, I know that.* You might even say it when things get really tough, but can you make it so that you don't have to hit the wall before you apply it as a last resort towards coping? Like having balance for a bicycle, can you develop it as an ongoing competence?

Stay with us for the ride. That's where we're heading.

You can't stop stressful events from happening, just as you can't stop thoughts and emotions. So, what can you do about them, and the reactivity they generally lead to?

Well, just as you can learn to observe and read your thoughts and emotions, you can learn to observe and read the stress in your life.

Now, let's get familiar with the steps you need to take to get there. These steps are defined by the three key elements of mindfulness: being aware, being nonjudgemental, leading to being nonreactive.

Being Aware | Stress Indicators

As you know by now, the first step towards solving any problem from a mindfulness perspective is awareness. In this case, becoming aware that you're stressed, and then moving to what's causing that stress.

Identifying your key indicators for when you're becoming stressed is a starting point. However, often that's too late, you're already in the cycle. The aim of this section is to support you to develop your awareness much earlier in the cycle so that you stay ahead of the experience of stress.

What are your typical stress indicators? We can break these up into four categories:

- **Behaviours** When you're stressed you're likely to notice yourself doing more or less of something. For example, eating more—especially the "bad" stuff, like sugar and other stimulants, or comfort eating—or not eating at all. Sleeping too much, or not sleeping enough—or not at all. Another behavioural indicator of being stressed is when you have some version of avoidance or procrastination, like burying yourself in reading, television or the Internet.

  Some people become more irritable and aggressive. They might take it out on others—the staff, those bad drivers, a shop assistant—anybody who's in the path. Others might withdraw, become more quiet than usual, or sleep, when the stress starts to pile up.

- **Cognitions** Under high levels of stress, your thoughts may tend to become quite extreme. You'll notice yourself having all-or-nothing thoughts, like, "I *can't* anymore." "I'm not coping at all." "I can't do a thing today." "It's too much."

- **Emotions** Emotions often overlap with behaviours as stress indicators. You'll feel more angry, and act out, or you might suppress your emotions and sleep, or bury yourself in distractions. If those distractions seem sweeter than usual, that might be an indicator!

- **Physical symptoms** You probably know that illness is strongly correlated to stress. There are numerous studies which indicated that stress may result in the development of gastrointestinal disorders such as peptic ulcers and ulcerative colitis, cardiovascular disorders such as hypertension or arrhythmia, respiratory disorders such as allergy, bronchial asthma or hyperventilation, musculoskeletal disorders such as lower back pain and tension headaches, and skin disorders such as acne, eczema or psoriasis.

Being Nonjudgemental | Equanimity

This is where mindfulness becomes particularly relevant to the experience of stress. In this section we'll look at equanimity (the ability to "be with what is") as a key to handling stress. This is not always easy as the situations generally seem so wrong. Don't stress, you're about to learn a powerful shortcut route to achieve equanimity!

In Chapter 4, in the introduction to the key element of being nonjudgemental, you will have read the statement, "It's not the thing itself, but your relationship to the thing." In that same chapter, in the panel on equanimity, we mentioned the Greco-Roman philosophical school, the Stoics, who held that "our feelings about life's events, not those events themselves, determine our happiness".

Yes, we are saying that a large part of your stress is in your mind. Remember the chair and your label for the chair? Therefore, being mindful, and taking care of your relationship to, and labelling of, events is a major part of dealing with stress. Taking care of the events themselves is also important and we'll get to that.

First, take a look at this issue of your relationship to the thing, or the emphasis you place on a thing. You can do that through two lenses.

Inner Problem / Solution versus Outer Problem / Solution

When your mobile phone battery dies halfway through the day, you generally regard that as a problem. The device has the problem, so it's an outer problem. So, what do you need? An outer solution. For example, find a charger. If you can't find a charger, you have a different problem. There may be nothing you can do about it until you leave the current venue and move to another one.

Any outer problem can also be reflected by a corresponding inner problem. Perhaps there's an important phone call you're waiting for. A sales prospect you're waiting to hear from, or someone you've just started dating. How you respond to the inner problem—whether you slam the phone or shout at someone—is something you can control. In other words, you have a choice with regards to the inner problem, even if you don't have a choice with regards to the outer problem.

The phone battery is an outer problem that needs an outer solution. Your response to it determines whether you turn that outer problem into an inner problem. Your response to the inner problem—your ability to provide an inner solution—can be greatly assisted by the development of equanimity.

Equanimity: being with "what is"

I noted in the panel in chapter 4 that equanimity is posited by practically every major religion and ancient philosophy as one of the primary—along with compassion—qualities or attributes towards which spiritual growth is directed. My personal belief is that life on earth is a training ground towards developing equanimity and compassion, among other things, like experiencing wonder and awe!

I also noted that equanimity is not mentioned in the leadership literature. The only quote I was able to find was this one by Debashis Chatterjee in the book *Leading*

Consciously: "Equanimity gives the mind purity of perception, clarity of vision and effective decision-making capacity."

A lot of your stress comes from your work context. And your work context—as indicated by the contemporary leadership lexicon—is a desert when it comes to fostering equanimity. Go figure.

As mentioned in the section on being aware, your cognitions are an indicator of your being stressed. Very often, these will contain an element that reveals your relationship towards the stressful events themselves—your lack of equanimity. They probably go something like:

- "This shouldn't be happening (to *me*)…"
- "This always happens (to *me*)…"
- "Why *me*, why now?"

Firstly, notice the presence of the label *my / me / mine*. You've seen this before, in the chapter on emotion regulation. The closer something comes to *my / me / mine*, the more intense the emotions you experience. Similarly, the more stress you experience. This may seem obvious—and the only way to be—however, as our mission statement makes clear, we're offering a *different*, better experience of life. It's also the key to a non-obvious solution.

Your cognitive—and consequently emotional and possibly even physical—reaction to stressful events can be drawn together under the common theme:

"Something's wrong!"

Usually, the thing is "wrong" because it's affecting *my / me / mine*! It's not in line with what *I* want, with *my* preferences. For example, when your sales or date prospect hasn't called back by the time you'd hoped. Of course, you might say, getting stressed about that is how life is and should be. Well, read on to find how and why this doesn't have to be the case and what you can do about it.

You were introduced earlier to the key concept of context versus content. You saw that thoughts are like Russian dolls. One thought arises out of another. Now you're going to discover how that applies to the subject of stress.

Consider, if your core assumption about a situation or event is that, "Something's wrong," where's your attention going to go, and what kind of problems are you going to create that might not even be there? Very often, you make decisions and take actions that are not necessary, thereby increasing your experience of stress.

Carl Jung said, "All modern people … assume that there is nothing … that they have not made up. We think we have invented everything physical—that nothing would be done if we did not do it; for that is our basic idea and it is an extraordinary assumption."

It's already been mentioned earlier that if you had to beat your own heart and breathe your lungs, work your spleen and digestive system, all by paying attention to it and thinking about it, you'd be dead within minutes. You just can't do it, and thankfully it takes care of itself. Yet you think that you can influence events outside of yourself to your exact requirements and specifications!

Many people come to me and say they're having trouble sitting down to meditate. Their thoughts are just too strong, too active. My response is often to invite them to check to see how much of that thinking is about the need to control. We really believe that our thinking is controlling events, and because we're so stressed, we need it even more, so we do more of it. We can't let it rest, even for a few minutes, and just allow life to go on without us, without our attempts to control it by thinking.

You have to act 100%, and allow life to act 100%, and make decisions at that frontier.

There is a brilliant TED Talk, available on YouTube, by the poet David Whyte called *Life at the Frontier: The Conversational Nature of Reality*. He points out that you "can't launch yourself like a missile" at life and expect everything to go your way. He points out that there is a "frontier" at which the things that you want and what the world wants or will allow—and vice versa—meet. He offers the analogy of a jet flying through the air: the interaction between the curve of the solid steel and the air, created by movement, keeps the jet airborne.

This is not to say you ought to do nothing. This may sound paradoxical, but you have to act 100% and allow life to act 100% and make decisions at that frontier.

A good real-life example of this is when sportspeople get interviewed after a stellar performance. Often, they can't explain what they did differently. They were pretty much doing what they always did, and it just happened. It's unlikely to happen in exactly the same way the next time they get out there to perform—even though they're doing their best and applying their skill and talent as much as they did the last time!

In the book *Leading Consciously*, mentioned earlier, Chatterjee quotes a former CEO of McKinsey, Rajat Gupta, as having said that he "allows some problems to lie undecided because he is conscious that a certain amount of inertia is more useful in solving a problem than is premature and aggressive action. He said, 'I tend to let things sort themselves out. Nine problems out of ten go away if you don't address them. You have to deal with the tenth. I often don't address things until I have to.'"

Here's someone who understands that situations, even problematic ones, are like those clouds in the sky. They come and go, they arise, change and dissolve, even without you having to do anything. Yet you think you're the only one who can determine what happens. How many times have things gone in a different direction from where you would have tried to steer them, and the result was even better for you than what you would have created?

Think about a time when you wrote that angry email and—for once—decided not to send it. Did that anger subside, and the situation resolve itself? Perhaps that person got their comeuppance in another way. Are there any other situations you can think of where leaving things alone had a perfectly good outcome—or one even better than you could have imagined? Go on, admit it!

REAL-LIFE EXAMPLE

Hitting the Magazine Deadline

I USED to edit a major national monthly magazine and the deadlines were quite fixed. If you missed the print deadline you missed the trucks. If you missed the trucks, you missed the supermarket shelves at month-end—the trucks only went out again two weeks later! The impact of a missed deadline was not something you could even consider.

As the advertising came in, so page counts went up in forms of 16 pages, then varied some more according to certain ratios.

Naturally, we planned ahead for such contingencies, and yet I found that stories would come in and things would happen that improved the overall editorial mix in ways that we could not have constructed, unless we were super-geniuses!

The end product often had elements that flowed together in a way that looked like we had planned a particular theme, or put ads opposite pages that just "worked"; yet, while we did our best to do this, a lot of the patterns just "happened". Occasionally there was the odd random "mistake" where things didn't work, but they were greatly outnumbered by the positive synchronicities.

I also learned that if there was a problem it would rise to the surface as long as I was paying *enough* attention. I didn't have to pay attention to *everything*. I didn't get stressed that "this should not have happened". It did happen, and we caught it—it doesn't matter how we caught it, as long as we caught it.

Of course, there are times when you still need to act, and you must. However, when your context is that "something's wrong", you tend to act on the wrong thing, in the wrong way, at the wrong time. Or you just act too much, or try to act on too many things—usually all at once.

You need to decide where to put your attention. Once again, remember that your thoughts are like Russian dolls and your outermost thought, or belief, provides the defining context for all those other thoughts.

Now, let's get clear: can you change your belief about something? Yes, you can. It may not always be easy, but you can. So, here's a suggestion that can help you deal with stress. What if you change "Something's wrong" to:

"Nothing's wrong!"

Note that creating this context, or perspective, doesn't negate the validity of your personal perspective that things do matter. If your house is burning down, it does matter. To you. Right then and there. And, if you pull back to the outer edge of the universe, and move forward a thousand years in time, well, this event is a tiny drop in a tiny ocean, isn't it? In a universal sense, it's just part of the movement of life and, even though it may hurt and may not make sense, nothing is ultimately *wrong*. It is what it is. So, your sports team lost on the weekend. It is what it is.

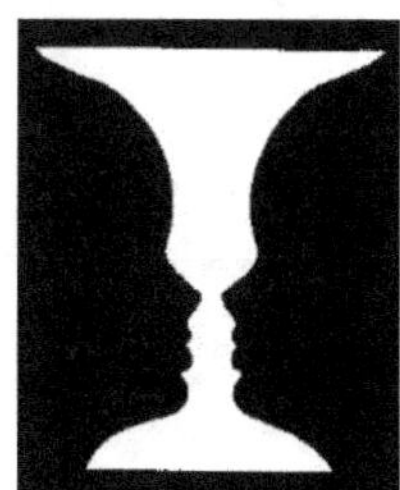

As you can see, we're not saying you should replace your personal perspective with an impersonal one; rather, consider the possibility of a dual perspective. Refer to the picture to the left. It's one of those famous dual-perspective images that you've probably seen before: you can see a vase, and if you shift your perspective, you can see two faces. Whether you're seeing the vase or the faces, can you remain mindful of the other perspective? It's still there, even though you're not perceiving it right now. Similarly, when your house is burning down, can you remain mindful that in a thousand years from now—or to someone on the other side of the world—this won't matter so much. OK, so that's an extreme example—and a figurative one. Mostly, you're likely to be dealing with less extreme situations. A business deal that you think is life-or-death. Your child's college entrance exam. Sometimes it's even less pointed. A meeting deadline. Your child's homework. A car repair. Traffic.

What if you didn't try to resolve it? Is it possible that it might resolve itself? You discover that the business deal was never going to happen anyway, and a better one comes along. The child is destined for something other than medical studies. The meeting gets cancelled. The child's teacher gives her an extension. The noise that the car was making suddenly disappears, or a friend of a friend comes in and fixes it for you.

There are two points to consider here. Firstly, while it's one hundred percent true that the event and the outcome matters to you, it's also one hundred percent true from a universal perspective that there's nothing wrong, except that you say so— except that it's happening to you.

From the inside-out things seem terrible. But if you can look at this moment from the outside-in, if you can pull back and consider how tiny the earth is within the scale of the universe, and how tiny this event is within the scale of everything that's ever happened, then things do seem tiny, trivial, irrelevant. And that's not to make them irrelevant, it's a *both-and* approach: this moment is both trivial and not trivial at the same time.

Holding both the personal and the universal perspectives enables you to maintain the balance of your mind, instead of going into that red zone reaction with the amygdala hijack where your executive faculty shuts down. You become more capable of choosing where to put your attention and to recognise what really matters in the situation.

That's how you can shift your perspective by shifting your context. Now let's look at how you can act differently, also based on thoughts arising from the context, *Nothing's wrong*.

Having taken every action you can, given your human capacity, you can now surrender control and trust that, *Nothing's wrong*. Things will take care of themselves, possibly to your advantage. And things that don't work out, well, perhaps you'll get another chance to do something about them.

Firstly, consider the possibility of things taking care of themselves. How many times have you heard someone say, "It was the hardest thing I ever went through, but the lessons were invaluable. They made me who I am today." You always get that in retrospect. What if you could open yourself to the possibility before it happens?

Secondly, on the possibility of having a chance to correct things, how often have you found that when you do something later than you had planned to, the timing turns out to be a whole lot better? When you finally get around to taking your car in, for example, there's a special on and you save a bucket of money.

Consider the possibility that everything is as it should be. With or without you.

As mentioned, gaining perspective, instead of having a red zone reaction, will help you to recognise what you can and can't change, and what does and does not matter.

How much value would that have for you, if you could recognise in any situation what does and does not matter and be able to put your attention in the right place, in the right way? Surely, your experience of stress—and of life—would change for the better and you'd be more effective?

As you do this more often, you can shorten your response time. Instead of taking a few days, or weeks, even years, to gain perspective, you can gain it in the moment. You can recognise in the moment what matters and what doesn't.

> *While it's true that it matters to you, it's also true that there's nothing wrong, except that you say so.*

When you relax and open up, you begin to see things in the situation that you weren't seeing before. You can find the gift in the situation. (There is a gift in every situation.) You can find the help that is probably there but which you weren't seeing. You can spot what's going to happen by itself and what needs your attention. Usually, what needs your attention will rise to the surface—as long as you're present and open.

As you can see, this is not to say that you should just suppress your feelings or thoughts. It's not that you should accept things as they are forever and become a "shoo-wow" hippy, or a passive vegetable. It's not an *either-or* choice, but a *both-and*. That's what we mean when we say that mindfulness is not a silver bullet; it's the salt in the mix. And by adding that salt, you can have a *different*, better experience of life.

If you have a particular problem with the phrase, *Nothing's wrong*, then consider changing it to something else that works better for you. Perhaps, "Everything is as it should be." In their book *The Art of Possibility*, Ben and Rosamund Zander propose that you look at every situation and go, "How fascinating! I wonder what will happen next?" The rule is that it should challenge your notion of what's possible. It needs to be outside the realm of things being right and wrong, but rather somehow immutable, if not perfect, right at this moment.

Being Nonreactive | Part 1: Crossing the Bridge

The shift from being reactive to being nonreactive (in other words, responding to the situation) can sometimes be more challenging than a simple mental switch.

As you saw in the section on the amygdala hijack, when something is perceived as life-threatening, your attention goes there again and again. Some situations are a little bigger than you and you may struggle to just change your context.

You need to "cross the bridge" first.

Below are some practices you can learn, then save and use in the situation.

PRACTICE - SAVE FOR LATER

Tools for Shifting Context

IN ORDER to arrive at the context or perspective of, *Nothing's wrong!* when the situation seems too big or too important, you might still need to do some work. Here are some steps you can use to break it down.

Remember, you're trying to move to a position of being nonjudgemental. You can do this using one of the following tools:

- **Surrender your preferences**
  Let go of all your ideas of what should be happening right now, or what must happen next. Let go means letting go; like the bungee jumper on the edge of the bridge, you may not feel like it or think it's a good idea, but you can surrender into the jump, surrender into the let-go.

- **Support questions**
  - What labels / judgements am I holding onto?
  - What outcomes am I afraid of?

- o Red zone: Is it really the end of the world / my life / my family's lives / the world (or does it just feel that way)?

- **The clouds are not the sky**

  Apply this to the event itself:
  - o "This too shall pass"
  - o "Most of these problems will take care of themselves, which one needs my attention?"

- **Treat the event as a messenger**

  Let the messenger go, take the message, which is usually:
  - o What do I need to complete / put in place? (Sometimes, the answer to that is, "Nothing, it just happened, and I/we caught it in time.")

- **Reframe the situation**

  Look for the unexpected positive outcome. Eckhart Tolle tells the story about the man who wins the lottery and, when people say how lucky he is, replies, "Maybe." He has an accident in the sportscar he bought with the winnings, and ends up in hospital. People say how unfortunate he is. He replies, "Maybe." While he's in hospital there's an earthquake and his house collapses. If he'd been home, he might have died. How fortunate you are, people say. He replies, "Maybe." And so on.

- **Red Zone check**

  Who is informed of your red flag indicators, and given permission to point them out to you? When you recognise that you're in the red zone, follow the above steps, including one more: play out the worst-case scenario. Keep asking yourself: And then? And then? You'll find that you're capable of dealing with whatever happens.

Sometimes it's not that easy to simply shift your context for the situation. This is particularly true when you're in or near red zone territory. Below are some presencing tools that you can use to ground and presence yourself when your thoughts and emotions are feeling a little out of reach or threatening to go out of control, even after you've applied the tools presented above.

PRACTICE - SAVE FOR LATER

Presencing Tools

AS YOU saw in the section on the amygdala hijack, when something is perceived as life-threatening, your attention goes there again and again. Some situations are a little bigger than us, and so asking the questions above may still not do it. If that's the case, then try any one of these physical activities, which only take a couple of minutes, to presence yourself:

- **Box-breathing**

  This technique physically interrupts the amygdala hijack—and it only takes two minutes!

  Breathe in for a count of four. Hold for a count of four. Breathe out for a count of four. Hold for a count of four. Repeat for two minutes.

- **The "Flop"**

  You know how, when you bend a ruler and then suddenly let go, it snaps back beyond its straight resting position before it settles. This is based on a principle called reciprocal inhibition and is a quick way to release muscle tension.

  Sit on a chair and put your hands behind your head, fingers crossed. Lift your knees up towards your chest and squeeze your abdomen. Simultaneously pull your head forward with your hands while also resisting with your head. Yes, you're creating as much tension as possible in every direction. Hold that position for a count of 30, then *flop*. Repeat if needed.

- **Sensation meditation**

  The recorded meditation available on the Practical Mindfulness website takes you through a nonjudgemental awareness of information from all five senses. You can use any slice of this meditation to presence yourself in any situation. For example, if you're in a noisy place, meditate on the sound in the way that you learn to do by listening to the recorded meditation. You can do this for as little as two minutes, or as long as you like.

- **Paying attention**

  In the same way that you lead in to the meditations by paying attention to the room that you're in, you can do that to anchor yourself in reality when you're having an amygdala hijack. Pay acute attention to the fine details of the room—shapes, colours, textures. Also notice how still everything is, how unaffected things are by your internal noise—your story of how things should or shouldn't be—and remind yourself that they'll probably still be there, unmoved, just like that, tomorrow.

You've already seen the benefits of presencing yourself. They are worth repeating here, in the context of handling stress and building resilience.

Firstly, presencing breaks the physical response of the amygdala hijack, which is causing that fight-or-flight response and the shutdown of the executive function. When that subsides, you're able to think clearly again and make better decisions.

Presencing anchors or grounds you in reality. This enables you to see that things are not always as bad as they seem. Remember, the body doesn't distinguish between thought and reality. It can have the same visceral response to a movie—or a fantasy—as to a real event. Presencing yourself makes sure you deal with the actual event and not imagined consequences.

It deals with the actual issue as it's occurring internally. Your body—and brain—are reacting as though it's a life-or-death matter. It's probably not and, if not, it's good to know that, to let your brain know that, so that it can deal with the situation as it is.

It creates space for choice. The definition of being reactive is that you have no choice. You're just reacting. You can't stop yourself. You just do that thing. Having choice—and exercising that choice—is the key indicator of being nonreactive. Presencing yourself creates that tiny gap in which you can recognise the possibility of choice, and then open it wider to actually explore and exercise that choice. Usually, then, you decide and act for the greater good of all, not just to defend yourself—sometimes unnecessarily and sometimes causing more harm than good, or, at the very least, wasting energy.

Being Nonreactive | Part 2: Choosing Your Focus

The key indicator for being nonreactive is being able to make a choice with regards to one's response. Instead of just that knee-jerk reaction, there is that gap that follows awareness in which you surrender your labels and judgements, and you then make a choice how to respond.

Responding mindfully in the context of stress results in you managing rather than reacting to the situation. You rise above the problem instead of becoming part of the problem—in which case somebody else has to come along and take your place in managing the situation.

Managing a situation may involve taking action and, very often, it may mean taking no action at all. This would not be a passive response but a deliberate, mindful, conscious choice.

In the context of stressful events, especially when demands overwhelm resources, being nonreactive enables you to choose where to put your attention. Most often, when you do this, you find that there is help at hand for those things that you can't handle. Often, you just haven't wanted to ask.

Have you noticed how some people are hopeless at organisational tasks, and yet somehow they'll have someone around them to pick up the pieces. If you look carefully, you'll see that whatever you need is always being provided in some form or another. You just need to see that it may not be in the predictable form. Like when you're looking for the stapler in the office; it's right there under your nose, but because it's in an unfamiliar place, you don't see it until someone points it out—or until you stop looking, relax and become present.

Similarly, the mother who has to rush a sick child to hospital might not want to leave work just before that all-important meeting. However, if she looks around, there's probably someone whose been waiting for a chance to prove themselves. And sometimes, when that's not the case, you find the client calling to change the meeting time. Or, someone else could take the child and that would not make you into a bad mother.

If you don't allow the help to come in some other form, then you may not be managing the situation. Instead, you're reacting to the situation and, when you do that, you become part of the problem. Somebody else now needs to intervene to get you to make a better decision.

Being nonreactive means treating the situation as it is, not as you'd like it to be. It means doing what's right for the situation, not just what's right for you. It also means rising above the situation and taking appropriate action—which may mean no action at all.

It opens you up to the forces of life that are always evolving and taking care of things. Those same forces that keep your organs functioning and trees growing, despite no effort or attention on your part.

The Red Zone

Some situations arise that activate your red zone trigger. So, apart from being aware of your normal stress indicators, you need to remain mindful of, and listen out for, your red zone indicators that will tell you when you're in the red zone.

When you recognise that the stress experience is arising out of a red zone trigger, the choice then is to consider moving in the direction of the fear that is threatening to cause a red zone reaction. For example, if your trigger is the possibility of getting into trouble for not getting things perfect, then perhaps try just doing your best and see if the world really does end. You might find that it doesn't, and that you survive. Then take note of that evidence and start building a case for being nonreactive so that, each time, you get to that point earlier in the cycle, until you're catching yourself in the moment, and even before it happens.

KEY CONCEPT – TAKE NOTE

Completion

YOU KNOW that experience of having too much to do and not knowing where to begin? For some people that happens occasionally, when the demands just get too much, and it's a temporary thing. For many people, this can be an ongoing experience.

The primary cause of that experience, especially when it's more chronic than acute, is that you've just left too many things undone—you have too many incompletions. You've let things pile up until your demands far outweigh your resources. That in itself is demotivating, and that adds momentum to the spiral.

Think about this scenario: you said you'd call someone and you didn't. Months later you see them at the mall and you remember that incompletion. It comes up in your mind. Whereas, if you had called them, nothing would come up.

These incompletions lead to further incompletions. You need to call someone for a business reason, but you put it off because you know that you first need to resolve a misunderstanding with that person.

One thing leads to another and soon you have a heap of incompletions. It even becomes normal to you, so you don't notice them piling up. Then, if you ever do decide to sort them out, you don't know where to begin.

Sound familiar? Read on.

In the illustration below, the black square in Fig. 1 represents your mind when it's full of incompletions. Imagine another, smaller, black square moving in front of that black square. It would disappear. This represents another incompletion entering your life and occupying your mind. You wouldn't even notice.

Let's say you call that old friend or colleague and resolve that misunderstanding. Then you clear out that library full of books you bought but will never read. Now you no longer have to think about all the reading you have to do. That's two big completion spaces created. These completions are represented by the two white shapes in Fig. 2.

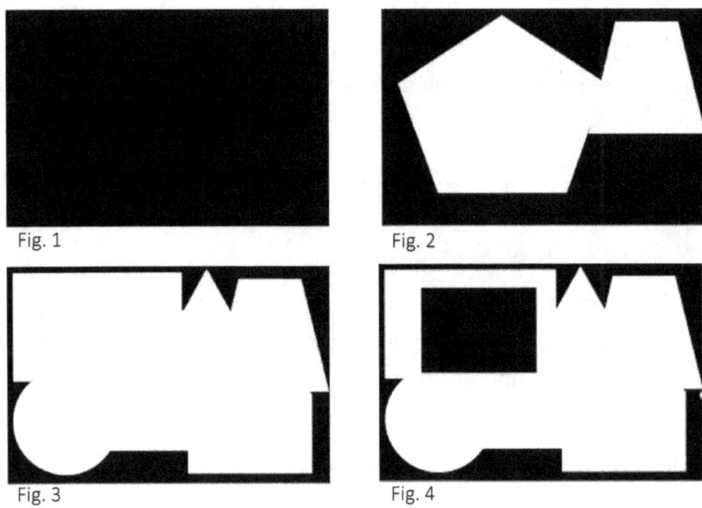

Fig. 1

Fig. 2

Fig. 3

Fig. 4

Let's say you clear out a few more areas of your life: your email Inbox; your garage that's being used as a storeroom; those arguments you've been having in your head with your father / mother / spouse / friend / colleague; you finally act on that business idea you've been nursing for years. Suddenly you have a whole lot of clear, white space, as in Fig. 3.

Now, imagine that black square coming into your space again, as in Fig. 4. You'll pick it up immediately as being something to deal with—to complete—right away. And, because you're in the habit of completing things, you'll do exactly that. You'll complete it—and create more clear space so that you recognise the next one.

You can say that incompletions occupy your attention and therefore reduce presence. You also know that they'll require energy (resources) and so they can be demotivating when they're in front of you; energising when they're behind you. Whether you're allowing incompletions, or creating completion, it gathers momentum and becomes a self-sustaining cycle. It becomes a way of life.

Examples of incompletions include: clutter (physical, digital, mental); postponements (repairs, phone calls, admin tasks, all the stuff you've been putting off until tomorrow); broken promises (things you said you'd do but haven't done— every single one gets remembered and processed from time to time); relationship stuff (withholds, resentments, unforgiven stuff, unresolved arguments).

As you can see, there's a lot of power in creating completion in your life.

If you pay attention, you'll see that those incompletions occupy a large chunk of your attention. They tend to come up quite randomly, but your instinctual and emotional centres—refer Chapter 8—will tell you where the energy is highest, and therefore where you need to start.

There are two phases to being able to live at the frontier of completion: *creating* completion and *maintaining* completion. Below are some exercises to support you to achieve both.

PRACTICAL EXERCISE – DO THIS NOW

Uncover Your Incompletions

AT THE end of this book is a table (TABLE B: Creating Completion) which you can use to identify the areas of your life where you are complete (i.e. you're sorted, there's nothing coming up for you as needing to be done) versus incomplete (i.e. you're not sorted, there are things you need to do).

For each area, list what needs to be done and by when you'll have done it.

The previous exercise was to support you in creating a lot of that white space— *creating* completion. The practice below is to support you to *maintain* completion.

PRACTICE - SAVE FOR LATER

Mindful Completion Walk

TAKE A mindful walk for 20-40 mins in a safe, comfortable place. Perhaps your garden, a familiar park, or a courtyard at work. Stay present by paying attention to your physical environment. Notice everything that comes up to distract you or that occupies your attention. Note it down and make a plan to complete it.

As an alternative to taking a walk, you may choose to be mindfully present while you sit in traffic and use voice memos to record the same.

In summary, you can say that anything that comes up and occupies your attention is incomplete. When something is complete, it doesn't come up. With too many incompletions, you cannot pay attention to, or deal effectively with, stuff that happens. In fact, you probably won't even notice the stress-inducing events piling up.

The more completions you create, the quicker you'll be to recognise new ones that enter your space. Then, if you pounce on them like a hungry hunter, you'll maintain that clear space which will be available for mindful awareness.

WHAT DIFFERENCE DOES IT MAKE?

THE GOOD news is that it is possible to reduce the number of problems you're experiencing at any one time, or to increase your level of resources. The not-so-good news is that life is, as Winston Churchill said of history, "One damn thing after another." Therefore, the bigger challenge is to keep pace with life, to keep up the momentum of dealing with every next damn thing as it comes in.

Resilience can be defined as your ability to get back up again after a setback, or to knock off problems without losing your stride. You could even say that your level of resilience is the speed at which you're able to do this, without losing momentum towards your main goal.

Here's a good analogy from the world of sport. The game of rugby has become as technical and data-driven as any sport. Players wear monitors so that coaches can measure every little detail of their physical state as well as their performance. Metres run. Tackles made. Gainline success. And so on.

One of the most successful coaches in the world is the Australian Eddie Jones. He took over the England team just after they failed to make the playoff stages of their own World Cup in 2015. Under his tutelage they then immediately won their next 17 consecutive games before they lost again.

At a media luncheon during this time, Jones was asked the question as to what data they considered most important. The reply he was reported to have given was that there's too much data in the game today. He only measures one thing: how quickly a player gets up after he's been tackled; and how quickly a player gets up after he's made a tackle.

A subsequent observation of successful teams told me that this was indeed a most important statistic. That competence certainly seemed to be a key feature of the most successful teams.

There's another factor too: the referee. There are many rules in the game of rugby that leave the situation open to interpretation by the referee. There's also the possibility of the "quick-tap" penalty in which a player can restart the game immediately by tapping the ball with his foot from the penalty spot.

If the players in the penalised team decide to remonstrate, as happens in football, they increase the likelihood of a quick-tap penalty happening. Given the speed of the game today, that can often lead to points scored against you. Rugby—both playing and watching—is therefore a good training ground for practising equanimity and being nonreactive. You have to let go of your judgements very quickly and move on.

As mentioned, resilience can be defined as your ability to repeatedly bounce back quickly after a setback. Life is less like football in this sense, and more like rugby. It doesn't wait for you to complain. It moves on, and you'd better move on too.

So you can live a life of complaining, feeling sorry for yourself, and trying to "process" and make sense of it all—in which case you'll get left behind, and the score will mount up against you. Or you can learn to get back up on your feet with no story, let go of your complaints, do what needs to be done—in which case you'll start to win more than you lose. It's your choice.

Hopefully you're convinced by now that at a good part of stress is not the events of life themselves, but your responses to those events. The solution, therefore, lies within you, and therefore it's manageable and controllable. Being more present and aware, nonjudgemental and nonreactive, you should find that you very quickly start to enjoy that different, better experience of life.

CHAPTER SUMMARY

THIS CHAPTER looks at the application of mindfulness to the subject of stress and building resilience. Key content includes:

- A certain degree of stress is necessary as it leads to the optimal level of performance based on Selye's stress curve.
- Dr Colinda Linde's Stress Equation model: stress demands—acute, chronic and hassles—and stress resources—inner and outer, current and ongoing—and how to balance the two.
- The notion that stress is the result, not of external events, but of one's reaction to those events, is supported by science.
- Being aware of stress means noticing key indicators in the form of either behaviours, cognitions, emotions, or physical symptoms.
- Being nonjudgemental begins with the distinction between what is an inner and an outer problem and what is an appropriate inner and outer solution.
- The next level of being nonjudgemental is recognising the level of judgement about the situation—the mental context, "Something's wrong!"—and the proximity to the label of *me / my / mine*.
- Coming from an outside-in, universal perspective enables you to create the mental context that "Nothing's wrong!" and thereby align yourself with *what is*, as it is *right now*.
- Tools to support you in shifting your mental context.
- Some physical interventions to break an amygdala hijack.

- Being nonreactive in the context of handling stress means mindfully choosing where to put your attention and focus your energy and efforts.
- Creating completion creates order and clarity and facilitates instant recognition of new stressors and the ability to prioritise.

8 | Complexity & Decision-Making

D O YOU sometimes find yourself feeling overwhelmed by how many decisions you have to make, and how quickly you have to make them? Do you sometimes wonder what the right decision is—at home, at work, for yourself, your employees, your children? Do you find yourself wondering who, or what, to turn to, in order to support you in making those decisions?

Let's face it, life is not as simple as it used to be, and the old rules don't apply anymore.

Think about it: a generation or two back, your place in society was quite well-defined in terms of race, religion, social class and gender. Whether you were the first-born son of an English aristocrat or the third daughter of an Indian municipal clerk, either way, the parameters of your life path—who you could marry, what work you would do—were, to a greater or lesser degree, handed to you. Likewise, your moral behaviour choices, the way you would raise your children, even your choices at the food market and how to spend your leisure time, were fairly limited.

In the post-consumer, post-truth, social media age, we're overwhelmed by choice. Women can become engineers or pilots as much as men can be openly gay and hold political office. Deciding on a career can be a major challenge, compounded by the fact that many people are now likely to have multiple careers across the span of their lifetime. Teenagers today have a range of gender identities available to them that were not even named a generation ago. That's not to mention the range of spiritual, religious, leisure and entertainment choices; the range of news sources; the range of product options.

That means, quite simply, that there are many more decisions to be made and, unlike the days of yore, they are not being handed to you by social or religious norms. Who, or what, do you reference?

At the same time, you need to make them more quickly than ever before. Meanwhile, science has shown that people have a stress tolerance limit when it comes to willpower, and willpower is required for decision-making. In addition, having too many decisions forced on you by life results in the experience of having no control, or a lack of autonomy, which is in itself a source of stress. You've also seen that incompletions play a big part in causing stress and incompletions arise largely out of unmade decisions. No wonder stress levels are so high, and depression so prevalent.

If your answers to the questions in the first paragraph of this chapter were a resounding yes, then this is likely to be a large part of the reason. The good news is that mindfulness can play a part in transforming that.

For example, being less attached to outcomes can reduce the intensity of the experience, and make energy available to make more decisions, more easily, in a day. Maintaining the balance of your mind means being able to assess situations more objectively and make purposeful rather than knee-jerk, reactive decisions— in other words, decisions that are based on your own highest values and intentions, instead of based on other people's potential criticisms or your own personal fears.

With this chapter you will:

- Gain an awareness and understanding of your dominant decision-making drivers;
- Learn to self-observe and balance the three "centres of intelligence";
- Be able to distinguish between what matters and what doesn't matter;
- Learn how to manage uncertainty and deal with paradox.

The "What Is" of Decisions

A DECISION is a mental action that leads to the elimination of one option—or range of options—for the sake of another. In fact, the Latin root of the word *decision* is most telling: *decidere*, meaning "to cut off". If you look at it, every decision—even a win-win decision—always involves a cutting off of one path, or course of action, over another.

All of life—and growth within life—is initiated by this separation of one thing from another. In the book of Genesis, the light was separated from the darkness; the sky from the water and the waters from the dry earth. In life, the offspring is separated from its mother; the young adult from the parental home; the pupil from the teacher; and so on.

Similarly, to move forward in life usually requires an elimination of options. To be with one person, you are asked to eliminate being with others. To pursue a career in one field, you have to forego others. To own a Windows PC, you have to walk away from a Mac.

You can see, then, that decisions are forced by the need to move forward. Similarly, decisions move things forward in a new direction. You decide to be with this guy / girl, not that one; next thing, you're meeting his / her family. You decide on this career option instead of that; next thing, you're moving to the city where you can study that subject.

No wonder that the world-famous life coach Anthony Robbins places so much emphasis on the importance and power of decisions. "Any action is a cause set in motion, and its effect builds on past effects to move us in a definitive direction and, of course, every direction leads to an ultimate destination—what we call our destiny."

He goes on to ask the all-important question: what precedes all our actions? The answer he gives is simply, "Decisions." Then comes his definitive quote: "It is in the moments of *decision* that your destiny is shaped," he says.

> *Control and resistance are indicators that the ego is trying to prevent the changes that it doesn't want.*

Right there sits the clue as to why you may sometimes struggle to make decisions. The ego, you've seen in the section on the red zone, starts out as a defence mechanism. Its very purpose is survival. It's also the storehouse for all your judgements and preferences, which it believes—and which you believe along with it—are necessary for your survival. The degree to which this is true is the degree to which your ego will naturally try to either control, or resist, any movement or change implied by decisions.

This means that, if you give way to reactivity, you're likely to either leap forward with decisions, in an attempt to control the situation very tightly, or, at the other end of that continuum, to resist change by avoiding decisions. Either way, those are indicators that the ego is trying to prevent the changes that it doesn't want.

The answer is not to just "go with the flow". A complete surrender of your power to decide is also an ego defence. Pretending that you're permanently chilled, or that you don't ever care about anything, is likely to be a form of denial.

In fact, as Napoleon Hill, author of *Think & Grow Rich*, wrote, "Life is a draughts board, and the player opposite you is time. If you hesitate before moving, or neglect to move promptly, your draughts will be wiped off the board by time. You are playing against a partner who will not tolerate indecision!"

Decisions are necessary, at the very least to keep pace with life—firstly to survive and function, and secondly to bring order in the form of ongoing completion. This reduces stress and improves your experience of life. At a higher level, decisions enable you to direct your life towards a purpose. As you'll see in Chapter 9, being decisive, maintaining a high level of completion and directing your efforts towards a purpose opens the way for the state of flow to occur, a state that is also termed "optimal experience".

THE SCIENCE

The Second Brain

YOUR BODY has a mind of its own. Literally. Scientists have begun to recognise that when people talk about deciding from the "gut" they may not be far wrong. In fact, they may not be wrong at all. There is, quite literally, a "second brain" in your gut. Yes, read on.

As strange as it might sound, within the tissues that line your "gut", and which run all the way from the oesophagus through the stomach, small intestine and colon, are millions of neurons—more than are in your spinal cord—all bathed in neurotransmitters and sending nine times more messages to the brain than they receive from the brain

You only have to think about how quickly your brain knows when you've eaten something bad, or how foggy your head can be when you're constipated—and how clear-headed you feel when you're not!—to recognise one level of truth in this. In fact, in its global marketing, Kellogg's All-Bran Flakes makes the claim that you'll feel "All-Bran New" in just five days from eating its product, which is designed to improve digestive health.

During the activation of this campaign in South Africa, the marketing manager Srinivas Adapa said, "The positive effects of [managing your digestive health] have proven added emotional benefits over and above achieving a sense of physical digestive wellness." (Quote from www.fastmoving.co.za – a site which is about fast-moving consumer goods—FMCG—marketing, not fast-moving bowels!)

Although it receives messages from the brain via the vagus nerve, studies have shown that the gut continues to operate—for example, performing the peristaltic reflex—even when that nerve is severed. In this and other ways, it qualifies as a self-regulating system that can send and receive impulses, learn, remember and produce feelings.

The gut is known formally as the enteric nervous system (ENS), as distinct from the central nervous system (CNS) and autonomic nervous system (ANS). It was first identified as far back as the nineteenth century by two English investigators, William M. Bayliss and Ernest H. Starling. This was picked up, first in the early 1900s by a Chicago-based anatomist named Byron Robinson, who wrote a book called *The Abdominal and Pelvic Brain*, and then in the late 1920s by Johannis Langley, who mapped out the ANS but also proffered the CNS and ENS.

However, it was not until Dr Michael Gershon—who is now Chair of the Department of Anatomy and Cell Biology at Columbia University—published *The Second Brain* in the 1960s that it started to gain even a mild amount of traction. Today, the field of *neurogastroenterology* is reckoned to be the new black of medical science.

The implications of this are enormous, and well summarised below in a 2017 article by Romesh Jayasinghe called *The Brain in the Gut*. He says: "Not only has research shown that our gut bacteria can manipulate our food cravings and behaviour in order to ensure their own survival (you can blame them for your junk food obsession), but the colonies in our digestive system also affect our mood. Studies suggest that people with healthy and diverse gut microbiomes are less likely to be depressed or anxious.

"The gut is no longer seen as an entity with the sole purpose of helping with all aspects of digestion. It's also being considered as a key player in regulating inflammation and immunity. ... In some ways, it seems like our second brain and its gut feeling is even more influential than our logical thought. ... In conclusion, the human gut has long been seen as a repository of good and bad feelings. Perhaps emotional states from the head's brain are mirrored in the gut's brain, where they are felt by those who pay attention to them."

Before we move to the application of the three key elements of mindfulness, there are two key concepts to introduce:

- Values & beliefs
- The three centres of intelligence

KEY CONCEPT – TAKE NOTE

Values & Beliefs

Remember the Russian doll example in Chapter 7 and how ideas are born out of other ideas? You can say that decisions are a particular form of idea—a choice—born out of another particular form of idea—a fixed idea called a belief. Those beliefs are based on what you value most. For example, you might value family more than money—or vice versa—or knowledge and learning more than being fit and healthy.

Decisions are generally congruent with what you value most—whether you realise it or not. Therefore, when presented with a choice of a job that makes you twice as much money, but it means you'll be far from your family, you might find it easy to say yes, or you may well turn down the job. Your decision will be based on—and will reflect—what you value most: money or family.

Or you might find yourself with a dilemma, being torn between the two and unable to decide. This would mean that you don't know what you value most, or that you can't admit it to yourself—you feel guilty, or somehow lack permission. Finally, you may take the job and convince yourself that it's for your family—you'll be able to fly home or fly them to visit you. In this case, you're quite possibly not being honest with yourself—or them.

Whichever of those is you, you'll probably find it's not just true for one decision, but for most, if not every, decision you make and have ever made. In other words, you've consistently decided to sacrifice making money for the sake of family, or vice versa. Or you were consistently undecided between the two, and tended to do what you were expected to do, or wait until someone made the decision for you. Or you consistently chose the job and convinced yourself it was to serve the family, but chances are you're a bit behind on making it up to them.

Dr John Demartini says, "The only thing we are truly committed to is our [highest priority] values." This is reflected, not by what we say, but by the facts: where we spend our time, money, energy and attention—and the decisions we make. For example, if you decide to spend more evenings and weekends working than with your family, you're expressing your priority of values through those actions, regardless of what you might profess verbally about your family being the most important thing in your life. It's tough, but it's true.

Most likely, your beliefs and therefore your highest priority values were inherited. They were most likely passed on directly by your parents, who emphasised money, or career success, or family, or ethics, or spirituality, or learning—yes, for ease of use, values can be categorised according the areas of life. If you've never stopped to question your family's values and your own, then this is probably the case.

If your beliefs aren't in line with the family's beliefs, then they're most likely in reaction to them. The family was religious and you became an atheist, for example. Either way, your beliefs and values are most likely either a result of alignment with, or reaction to, your family's beliefs and values.

Below is an exercise that you can use to determine your priority of values.

PRACTICAL EXERCISE – DO THIS NOW

Your Priority of Values

USE TABLE C: Priority of Values at the end of this book to score your own personal priority of values.

Ask yourself:

How much do you prioritise each area of life by thinking about, planning and spending time and/or money on this activity?

Would you sacrifice time or money spent elsewhere for the sake of time or money spent in this area? Score 1 if very low; 10 if very high, then rank them from 1 to 8.

***NOTE** If you're in a job you love, and you'd stay regardless of how much you earn, you can mark **Meaningful Vocation** as high, even if you do earn well. If you're in a job you don't love, but you do it for the money—even if that money is intended to set you free so you can follow your passion—then you'd give **Meaningful Vocation** a lower score and **Making Money** a higher score.

You can score **Immediate Family / Significant Other** as higher than **Making Money** only if you've proved that you sacrifice your earnings—eg. by moving to a lower-paid job—specifically to spend time with them, even if all or most of your money is spent on them. It's tough, but it's true.

Now write down each area of life in order of its ranking.

My Priority of Values (in order of ranking)
1.
2.
3.
4.
5.
6.
7.
8.

Can you see how these have informed and even driven the decisions that you've made?

Now that you have a list of your own priority of values, hopefully you can start to see a picture emerging of what you value most and how that has driven your decisions up until now. If you're still unclear, continue to reflect on it, and perhaps ask somebody who can give you feedback on what they've observed.

Clarity of values is important for effective decision-making. The thing that often prevents you from being clear about your own values is that you feel guilty about what you really value. You may feel that you should value family, or friends, for example, more than you do. If you're struggling with this, read on, read the real-life example of Nelson Mandela later in this chapter.

Work-life balance is another subject that emerges out of the values exercise. Having done the exercise, you'll probably have realised that there are some areas of neglect. Perhaps you've been neglecting your health, or your social life. One thing you can be sure about is that whatever you neglect will eventually become the only thing that matters. For example, when you're sick, the only thing that matters is getting better.

That said, I'm not an advocate of balance so much as being clear about your values. Sure, you should not totally neglect any area; however, most of my clients are relieved when I say you should also not drive yourself crazy trying to do everything.

Once you're ready to move on, hang onto this list. You'll get a chance to refer back to it when you learn to apply the three key elements of mindfulness later on in this chapter.

KEY CONCEPT – TAKE NOTE

The Three Centres of Intelligence

Some people are quick to make decisions. They get an instinctive sense of what's needed, or what they want, in a situation and they decide, and act, based on that. If you ask them, they'll usually say something about using or listening to their "gut".

Other people may get the same instinctive feeling, but they'll have a bit more concern about how their decision might impact others—what other people might feel or say. This concern may be great enough to cause them to not make the decision, or to make a different one than what the person above would make.

For example, let's say a manager needs to take someone off a team to save costs. The gut-based person is more likely to just make the call—and the announcement. They might even do it publicly, with little regard for the affected person's feelings. The person in the second group described above may hesitate because they don't want to hurt the other person's feelings. They may decide to take the person aside and do it with greater sensitivity. Or they may even decide to leave the person and try to solve the problem of costs in some other way.

We're not evaluating which of these approaches is right or wrong. Each one has its merits and it depends on the situation. At the moment, we're more interested in describing the different styles.

You could say that the first style mentioned above is a more instinctive or gut-based style of decision-making. The person who relies on that is likely to sense the decision in their body and be instinctually driven to decide and act in line with that sense. Notice the use of the word *sense* in this description, which is distinct from the word *feeling*.

The second style described above, you can say, is more heart-based—they are more about feelings—what they and other people might feel. The heart is the seat of emotion, which as you have seen, is all about motion, or movement.

You can also say that the heart gives you courage to take action, with empathy—so you do things, but you don't hurt people. Too much heart, however, and that courage can turn to recklessness, while empathy can turn to sympathy, even guilt, perhaps fear, in the sense of being afraid of what others might think, feel or say.

There is a third type of decision-making style, one that tends to ignore the messages of instinct and heart and chooses instead to spend time researching and weighing up the facts. You could say that this is the head-based style of decision-making.

The head-based person would tend to spend time gathering and analysing data. They would also be less sensitive to people's feelings. In the team costs dilemma described above, they would similarly tend to make the hard decision based on facts, although they would have spent the time and taken the trouble to check the data. They wouldn't just jump to conclusions as the gut-based person might do. They'd similarly expect people to deal with any decision without being emotional—the head-based person might *understand* emotion, but will be less likely to actually feel it, or to express it.

The challenge for the head-based person is that, without a feeling sense for when enough is enough, they can tend to continue gathering data—and put off making a decision—forever. As you've seen, it's the emotions that create movement, the heart that gives courage, and the gut that expresses the will or life force. Without some element of those, the head-based person can get rather stuck in analysis paralysis.

Of course, everybody uses a combination of all three centres. Some people are quite well balanced between the three, and others can lean more strongly to one or the other.

Now let's move on and see how these concepts come up when you view them through the lens of the three key elements of mindfulness.

THE SCIENCE

The Heart of the Matter

EMOTIONS HAVE received a bad rap when it comes to decision-making. They've been seen as interfering to the point that, in business, it's often said that you need to "keep emotions out of the decision". Women, in particular, have borne the brunt of this prejudice. Yet, a number of studies have shown that emotions are essential to good decision-making—and that you use them in ways that you don't even realise.

Back in the 1950s, the prefrontal lobotomy was a widely used "treatment" for people who had been diagnosed as schizophrenic, or who had severe OCD or depression. Essentially, it involved severing the fibres that connected the prefrontal cortex to the rest of the brain. The prefrontal cortex is the area recognised for, *inter alia*, complex cognitive behaviour, decision-making and social behaviour.

However, diagnosis was not that rigorous back then, and many people received the treatment simply because they showed abnormal behaviour that included strong emotions that the family were not able to deal with.

In general, it was recognised that, "following the [lobotomy], spontaneity, responsiveness, self-awareness and self-control were reduced. Activity was replaced by inertia, and people were left emotionally blunted and restricted in their intellectual range." (https://en.wikipedia.org/wiki/Lobotomy)

The point of telling you all this is that the prefrontal cortex is seen as the seat of the executive function and not the seat of emotion, and yet these operations removed, not only intellectual capacity, but also emotional capacity. This served as an early clue that emotions and decision-making were bound up.

In addition, studies done with lobotomised people showed that they were unable to choose between two different times in a blank diary, the reason being that they could find enough evidence for and against both options to continually cancel out either one.

Many years later, one of the world's leading neuroscientists, Dr Antonio Damasio, made a similar finding with one of his patients, a successful businessman whom he named Elliott.

Elliott had suffered brain damage as a result of a tumour and subsequent surgery for removal. According to Damasio, "Elliott emerged as a man with a normal intellect who was unable to decide properly, especially when the decision involved personal or social matters." Apparently, it took Elliott 30 minutes to choose an appointment time, and even longer to decide where to have lunch, and he even struggled to decide what colour pen to use to fill out office forms. All this despite the fact that he remained in the 97th percentile in terms of his IQ score.

The other factor that Damasio noticed was that, as Elliott's life fell apart, he seemed to show no emotion. "He was always controlled. Nowhere was there a sense of his own suffering, even though he was the protagonist. I never saw a tinge of emotion in my many hours of conversation with him: no sadness, no impatience, no frustration." Damasio also noted that Elliott lacked motivation to the extent that he called him an "uninvolved spectator" in his own life.

Damasio provided Elliott as a case study in his 1994 book, *Descarte's Error*, in which, according to the Amazon blurb, Damasio "challenged traditional ideas about the connection between emotions and rationality" and proffered that "emotions are not a luxury, they are essential to rational thinking and to normal social behaviour".

In fact, far from excluding them, we can't do without them, he insists.

The orbitofrontal cortex is a region within the prefrontal cortex of the brain which is involved in the cognitive processing of decision-making. The amygdala, we know, is the seat of our most primitive reactions, in particular our fight-or-flight response, and therefore the wellspring of our emotions.

Damasio's somatic marker hypothesis describes the interplay between the two. It has the amygdala and the orbitofrontal cortex being intricately linked to form a neural circuit critical for judgment and decision-making.

"Nature appears to have built the apparatus of rationality (the orbitofrontal cortex) not just on top of the apparatus of biological regulation (the amygdala), but also *from* it and *with* it," he wrote in *Descarte's Error*.

This statement implies that emotions provide additional information, for example in the form of motivation and meaning, to rational factors when making decisions. Without it, for starters, we'd get stuck in analysis paralysis. Then, as the author of *How We*

Decide, Jonah Lehrer, points out, "Emotion and motivation share the same Latin root, *movere*, which means *to move*. The world is full of things and it is our feelings that help us choose [and therefore move] among them."

Lehrer postulates that our best decisions are a finely tuned blend of both feeling and reason—and the precise mix depends on the situation. He states that "Emotions are profoundly smart and constantly learning, they are not simply animal instincts that must be tamed."

# Applying the Three Key Elements

MAKING DECISIONS mindfully doesn't mean being passive. It means making decisions in line with something other than your ego needs—those pesky judgements and preferences. For most people, making decisions according to your ego needs seems to be the only viable, and the most common sense, course of action. However, as you've seen, it's a primary source of conflict and misery. If your ego is good at making you feel guilty for wanting what you really want, then making decisions according to your ego needs can also lead you on a path that is not authentic.

With mindful decision-making, you can still express your preferences, yet you'll see the possibility of not holding onto them so tightly—because it opens you up to those unexpected positive outcomes as per the "Maybe" story recounted a few times in this book. You'll also be aware of what's driving you versus what the situation needs and you'll be more open to doing what's right for the situation, rather than just focusing on what you want. All of this puts you in touch with life as it is, and enables you to make decisions based on what's real and what matters—to treat the situation as it is, and not as you are.

By applying the three key elements of mindfulness to decision-making, you can find a way to increase the ratio of mindful or conscious decisions—those ones you know you made with full awareness—to decisions that are forced on you, or are made from a reactive standpoint. Autonomy is a major factor in the experience of stress and so, by increasing your sense of control over your decision-making, you can also reduce your experience of life as being stressful.

Excited? Let's move on and apply the three key elements of mindfulness—being aware, being nonjudgemental, and being nonreactive—to the subject of complexity and decision-making.

Being Aware | Values & Centres

Being aware in the context of decision-making means, firstly, being aware that there is a decision to be made.

In some cases, you may not know that you have a choice in a situation because your reactivity is so high. For example, your boss asks you to do something and you feel an obligation to do it right away. You don't realise that you have a choice, even if the choice is simply to ask him or her what they would like you to prioritise, given your heavy workload. Or perhaps you'd like to leave your job, but your fear of the unknown, or of what people might say, overwhelms you and so you don't even go there.

Or you may know there's a decision to be made, and you're very busy putting off making it. You can look to your typical procrastination behaviours as a strong indicator of this. When there's a difficult work decision, for example, you might find yourself suddenly tackling the "long read" stories on your favourite news app, or clicking through to the full articles on LinkedIn.

In fact, it could be more than just behaviours, you can also identify your typical cognitions, emotions and physical symptoms that show up when you're unconsciously avoiding a decision. Some people like to rationalise things away, for example making excuses for other people, or telling themselves that things will get better. Some people withdraw. Some even sleep to avoid making decisions.

Awareness of Values

Once you're aware that there's a decision to be made then it's about being aware of what values usually drive your decisions, and whether those are relevant in this situation.

If you stand back far enough from your life and observe yourself, you'll see that as events have passed through your life, you've most probably made the same decision, in the same way, again and again, each time with different content. It's that last bit—the ever-changing content—that gives you the illusion that you're in control and that you're really making a different decision each time.

Let's look at what that means, to be making the same decision, each time with different content. You can probably recall that scene in a movie or a television series where the father is so committed to—or obsessed by—his work that he misses his child's birthday party once again, or the rugged cop is so fervent about justice that he has to have one more go at getting the criminal, or the young lawyer is so ambitious that she makes one more deal that compromises her firm's ethics.

Each time they'll offer a reason why *this* job, or *this* criminal, or *this* deal, is so important. What they're not seeing is that they've done that before, and last time it was just as vital. Last time it was *that* case. Now it's *this* one. Next time it'll be the next one. (Can you also see how those life-or-death red zone reactions could possibly be driving each of these people?)

The bottom line is that if you're not aware of your priority of values and how those drive your decision-making, you'll tend to make the same decision all the time, based on beliefs that were handed to you, or which you took on as a reaction to how you grew up.

More importantly, without awareness, you'll tend to risk your family, your life, or your career for the sake of those values. In the previous examples, the absent father's wife leaves him; the cop gets shot; the lawyer gets caught and disbarred.

Being aware of your inherited values means that you can start to notice the impact they have on your life. With awareness, you can start to choose what's important in different situations and modulate your behaviour accordingly. Or you can stop fooling yourself and everyone else and just declare what matters to you so that there is no self-deception and no mismatched expectations from others. (Read the *Real-Life Example* panel about Nelson Mandela later in this chapter to get a full grasp of what this looks like in real terms.)

You'll find more about working with values in the section on being nonjudgemental.

Intuition, "wise mind": Balancing the centres of intelligence

Being aware also applies to how you use your three centres of intelligence, the head, heart and gut. Without awareness, you'll tend to make a decision again and again *in the same way*.

For example, if three people, each with a different dominant style of decision-making, were deciding whether to buy a house, the instinct-based person would decide based on a "gut feel". They'd probably get this the moment they walked into the place and everything they saw would just corroborate that sense.

The heart-based person would probably weigh up the things they like against what they don't like—these would most likely be aesthetic things: the light and the airiness versus the colour—as well as the more empathic considerations, like how other people will feel. If their buying it made someone else feel bad, for example, they'd struggle to decide in favour of buying it. They'd probably take a bit more time than the gut-based person to reach the point of decision.

The head-based person would not care much for any sense or feeling. Instead, they'd probably want to know what the sales values of all similar properties in the area were for the past five years—and how much the municipal rates are and whether they're likely to increase in the next five years. They'd have to go away and do this research.

You can see that the instinctual style of decision-making is quick, even instant. The heart-based style is probably a little less quick. Instead of just making and delivering the decision, regardless of the consequences, this style is more sensitive and tries to get the overall balance, timing and placement right. The head-based style generally takes longer than both. After all, gathering data takes time. And how do you know when you have enough?

Now, everybody has a mix of decision-making styles, for sure. Yet most people also tend to lean towards one over the other, especially for those bigger decisions. Some people are quite pronounced in their preference for one style. You can see for yourself that if you're a dominant head-based, heart-based, or gut-based decision-maker, you tend to use that for all or most of your decisions. Hence the statement that you always make decisions in the *same way*.

With awareness, you can shift your decision-making style to one that is more balanced, or more relevant to the situation. The question is, why would you? Well, if you're quite extreme in one of the centres, you'll probably have had the experience that too much of a good thing becomes a bad thing. In other words, a strength, overplayed, becomes a weakness.

For instance, if you're an instinct-based person, you may have found yourself in trouble more than once for offending people, or taking unnecessary risks, because of your impulsivity. If you're quite strongly heart-based, you may find yourself overburdened by everyone else's troubles, which you've taken on instead of making some tough decisions. As the head-based person, you might have missed out on a few good opportunities or find yourself constantly butting up against some more adventurous team or family members.

These are all indicators of making decisions based on the way you are, rather than based on what the situation requires. The ability to flex between decision-making styles—to sometimes move into the head, sometimes into the heart, sometimes into the gut, can benefit you.

The possibility being presented here is for you to be aware of all three centres, to be able to balance them, and to turn up the volume of any one centre based on the situation you find yourself in. If you're buying shares, for example, you may want to turn down the volume on your instinctual, or "gut", centre, and stay tuned into the head. If you're president of a country and having to decide whether to go to war, you may want to turn up the volume on the heart centre a little before you unlock the briefcase with the red button. Or not.

You would term this integrated use of all three centres as "intuition", a "wise mind", a "knowing response". It is one of the manifestations of "maintaining the balance of your mind".

REAL-LIFE EXAMPLE

The Essence of Mandela's "Madiba Magic"

NELSON MANDELA is one of the most revered statesmen and leaders of the last century. He was very charismatic, and his charm was often referred to, using his affectionate clan name, as the "Madiba Magic". However, it wasn't just his charm that won him universal respect. Perhaps the primary attribute that earned him that admiration was his level of clarity of values, and his degree of adherence to those values.

You can view his life from a number of angles. Firstly, according to some people's standards, he can be said to have "failed" horribly as a husband and father. After all, he was hardly ever home. Firstly, he was in jail for 27 years. This statement is not intended to make light of that. Seriously, how many people would shrink back from joining a political struggle for fear of what it would mean in terms of not being home for their family?

Once again, there's no judgement here. We're just looking at what is. After all, even before he went to prison, Mandela was often on the run from the security police. And prior to that, he was out rallying people to the cause. In fact, his late ex-wife Winnie has been quoted as having said, "To be with him was to be without him."

If he had been on a modern-day leadership program that talked about work-life balance, he would probably have laughed. He was clear on his values of social transformation and he had no hesitation in putting these first, even if it meant putting his life at risk, let alone time with his family.

During the Rivonia Trial, in which he was ultimately sentenced to life in prison, he famously said, "During my lifetime I have dedicated my life to this struggle of the African people. I have fought against white domination, and I have fought against black domination. I have cherished the ideal of a democratic and free society in which all persons will live together in harmony and with equal opportunities. It is an ideal for which I hope to live and to see realised. But, my Lord, if it needs be, it is an ideal for which I am prepared to die."

This was not the kind of willingness to die that most people have when they unconsciously let their health suffer because they are slaves to a stressful job, or slaves to bad eating habits. This was the kind of grand vision that transcended self and family. It was a conscious, deliberate choice, and he proved himself willing to live true to that value.

Even so, all of this would have defined his legacy as a great and ethical warrior, but it was his legacy after he was released from prison that earned him the kind of reverence that he received from others later in his life. One particular aspect of this was his commitment to reconciliation and non-racism.

This commitment, and his actions in alignment with those values, was represented in the movie *Invictus*. One scene showed his grandson making reactive comments to two white policemen, at which Mandela senior reprimanded him. He was clear that being nonracist ran both ways and he acted on that principle. The movie also showed Mandela pressing forward with his commitment to support Springbok rugby and its right to maintain that name and emblem, despite both being one of the ultimate symbols of white male dominance.

He met with strong opposition from within his own party for this and yet he persisted. From a unification point of view, it was a masterstroke. South African went on to win the 1995 Rugby World

Cup and that achievement brought people together in a way that nobody could have anticipated.

A lot of that good has been undone by the more recent president of South Africa, Jacob Zuma, who did not represent any higher or transcendent values. By the end of his time in office, there was a general consensus that Zuma had no real values, and that he was in it just for himself. The level of corruption, as well as racial conflict, had escalated to dangerous levels during his time in office and he was eventually ousted by his own party under a cloud of scandal.

Mandela's actions give credence to this quote by Anthony Robbins from his book *Awaken the Giant Within*: "Who are the most universally admired and respected people in [your] culture? Aren't they those who have a solid grasp of their own values, people who not only profess their standards, but live by them? We all respect people who take a stand for what they believe, even if we don't concur with their ideas about what's right and what's wrong. There is power in individuals who congruently lead lives where their philosophies and actions are one."

Being Nonjudgemental | Making Right, Not Wrong

At first glance it may seem odd to suggest that you could apply being nonjudgemental to the context of decision-making. After all, isn't decision-making all about discernment, and choosing one option over another, which requires judgement? Quite right. Making judgement calls while maintaining the balance of your mind is exactly what it's all about.

However, our use of the word judgement in this context refers back to Chapter 4, where you learned that it's your labelling and judging of things as good or bad, right or wrong, desirable or not desirable—your set of preferences, in other words—that causes you to lose the balance of your mind. When you become lost in the idea of things having to be a certain way, you lose presence, and, in turn, you lose touch with reality and you can make bad decisions.

As a child I would lie on the grass and watch the clouds. Yes, those days existed, once! I could create the illusion for myself that it was me and the earth that was moving, not the clouds in the sky. See if you can picture that—or actually go out and experience it—for yourself right now.

You can think of situations and events in your life as being like those clouds. You can create the illusion that you're moving past them as a result of your decisions, but in fact they're just passing into and through your life. You think you're choosing them, but what if you're not? You think you're directing them, but what if you're not? What if you could just as easily stand back and smile and wave and get the same results?!

Yes, that's a scary thought, and it's not 100% the case, yet it's a lot closer to reality than the illusion that you control everything. I already referred to this, and gave a quote by Carl Jung on the matter, in Chapter 7.

Being nonjudgemental enables you to mindfully balance your own beliefs, judgements and preferences against the situation and thereby make decisions based on what's real, what matters and what you can and can't influence.

There are a number of areas in which the word judgement—and being nonjudgemental—can be applied within the context of decision-making:

- Your preferences
- Your values
- Your decision-making style
- Your red zone triggers

Let's look at each one in turn.

Your preferences

Your decisions are strongly informed by your beliefs and you generally hold your beliefs to be right and other people's beliefs, if they disagree with yours, to be wrong—a judgement, in other words. To make matters worse, as you saw in the red zone section of the previous chapter, you hold onto your beliefs, and their associated judgements, at pain of death—yes, to the point of being willing to die for them.

One outcome of this strong attachment to your own beliefs—or judgements—is that you may make decisions that don't consider the full scope of the reality you're dealing with. For example, you might decide to punish someone because what they did was "wrong" or "not up to standard". Meanwhile, other people are telling you that those standards are insane, or that you're too inflexible with them. You might know this, but you just can't stop yourself. For sure, there are times when you are right, that people should measure up, but do you know the difference, and can you act differently in different situations? Because, if not, you're probably being reactive.

Other judgements you can probably notice in yourself include the judgement that one outcome will be good, and another one bad, or that one outcome you will like; another, you will not.

When you become too focused on your preferences, you lose touch with reality, and you try to force your agenda on the world. You become a bit of a tyrant where you could be more like the scientist. The tyrant says, "Things *must* happen like this!" The scientist, on the other hand, says, "I wonder what will happen if I try this?" The scientist weighs things up and tries things out, tweaking one variable at a time and then observing with a sense of fascination. As the scientist, you're in a dance with reality, responding instead of reacting.

To bring this closer to home: if you are or have been a parent, especially of teenagers, think about how many times you tried to force your agenda on your child and it didn't work. The challenge is to be more like the scientist and see what happens. Of course, your ability to do this is affected by how much the decision is likely to impact the all-important *me / my / mine*.

As you can see, being nonjudgemental in the context of decision-making, firstly, means holding your judgements about the situation (*good / bad, right / wrong, like / don't like*) and your preferences for the outcome lightly. This can also be termed as being *non-attached*, or, as some people say, *detached*. However, you're not detached as in not caring and not doing anything. You care very much, but you're more open to what happens, and ready to respond if it doesn't go your way.

This is a good place to once again reference the "Maybe" story and the fact that sometimes things happen that turn out better than your decision would have.

A good analogy for being non-attached would be a politician who campaigns for an election wholeheartedly, and then accepts defeat at the polls gracefully. The tyrant doesn't accept losing at the polls, and takes over by force. He (it's usually a he, isn't it?) becomes a dictator. We've seen examples of this type of decision-making by, for example, a number of African leaders. Idi Amin. Mobuto Sese Seko. Robert Mugabe. Conversely, Nelson Mandela did not seek a second term as president of South Africa. You can be sure that he probably still wanted the position, and was just as passionate about his beliefs, and yet he stepped aside with grace.

Your values

In addition to the above, being nonjudgemental in the context of decision-making means recognising that your priority of values is personal, and not an absolute truth. Therefore, you don't judge people who have a different priority of values; you recognise that they are not wrong, they are merely different.

This enables you to choose which values you're going to serve in each situation. For example, when your spouse asks you to attend a school event for the kids' sake, at a time when you think you ought to be working to make money, or change the world, you can both choose to actively let go of your judgements about what matters most and look at the situation. Sometimes it may be appropriate to go; on another occasion, it may not.

Similarly, knowing and being clear on your priority of values is important for being able to deal with the complexities mentioned at the beginning of this chapter. Without the strong reference points that were provided by social norms and religion in past generations, you need to be clear on your own values and have the strength to remain committed to those. An important aspect of this is to be nonjudgemental about your own values in the face of judgement from others. The example given earlier of Nelson Mandela speaks directly to this.

A lot of confusion disappears when you get clear on your priority of values. Anthony Robbins says, "If you've ever found yourself in a situation where you had a tough time making a decision about something, the reason is that you weren't clear about what you value most within that situation. ... All decision-making comes down to values clarification."

Sometimes, this may put you at odds with your world. However, as the Mandela example illustrates, the world also admires people who are clear on their values and live by them.

Your decision-making style

When you are being nonjudgemental, you are also able to "listen" better—to what your gut is telling you, to what your heart is telling you, and to observe and manage your thoughts. This means you can integrate your different decision-making centres and not rely so strongly on that one centre that you insist has always worked for you.

If you're considering a major investment, for example, and you want to just "go on gut" as you always have, you might be willing to give time to the head that whispers the need to do more research, or vice versa.

You can then decide to treat each situation on its merits: some situations require speed; others require caution, and research.

Being nonjudgemental can also mean surrendering any judgements you may have based on your style of decision-making (head-based, heart-based, or gut-based) versus that of the other person. You can tolerate, and perhaps even learn from, the other person's style.

Letting go of your judgements that your style is the right one, that the other person's is wrong, creates the space for this to happen.

Your red zone trigger

One more area in which it will be useful to surrender the judgement that your way is the right way, is with regards to your red zone trigger, identified in the previous chapter. If your red zone gets triggered when people break the rules, or don't comply with procedures, for example, and someone is suggesting you tolerate that, you may want to take a moment to see whether it really matters, or not. In some cases it will; in others, it won't.

Some people are ardent peacemakers and their red zone gets triggered when they have to speak up, or assert their own will on the world. They find it as hard to speak up as some people do to shut up. If you're that kind of person then you need to let go of the fears and judgements you have about making decisions, and step out onto the playing field and announce yourself.

Some people's red zone trigger is hearing the word *no*, or being told that there are restrictions of any kind. They see this as being negative in some way. Once again, if you decide to rebel every time you hear this, it's probably about you more than it is about the situation. You'd need to assess your judgements and fears with regards to people saying no.

In all of the above, if you recognise and let go of your judgement, you are better placed to make a mindful, conscious decision. You can decide based on the situation, and not based on your fears—or judgements—about the situation.

If you recall the "Maybe" story once again, you can see that outcomes you may have dreaded very often contain their own silver lining. Yet you usually only see that in retrospect and after much resistance. What if you could see that up front, every time you made a decision, no matter how serious it was? Take life seriously, and, at the same time, treat it like an experiment, even a game (albeit a serious game), and be open to what might happen. You never know, life might provide a better outcome in the long-term than you could ever conjure up.

PRACTICE - SAVE FOR LATER

Daily Decision Check-In

DO A daily check-in for any decisions you need to make, and make them, while considering the following questions:

- What decisions do I need to make?

- If I am unable to decide something, where is my priority of values conflicted with regards to that issue? Which set of values do I choose to prioritise in this instance?

- If I am in conflict with someone else over a decision I need to make, what judgements or preferred outcomes am I (or, could they be) holding onto that we can both hold less tightly?

- What wants to happen in this situation that I can align myself with, instead of resisting it?

- What positive outcomes could emerge even if things don't go my way (as in the "Maybe" story)?

Being Nonreactive | Paying Attention to What Matters

Being nonjudgemental—and non-attached—opens up the possibility of being nonreactive. As you know by now, the indicator of being nonreactive is that you are able to exercise choice, instead of just having a knee-jerk reaction. The choice you have, with regards to decision-making, is to decide based on the situation, and not based on your judgements, preferences, fears, or blind beliefs.

The first step in being nonreactive is to maintain the balance of your mind. This means managing the paradox of having an intention, but not trying to control outcomes. Other paradoxes to manage include: not having to act, but being ready to; not having to be right, but supporting your own point of view; not having to win or have things go your way, but still proposing them.

To achieve this in some situations, which border on being red zone issues, where you want to start treating the matter like it's the end of the world, it may be useful to use the techniques introduced previously to ground yourself. Place yourself in space and time. Recognise that the sun won't fall out of the sky.

You can take this a step further and consider the vastness of space and time (or, to be technically correct, the vast infinity of this moment). Consider how much has happened on the infinite canvas of history and how insignificant the events of this moment are. Remember that events are passing through this moment the way those clouds passed over you in the experiment mentioned earlier.

When you see yourself within the context of the infinity of space and time, you gain the other perspective that you were missing when you were treating the situation like it was the end of the world. You regain the balance of your mind. You can do your checks. What is my priority of values and how is that being impacted by this situation? What are the priorities of values of the other people involved? Can I get myself and them to each hold our own priority of values a little less tightly? What about my decision-making style? What about my red zone trigger? Can I put all of those mindfully on the table and then decide based on what the situation needs?

That last question is important, and you may want to consider that for a moment. Every decision is ultimately an answer to a question. Often you are answering the question, *What do I want to have happen?* There is that all-important *me / my / mine* identification that is linked to the loss of presence and hence the loss of perspective. Yet you are part of the situation and, as you've seen, far less able to direct the situation than you like to believe.

A better question that can guide your decision-making is, *What wants to happen in this situation?*

This implies a *teleological* approach to the situation. Teleology is a concept that originates out of the writings of Plato and Aristotle. It means that things that are happening now can be explained in terms of their ultimate end goal, or purpose. For example, a child wants a chemistry set and goes on to become a great chemist who produces a cure for cancer. Something in the child, or the situation, knows what wants to happen.

Clearly, teleology is not a perspective that modern science and business will easily endorse, however, the discovery of quantum physics confirmed what the Buddha said 2,500 years ago: that reality is made up of tiny elements which he called *kalapas*, which are constantly vibrating in and out of reality. So we'll use a teleological approach, which is very hard to prove, except anecdotally, and wait for modern science and business to catch up.

Seriously, on a purely practical level, asking, *What wants to happen?* causes you to pull back and see the bigger picture, with yourself in it, as a part of it. It enables you to gain perspective on what you can and can't impact. It creates a context for you to consider the notion that most situations take care of themselves. This can lead you to consider which one, or which part of one, needs your attention, and therefore your decision.

Being nonreactive with regards to decision-making can mean forcing yourself on reality a whole lot less. For some, this may seem counterintuitive. I'd point them to the series *The Crown*, in which the young Queen Elizabeth learns that her power lies in *not* choosing sides, in *not* stating her preferences, but in being a neutral outsider. By exercising this, she gained tremendous power, firstly over herself and, secondly, she retained her political power in a way that no other modern monarch has done.

Each person is different and there's no single, hard-and-fast rule being applied here. Discernment is needed for each situation. If you've been a control freak, then being nonreactive may see you consistently deciding to stand back and observe—deciding to not decide, but to see what happens. Except sometimes. Or making decisions that only affect one variable in a situation, rather than trying to affect them all, and then watching to see what happens. Of course, for some people, it may mean making *more* decisions, being *more* proactive, getting themselves *onto* the playing field.

Another aspect to bear in mind is that once you've made a decision, further thoughts and feelings might come up. These will naturally contain judgements and preferences that may tempt you to go back on that decision, or to undo it by another contradictory decision. Being nonreactive means letting those thoughts and feelings pass and staying with your decision. Except sometimes. Like if there's significant new information or input. Or you just know you were wrong—be careful now, this should not happen too often, and yet you should always be willing to consider it.

WHAT DIFFERENCE DOES IT MAKE?

THE POWER to decide is the power that separates humans from all other life forms. It gives you the power to create anything you choose—and the power to destroy, both your own life and the lives of others.

It could be the characteristic that is referred to in the Biblical writing that says we are made in the image of God. Certainly, it elevates us to the level of gods in the secular sense.

If you don't know that you have that power, then it's dangerous in your hands. If you know you have that power available to you, but you don't find out *how* to use it, that's not only dangerous, but irresponsible.

The performance of modern sportscars has reached a level that would have challenged the skills of most racing drivers a generation ago. Yet they are sold without any additional driving skill requirements. In South Africa, there are frequent media reports of one of these expensive cars—often very recently acquired—being in accidents where people get injured or even killed.

As the saying goes, with great power comes great responsibility.

Animals don't have the power of decision and so they cannot create, they can only react. Notably, animals have not destroyed the environment—and don't destroy their own lives—as we humans are currently at risk of doing.

Having this tremendous power available to us, and then being in a constantly reactive state while we use it is quite possibly the source of the destruction we are wreaking on the world. Not to mention the destruction that each person wreaks in their own life. Conversely, being mindful of this power and using it with nonjudgemental awareness is the ultimate exercise of your power and the height of your responsibility.

You can't control outcomes, but you can control your inputs. When you live in this way you come as close as you can to the experience expressed in the poem *Invictus*, which so inspired Nelson Mandela: "I am the master of my fate; I am the captain of my soul."

One of the major problems of the modern, technological society, is that everything has to be done now. We treat everything—every text message, every email—like it's the end of the world. Technologies that were supposed to save us time have made us slaves to this kind of unconscious reactivity. Things have to happen *now*.

This brings us to one final point about being nonreactive with regards to decision-making: How much time do you really have to make a decision? Well, the deeper question is, how do you want to live your life? Do you want to run around in a blind, mindless, reactive panic?

If not, perhaps you can start to practice being nonreactive by not leaping onto your phone every time you hear a message tone, and by not checking your email every ten minutes. Leave it. Go outside. Look at the sky. Remind yourself that the world will not end. And then decide when you will read the message or the email.

Once you've read the message, decide if, when and how you will respond. Indeed, some decisions need to be made quickly. However, many don't. Once again, responding is different from reacting in that it implies choice. Mindfully choose what needs your attention right now, and what may be left for later—or left altogether to sort itself out. Then welcome yourself to a different, better experience of life.

CHAPTER SUMMARY

THIS CHAPTER looks at the application of mindfulness to the subject of complexity and decision-making. Key content includes:

- Decisions shape your destiny. You can wait until they're forced on you, or get ahead of the curve and make them mindfully.
- The gut as the "second brain": how the new field of neurogastroenterology is linking the gut to mental health.
- Being aware begins with recognising how you tend to make decisions based on your priority of values and how you use the three centres of intelligence—head, heart and gut.
- Scientific references to the vital role that emotions play in decision-making.
- Nelson Mandela as a real-life example of values-based living and decision-making.
- Being nonjudgemental in the context of decision-making means not trying so hard to control outcomes and not being so attached to your own preferences.
- Being nonjudgemental also applies to your values, your decision-making style and your red zone fears.

- Being nonreactive in the context of decision-making means making decisions based what the situation needs, or on what wants to happen. This implies a teleological approach.
- It also means deciding what needs your attention and when.
- Decision-making is a power that belongs uniquely to human beings and therefore implies a responsibility to use that power wisely.

9 | Flow for High Performance

D O YOU experience life as a constant struggle where very little seems to go your way? Do you find yourself having to apply a lot of effort, even force, to get things done? Do you struggle to come to terms with the tide of events and the way things are going?

The fashionable approach to this subject is to say that the entire universe is always conspiring in your favour—you only have to get into the right "hum" and you'll attract everything you want and need. Well, that's if you believe *The Secret*. But let's face it, the universe has been around for billions of years. It wasn't waiting for you so that it could serve you like it was some giant slot machine.

That took you by surprise, didn't it? OK, let's get serious. What if both views are true at the same time? In other words, it's another of those dual-perspective challenges. Whichever you're looking for is what you'll see. In other words, if you approach your position in the universe from an outside-in, statistical probability perspective, you shouldn't even exist, and the universe, with its exploding stars, cares nought for you. However, if you look from the inside-out, you could say that this entire creation, from start to finish and from limitless end to limitless end, had to exist in order for you to have the experience that you're having right now. Isn't that a marvellous thought?!

From the outside-in perspective, life appears to be a dangerous and meaningless struggle. From the inside-out perspective, it's a nurturing and meaningful miracle. (Ever wonder where heaven and hell are? What if they're all around you, and your perspective creates them?!) What if life is both dangerous and nurturing at the same time and, whichever it is for you, depends, not only on the perspective you choose, but also the actions you take?

That last point is potentially very empowering—it implies that there's something you can do about it. Well, according to years of scientific research, in particular by psychologist Mihaly Csikszentmihalyi, it's apparently true. There is something you can do about it. The state of flow—that optimal experience where you feel in tune with and supported by all of life—is real and it's within your power.

The even better news is that it's a self-fulfilling prophecy: the more flow you experience, the more inclined you will be to believe—based on evidence—that all of life is designed to support you having this experience right now and, consequently, the more meaning and fulfilment you will experience.

This doesn't mean that it's easy or that it falls out of the sky. It's more like the concept of a flywheel. Getting a flywheel to turn requires the input of external energy—which requires effort and commitment—at first. Once it's gained momentum, it spins easily on its own without having to add more energy or effort. Instead, it can deliver energy more smoothly and beyond the capacity of its energy source.

Similarly, the state of flow can be activated and sustained by your own actions, which, yes, requires an initial input of effort and commitment.

Read on and discover how to apply your mindfulness experience in a way that can activate and sustain the flow state, and thereby transform your experience of life.

With this chapter you will:

- Gain an understanding of the power of presence and the nature of flow;
- Learn how to recognise—and to activate—the state of flow;
- Learn to integrate "making happen" versus "letting happen";
- Discover the main obstacle to remaining in flow when you find yourself in flow.

The "What Is" of Flow

A LOT has been written about the subject—and the state—of flow, and most people seem to know what it is when you talk about it. Almost everybody, it seems, has had a flow experience at some point in their lives: that "state of joy, creativity and total involvement in which problems seem to disappear and there is an exhilarating feeling of transcendence".

The quote above comes from the definitive book on the subject, *Flow: The Psychology of Happiness*, written by Mihály Csikszentmihalyi (pronounced shik-shunt-mi-hal-yi), professor and former chairman of the Dept of Psychology at the University of Chicago. He is generally recognised as the person who has done the most to lend scientific credibility to—and to popularise—the phenomenon, which he also termed "optimal experience".

Perhaps his most remarkable finding is that the state of flow is not random. It arises when a distinctive set of factors are present. It may appear to arise randomly for those who don't know this, and who find themselves in a situation where the relevant factors are present. However, for those who do know, the state of flow, or optimal experience, can be: (a) recognised by the presence of those factors; and (b) deliberately activated by bringing those factors into play.

The factors, or "elements of enjoyment", that are generally present when one is experiencing the state of flow are:

- **A challenging activity that requires skills** You're unlikely to experience that state of flow while sitting on the couch watching TV. It's more likely to happen while you're engaged in a task that is at the outer range of your level of skills for that task. You need to believe that you have the potential to succeed, and some doubt that you might not (otherwise it's too easy).

- **Clear goals and feedback** The activity is not random. You have clear goals, you know what those goals are, and you get consistent, immediate feedback as to your progress towards those goals. For example, if you're playing sport, your goal might be to win, and you're either hitting the ball and scoring the points or not. If you're playing music, your goal might be to play a song perfectly and with feeling, and you're either hitting the notes or not.

- **The paradox of control** It's often the riskier activities that elicit the state of flow, eg. mountain climbing, surgery. This is because you are confronted with a doubtful outcome, yet, through your skill level, you're able to influence that outcome. If genuine physical risk is not for you, then any task that is both challenging and important enough can offer this for you.

- **Intrinsic reward (the activity is done for its own sake)** Although the goal may be to win, or to get to the top of the mountain, that goal becomes forgotten for the sake of the experience of doing the activity and doing it well. When this is the case, the activity becomes known as an *autotelic* activity—one that is done for its own sake. The goal becomes secondary or peripheral to using the activity to learn, improve, stretch your skills, perfect your craft, and master your attention.

- **The merging of action and awareness** For the reason that it requires all the skills you currently have available for that task, your attention naturally becomes fully absorbed by the current action you are taking.

There is no attention left for anything else. This results in two by-products:

- o **Concentration on the task at hand** This one is great. It speaks directly to mindfulness! In the words of Csikszentmihalyi, "When an activity is thoroughly engrossing, there is not enough attention left over to allow a person to consider either the past or the future, or any other temporarily irrelevant stimuli." This is probably one of the main reasons why flow is so enjoyable. Because your attention is focused purely on the task, you forget all your worries and everything else about your life.

- o **The loss of self-consciousness** "One item that disappears from awareness deserves special mention, because in normal life we spend so much time thinking about it: our own self," says Csikszentmihalyi. This temporary suspension of awareness *of* the self is perhaps another reason why the experience is so enjoyable. It's similar in that sense to what happens when you watch an enthralling movie in a cinema with no distractions. If the task has been sufficiently challenging, then the self is further "enriched by new skills and fresh achievements". This "expansion of the self" clearly adds to the enjoyability of the experience.

- **The transformation of time** Most often, people who have been in the flow state report the compression of time: hours seem to last minutes. Some ballet dancers in Csikszentmihalyi's study reported that "a difficult turn that takes less than a second in real time stretches out for what seems like minutes". Either way, the transformation of time into a wholly subjective experience is a by-product of being in flow, while being free from the tyranny of time clearly adds to the enjoyment that you derive from the state.

To summarise, flow arises when there is intense focus at the outer limit of your skill level on a task or activity where the outcome, and the activity itself, really matters to you. This could mean, for example, putting up shelves at home, or creating a mosaic. It could mean hiking, running or cycling a challenging new route. It could imply a career project, like writing a book and getting it published. It requires a goal, and an activity that can provide immediate feedback. It should be an activity that you enjoy or that produces an outcome that you're passionate about.

Author and spiritual teacher Eckhart Tolle uses the word *enthusiasm* to describe something similar: "Enthusiasm means there is deep enjoyment and what you do plus the added element of a goal or a vision that you work toward." His use of the word *enjoyment* is specific. By his definition, the joy "does not come from what you do, it flows into what you do". In other words, you will enjoy any mindfully chosen activity, done with full presence, that is not just a means to an end.

Tolle's definition points to an important caveat noted by Csikszentmihalyi, who said, "Some things we are initially forced to do against our will turn out in the course of time to be intrinsically rewarding. ... Often children—and adults—need external incentives to take the first steps in an activity that requires a difficult restructuring of attention. Most enjoyable activities are not natural; they demand an effort that initially one is reluctant to make. But once the interaction starts to provide feedback to the person's skills, it usually begins to be intrinsically rewarding."

This is well illustrated by one of the world's leading ultra-marathon runners, the South African Bruce Fordyce: he has said that he would run past the second lamppost before he made the decision whether to train each day or not. On a more general level, when you take up running, there is difficulty, pain and stiffness to contend with. Once you start getting fit, you can become enthused to the thrill of challenging your best time.

As you can see, a challenging goal is an essential element for initiating flow. Enjoyment is an input and enthusiasm is an outcome. Activity is the axis. So often, people look for the activity or career path that will "make" them happy. What this shows us is that you can find enjoyment and flow by doing any activity. As Tolle says, "It isn't the action you perform that you really enjoy, but the deep sense of aliveness that flows into it."

Of course, there may be some things you detest, so you're allowed to exclude things. The point is to not sit back and wait until you've figured out which activity you enjoy most. Chances are, you can get into a state of flow while doing any activity.

What's clear is that the flow factors are under your control. You can choose to create activities—and even work scenarios—for yourself that match the first four criteria above, and then invest in them fully. Once you're up and running, the other factors—the merging of action and awareness, the transformation of time— will arise of their own accord, and can be promoted through mindful awareness.

This becomes easier as a result of mindful living. "When you make the present moment, instead of past and future, the focal point of your life, your ability to enjoy what you do—and with it the quality of your life—increases dramatically," says Tolle. You might decide to start by applying this at a micro-level, for example by engaging in a hobby on weekends. Then you may choose to expand it into all your activities until it becomes a way of life.

THE SCIENCE

The Flowiness of Flow

FLOW SOUNDS like a very unscientific topic. Instead, it conjures up images of 1960s hippies in California just "going with the flow", like, being all groovy, man.

However, the term was chosen by Mihály Csikszentmihalyi because that was the word that people most commonly used to describe the state when he began to research it, using scientific methods, in Chicago in the 1970s.

Abraham Maslow had already delved into the subject back in the 1940s, when he identified states that he called "peak experiences". The idea had even older roots in psychology and physiology through the William James protégé, Walter Bradford Cannon, who in the 1900s, identified the fight-or-flight response that was seen to result in heightened levels of performance. Of course, most ancient religions and martial arts forms had long laid claim to such states, and offered practices, such as chanting, or the kata, designed to induce them.

Csikszentmihalyi's research began with various experts—chess players, surgeons, dancers—in and around Chicago and expanded globally to include a vast range of professions and activities: Navajo shepherds, Italian farmers, old women from Korea, teenage bikers in Tokyo. Researchers in Canada, Germany, Italy, Japan, and Australia took up its investigation. It became one of the largest psychological surveys ever conducted.

In the beginning the data consisted of interviews and questionnaires. To achieve greater precision, they developed a technique called the Experience Sampling Method, in which people wore an electronic paging device for a week and wrote down how they felt and what they were thinking about whenever the pager signalled, which was about eight times a day, at random intervals.

By the time he published the second edition of his book *Flow: The Psychology of Happiness* in 2002 (the first edition was published in

1992), over a hundred thousand such "cross sections of experience" had been collected from different parts of the world.

These studies suggested that "optimal experiences were described in the same way by men and women, by young people and old, regardless of cultural differences".

However, a major shortcoming of this research, despite its statistical validity, is that it was based on reported experience. At a scientific level, this is always less desirable than empirical evidence derived from physical measures like heart rate or brainwaves, which are less subject to interpretation or influence by the subject.

Advances in brain imaging technology have changed all that and, as a *Time* magazine article by Steven Kotler pointed out in 2014, the results have shown that the term "flow" was well-chosen: it accurately describes what happens in the brain when the state of flow, or optimal experience, is achieved.

For example, a study of jazz musicians done in 2008, and reported in the aforementioned *Time* article, found that the dorsolateral prefrontal cortex deactivated when they played. That's the area of the brain responsible for self-monitoring, i.e. where your inner critic lives. With that switched off, the mind stops second-guessing and allows the free flow of creativity, automatic problem-solving and risk-taking. The more efficient subconscious, intrinsic processing system takes over.

Further studies reported in the same *Time* article, showed that brainwaves slow down too: from the high-paced beta waves of your normal waking state down to the much slower alpha (day-dreaming mode) and theta (pre-sleep mode) waves. This may sound dangerous, but the benefit is that, as in dreams, ideas begin to combine in more radical ways—ways that wouldn't happen when the mind is under conscious control.

Finally, the neurochemistry of the brain has also been shown to change: there is an increase in endorphins, norepinephrine (noradrenaline), dopamine, anandamide and serotonin—a cocktail of performance-enhancing, pleasure-inducing neurochemicals.

As the *Time* article concluded, "Csikszentmihaly was more right than he could have known. Not only does flow *feel* flowy; neurobiologically, it actually *is* flowy."

Applying the Three Key Elements

AS YOU can see, flow is not random. Instead, it arises when, as Csikszentmihalyi puts it, there is "order in consciousness". In past generations, there were many activities that people naturally engaged in that generated a state of flow. Simple things like mending clothes or fixing machinery, baking, gardening, DIY. These days, you tend to outsource those things, or you buy ready-made mixes and bang them in the microwave. Machines are digitised, so when they break you need a specialised programmer, or they consist of replaceable parts, so you don't spend enough time engaged in the repair activity to generate a flow experience.

You end up sitting on the couch, looking at your phone a hundred times a day, which is a very fragmented experience. Or you watch TV. Perhaps the people who have the best possibility of a flow experience in this day and age are PC gamers— and then they get addicted, so it's one extreme to the other.

If your environment is not naturally producing opportunities for flow experiences, then you have to deliberately create them. In addition, bringing mindful awareness to those activities is needed to produce the state of flow, or optimal experience.

Read on to discover how you can apply the three key elements of mindfulness to the context of flow.

Being Aware | What Is My Motivational State?

Being aware in the context of flow means paying attention to your current motivational state as well as your relationship to the present moment, which includes present events and present activities.

There are five broad motivational states that you may find yourself in: rest (active recovery); ennui (boredom, which if sustained can develop into depression); animation (being in positive mental or physical action towards creating something or resolving a problem, which if sustained with the right variables can lead to flow); agitation (pushing to make things happen faster than reality will allow, which destroys the possibility of flow); and flow (which cannot be sustained indefinitely for any single activity, but must be constantly created and recreated).

One thing that shifts you from ennui to animation is the imposition of external factors. For example, a danger enters your environment, or your boss, or spouse, is on his or her way and you need to catch up on tasks you agreed to do. That would be a reactive ignition of the animated state—reactive because it's reliant on external factors.

Humans also have the capacity to consciously and deliberately activate the shift from ennui to animation. In other words, it can be a conscious decision. To do this, you decide on a desired outcome, commit to take the action that will produce that outcome, and then you act on that commitment. This would be proactive, or, in our terminology, a conscious, mindful response.

For example, when my son was little, I'd come home from work and he'd want to play. Naturally, I often didn't have the energy to keep up with him as a five-year-old. So I'd play, but I'd do it half-heartedly and the time seemed to stretch out forever. One day I decided to apply this principle. I needed an inspiring outcome, so I decided that, from now on, it wouldn't be me who asked to stop, it would be him. I would play with so much gusto that *I* would exhaust *him*!

It was a tall order and as you can imagine, I played with a lot of intensity after that! Remarkably, time flew. Plus, ironically, it never took as long as I'd feared before he was ready to turn to some other activity and I could, with good conscience, say no. I felt better for it afterwards. It was good for him and for our relationship.

Whether it's ignited by an external factor or internal decision, you become animated by the activation of an internal energy, which for our purposes here we can call the *life force*, or *will*.

In the reactive approach mentioned above, that life force would be ignited by an external event and would probably be described as some form of anxiety, fear or anger. In the case of the mindful response, the same life force would be activated internally by a conscious choice. Once it gathers momentum, it would probably look a lot like, and be described as, *passion*, or Eckhart Tolle's *enthusiasm*, mentioned earlier.

"When you add a goal to the enjoyment of what you do," says Tolle, "... [a] certain degree of what we might call structural tension is now added to enjoyment, and so it turns into enthusiasm. At the height of creative activity fuelled by enthusiasm there will be enormous intensity and energy beyond what you do. You will feel like an arrow that is moving toward the target—and enjoying the journey."

As you can see, the action is fuelled by the same energy; the energy is transformed according to whether it's sparked reactively or creatively. Remember, *creative* is an anagram of *reactive*! Just as fire and nuclear energy can be used destructively, they can also be used constructively. Similarly, passion or enthusiasm—that state of flow developed through mindful action—is a positive expression of the same life force energy. Perhaps this is what the alchemists were pointing to all the time when they talked about transforming lead into gold: the transformation of energy through a conscious act of will.

Csikszentmihalyi says, "The autotelic experience, or flow, lifts the course of life to a different level. Alienation gives way to involvement, enjoyment replaces boredom, helplessness turns into a feeling of control, and psychic energy works to reinforce the sense of self, instead of ... being held hostage to a hypothetical future gain."

So, the next time you find yourself feeling down, become aware of your motivational state. Identify in what area you're suppressing or denying the life force. Then decide what to do about it. Take action—or adjust your current actions—in a way that meets all the elements of flow, with a view to potentially igniting the state of flow, or optimal experience. As Tolle says, "You don't have to wait for something 'meaningful' to come into your life so that you can finally enjoy what you do." Essentially, you want to set yourself a task that has a meaningful outcome, which challenges your current skill and risk levels, and then immerse yourself in it.

When people experience low motivation as a result of a lack of meaning in their lives, their response is often to withdraw further into themselves, to reflect, or "process", as though the solution might be found by thinking about it. If that's you, then you're invited to test the veracity of the following statement: "If you haven't solved the problems of the world (or your own problems) within 20 minutes, go and wash the dishes."

It sounds trite, but there is a world of truth behind that statement—and, most people report back, it works. Of course, washing the dishes is an analogy for engaging in any activity, but it implies that you start small, with manageable tasks. Ironically, people struggling with low motivation or depression often do have unwashed dishes, and cleaning up your physical environment is a good place to start.

The ongoing denial or suppression of the life force energy leads to depression. Conversely, being aware of and connected to one's life force, and being able to activate it consciously, lifts and sustains one's energy to accomplish tasks, goals and objectives. If you allow this to happen it creates a positive feedback loop. More energy begets more energy. Depression fades away like the mist before the sun.

"Expansion and positive change on the outer level is much more likely to come into your life if you can enjoy what you are doing already, instead of waiting for some change so that you can start enjoying what you do," says Tolle.

REAL-LIFE EXAMPLE

Vasbyt! – The Mother of All Challenges

I SERVED my mandatory national service in the South African military during the late 1980s. On the officers' course, you knew that one day you would be woken up for the endurance hike that was commonly known as *Vasbyt*.

Vasbyt is an Afrikaans word that translates to "bite the bullet" and it's a perfect moniker for this activity, which is an adventure race on steroids in which the training officers do their very best to break you psychologically.

To kick it off, they woke us with sirens in the middle of the night. They allocated equipment for us to carry, but insufficient materials to make the braces we needed to carry it on. Even so, we had to lug this equipment along a narrow crevice of space that ran between a steep embankment and a railway line. For miles. For hours. For a whole day, it turned out.

Towards sunset, we were allowed to drop our load and we marched on easier terrain. Up ahead was a luxurious-looking tent. Ah, this would not be so bad, we all thought. We were directed past the tent, down the road and into the night.

All through the night we were given scouting exercises to do. If you returned without the right information, you were sent back. It was freezing cold, so that if you sat still for too long you froze. All the while, officers drove along the route in trucks offering you a ride back to camp if you wanted to give up. Many did.

Eventually, in the early hours of the morning, we were given time to sleep out on the open *veld*. Just as we'd settled into our sleeping bags, they began to play music, backwards, through loudspeakers, while blue emergency lights flashed. Needless to say, we didn't sleep much. The next day things got tougher, and more pointless, and the encouragement was still there for you to give up and hop on a truck and go home.

Today, thirty years later, I still remember clearly the moment on that second day when I decided that I would not give up. I would finish this. It was pointless, but I would own it. I would make it my own. I would conquer this thing, whatever it was. At that moment I felt a surge of energy flood through me. I felt alive and powerful in a way that I had never known, even though I'd played competitive rugby at a high level.

I had kept my tiny portion of rations but shared them with a guy who had run out of his own, so that by day three I had no food left. By day four, it was each to his own and you had to find your way home, before cut-off time.

For the last half a day we walked back along that railway line. Everyone was too exhausted and hungry to even speak. You just put one foot in front of the other and dared not stop. If you made it before the first cut-off time you could gain the honour of "flying colours". Some guys took to running to make it.

I just missed that cut-off, but I made the main time and, soon after, I found myself back in my bungalow, standing alongside my bed, reluctant to remove my backpack. *Is that all*, I thought. *That wasn't so bad! I could go again!*

I never imagined that I would have been able to endure what I had just been through, and yet I felt that I could do more. The four days seemed to have flown by.

Before the army, I had always enjoyed running for fitness. I had run a distance of five to eight kilometres, almost daily, throughout my teenage years. When I returned home after having completed *Vasbyt*, I noticed that my running times dropped by a quarter.

The reason? I had always paced myself and kept something in reserve. After *Vasbyt*, I knew that it was all in the mind, that you could push yourself so much harder and that, when you did, you entered the zone, that place where nothing mattered, where pain was pleasure, and you could go forever—and all because of a decision to totally own an apparently impossible activity!

 # Being Nonjudgemental | Letting Go of Outcomes

At the risk of overstating it, flow is an active process. It requires initiation by decision, followed by sustained action within certain parameters, eg. challenge and concentration. However, as you've seen, you often don't feel like doing the activity that is required to generate the state of flow. Or you don't think it's the right one. You're not sure if it will really bring you the enjoyment that you're after.

From a mindfulness perspective, you can say that your judgements, or preferences, are in the way. If it's not the wrong activity, it's the wrong time. The weather—or other conditions—are wrong. For example, you wanted to go running, but now it's raining. You wanted to host a dinner party, but now's not the right time for everyone you'd want to invite. You wanted to do some writing or studying, but now you just don't feel like it.

If you heard those reasons from someone else—your friends or your own children, for example—you might call them excuses. Coming from yourself, you tend to believe them. In most instances, the conditions don't matter. You can run in the rain. There's never a good time to host a dinner party. You never really feel like studying. Once again, how many times has it happened to you that you did something you didn't want to do, or at a time that didn't seem to suit you, and it turned out to be fun, or beneficial in some way?

In fact, you might even say that passing through some kind of a dip, or overcoming some kind of resistance or inertia, is a necessary condition for initiating flow. This is illustrated in the Flow Experience Ladder diagram below, which is based on the work of Georg Simmel, who described four categories of human experience.

Lazing around and being in that ennui state may feel good, but you know it's not good for you, it's not good for others and doesn't serve a higher purpose, like getting you fit. That would be Level 1 on the Flow Experience Ladder. Where you want to be is at Level 3, which is that flow state. It feels good, and it's good for you, good for others, and serves a higher purpose. To get there, you have to pass through Level 2, which—you guessed it—doesn't feel good, yet it's good for you, good for others, and serves a higher purpose.

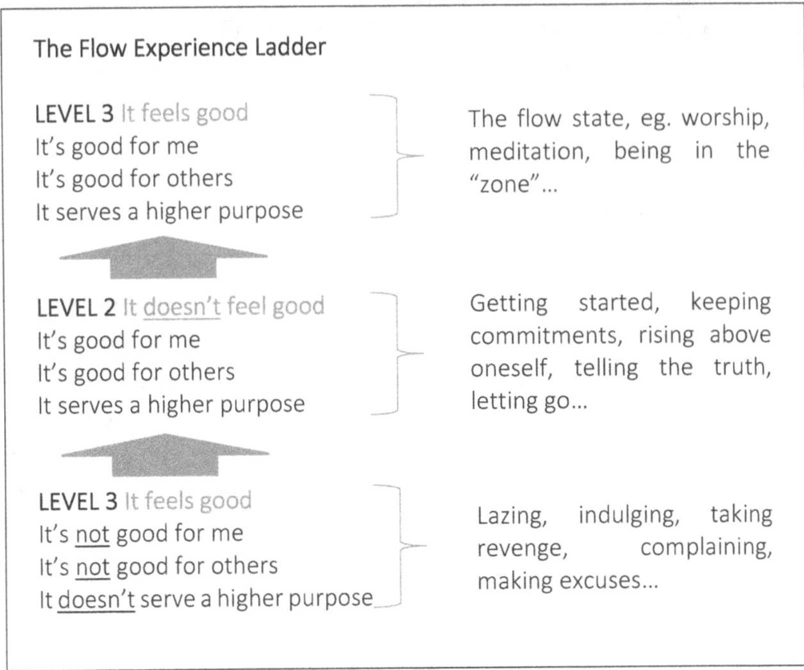

So, you can say that when it comes to creating flow experiences, you almost never feel like it. Yet you can do it. Your ability to decide and to act is independent of your judgements—those pesky thoughts and feelings. The bungee jumper standing on the side of the bridge often doesn't feel like it and doesn't think it's such a good idea anymore. Yet she can still jump. Giving up your attachment to your preferences, or judgements, about the situation or the activity, is the key.

When you give up your judgements, or preferences, any activity—even washing dishes, or playing a seemingly endless game of hide-and-seek with your child, or studying—can turn out to be enjoyable and even beneficial. Your whole life takes on meaning and it's not based on getting your way, or getting what you want, but on your attitude towards what you're getting.

As Eckhart Tolle says, "When you say, I enjoy doing this or that, it is really a misperception. It makes it appear that the joy comes *from* what you do, but that is not the case. Joy does not come from what you do, it flows *into* what you do and thus into this world from deep within you."

Another obstacle to initiating action at a more macro level is when you're strongly focused on your preference for the outcome, and you're not sure that the options that are available to you will produce that outcome. You're not sure whether *this* exercise regime, or *this* diet, *this* coach, *this* degree, *this* job, will bring you the results you're after.

Your judgements may be valid, and they may not. It may be true that one option won't produce a particular result, or defined outcome. A sprint coach is probably not the right one to help you with your marathon running. However, for the most part, what you're really after is not the defined outcome, but the sense of enjoyment that the activity will bring you—the state of flow, or optimal experience. And as you know by now, any option can be used to create a state of flow. Incidentally, and mostly because you're enjoying it, it will also produce results—sometimes, unexpectedly pleasant ones. So be careful to notice whether your choosiness really matters, or is just another way of avoiding the activity required to get into flow.

Once you've initiated action, being nonjudgemental can be applied to the activity itself. That means, firstly, not doubting that it's the right activity and, secondly, not being too critical about how well you're doing. If you're running and not hitting your time markers, just drop the judgement and keep going. Do the best you can on that day. If you're learning a martial art, or to play a musical instrument, and you're making mistakes, let go of the self-criticism and the voice that says, "I'm no good at this, it's no use." The more quickly you can do that, the more you can remain in the zone that enables the flow state to develop, even when you're not performing that well.

PRACTICAL EXERCISE – DO THIS NOW

Finding Flow by Letting Go

FOR THE areas of life listed in the exercise in Chapter 8, identify a short-term (three to six months) and a long-term (two to five years) goal for each.

Now break those down into tasks or activities that meet the conditions for generating flow:

- It challenges you to learn or develop your skill level;
- You're able to set goals and get immediate—or at least short-term—feedback;
- It's out of your comfort zone in terms of being able to control the outcome (this doesn't have to mean danger, just that you may or may not achieve it each time and that your skills are what will make the difference—in other

> words, it doesn't have to mean climbing Kilimanjaro; just getting to the gym and learning and completing a new routine may be far enough out of your particular comfort zone);

- It's interesting enough to you that you'll be able to do it for its own sake once you get going (be careful, there's a lot more in this category than you might think).

Set yourself deadlines and/or commit to how often or frequently you will do these activities.

If you get stuck in identifying goals, or find that you're not moving forward with planned or needed tasks or activities, ask yourself what preferences or judgements you're having difficulty letting go of, or what outcome you might be resisting, or what conditions you're blaming.

If you've been trying things and not getting anywhere, look to see in what way you may be using force to try to make things go your way, instead of responding to what is, even if that means pivoting or moving in a new direction. What would you need to let go of in order to be able to commit to an action that would challenge you and move you forward in that area?

Being Nonreactive | Remaining in Flow

Being in flow is a wholly nonreactive state. Eckhart Tolle inadvertently describes the flow state when he talks about enthusiasm: "Enthusiasm knows where it is going, but at the same time, it is deeply at one with the present moment, the source of its aliveness, its joy, and its power. … [There is] always a still but intensely alive space at the centre of the wheel, a core of peace in the midst of activity that is both the source of all and untouched by it all."

As you can see, there is presence, awareness and being nonjudgemental, which is what we say results in a nonreactive state. Naturally, remaining in the flow state means remaining nonreactive. You can look at this at a micro (activity) level and at a macro (lifestyle) level.

At the micro-level, there is a saying that, "The moment of beauty is destroyed when 'I' walks into the room." That means that the flow breaks down when you suddenly become aware, "Ah, it's me, *I'm* doing this!" If you don't recover or return from that thought quickly enough, you'll probably start to self-evaluate. You'll think about the goal and how well you're doing, and whether you're going to achieve it or not.

You've probably seen this in sport. Take tennis, for example, when two players get into one of those long rallies. Eventually, one of them makes a mistake. Is it because they became aware of themselves doing the action? Did they become self-evaluative as a result, or just think too much about what they were doing?

According to Csikszentmihalyi, when the *perceived* challenge level rises too high relative to the *perceived* skill level, then anxiety is likely to ensue and the flow state is lost. You usually see this when the one player or team starts to lose ground. Their ability to regain their performance will depend on their *perceived* ability relative to the other player or team, who represents the *perceived* challenge.

A good example for this is provided by the New Zealand All Blacks rugby team. Consistently the best rugby team in the world for the last decade, they have proved time and again their uncanny ability to win from any position, even if they're well behind on points with little time left on the clock. In response to an interview question after one such come-from-behind win against South Africa's Springboks, their captain, Kieran Read, said, "Ah you don't really think about [the prospect of losing] as an All Black." This statement shows how their *perceived* ability relative to the *perceived* challenge remains in balance; they don't panic, and so they remain in flow, which means they don't make the kind of mistakes that other teams make in the same situation.

Eckhart Tolle describes it like this: "When you want to arrive at your goal more than you want to be doing what you are doing you become stressed. The balance between enjoyment and structural tension is lost, and the latter has won. When there is stress, it is usually a sign that the ego has returned, and you are cutting yourself off from the creative power of the universe. Instead, there is only the force and strain of egoic wanting, and so you have to struggle and 'work hard' to make it. Stress always diminishes both the quality and effectiveness of what you do under its influence."

At the beginning of this chapter you read about five motivational states, one of which was agitation. This arises when you're pressing too hard to make a goal happen, in spite of what reality will allow. It can be likened to shouting or revving your engine when you're stuck in traffic. It doesn't achieve anything, other than to make you upset and destroy any possibility of the state of flow. You can see that this is the state that has been described in the preceding quote. You will probably also recognise that this level of operating is quite prevalent in today's business environment where everybody wants everything done now, as a top priority.

Talk about maintaining the balance of your mind! As you can see, this is quite an accomplishment in the modern world. The key is to remain nonjudgemental, or, when you see that you are being judgemental, to return as quickly as possible to that nonjudgemental state. Practising a meditation like Vipassana, or the Sensation Meditation that was introduced in Chapter 4, is a good way to develop this competence at the deepest level of the mind.

Conversely, if the challenge becomes too easy, then boredom may result. In a sports context this may show up as complacency and we all know how dangerous that can be for a player or team.

If we bring this a little closer to home, you can see that if you set yourself unrealistic goals, or if you grow impatient when learning or doing a task, you're going to lose the experience of flow. In the world of instant gratification, we've become habituated to getting quick, easy results, so this may be a common problem.

Conversely, when you become skilled at something and no longer find it challenging, you may also lose the experience of flow. The challenge then is to up the ante—to define a new, inspiring goal or reason for doing the activity. Or it may be time to move on to something new.

PRACTICE - SAVE FOR LATER

Finding the Extraordinary in the Ordinary

IN YOUR daily activities, always remember that whatever you're doing is an opportunity to get into the flow state, or to have that optimal experience. You don't need to go and climb Kilimanjaro.

Whatever you are doing, do it mindfully, and set yourself some parameters that will enable you to turn it into a flow experience. For example, to complete it within a certain time, or to a particular standard, or with one hand tied behind your back! The more you do this, the easier and more natural it will become. You'll get into the flow state more quickly, more often, and that will take you closer to that different, better experience of life that we promised.

You can also look at flow from a macro point of view. This means enjoying the experience of flow in your life as a whole, not only within a particular activity or task. For example, when you have a high level of completion (as defined in Chapter 7), when you're busy but not too busy, when your work is stretching you just out of your comfort zone and your relationship is challenging you to grow in a positive way, then you'll probably have the experience of your life as a whole being in flow.

A key feature of that state will be the experience of things "going your way". You bump into the right person at the right time. Problems at work seem to take care of themselves more often than not. You're in a groove with your relationship partner. You're switched on to knowing what needs your attention and what doesn't, and you consistently get it more right than wrong. You consistently get a lot done and still feel energised, rather than stressed or tired. You'll probably also find that, in this state, you experience a lot more of what Carl Jung called synchronicity, or "meaningful coincidences". For instance, you think about starting a project and within a day you bump into someone who links you to a person who has the skill set you need.

This seldom happens when you're using force. In fact, if you're using force, you're likely to bump into someone or something that tells you to slow down—like someone else's car! Using force, if you remember the earlier quote by Eckhart Tolle, is "when you want to arrive at your goal more than you want to be doing what you are doing". This is when you lose the balance between enjoyment and striving. This is when you experience stress.

Naturally, the more your life is filled with flow at the micro (task) level, the more it will aggregate into a flow-filled experience at a macro (lifestyle) level. If you set yourself challenging goals in all that you do, and keep your attention on what you're doing at any one moment and do it mindfully, you'll be creating the conditions for flow to happen, within and beyond each task. If this sounds exhausting, well, there's that judgement again! Think about the benefits of a life lived in flow. When you really connect to that, then setting both micro and macro goals and getting active in service of them will become a natural way of life.

The key feature of synchronistic events—those meaningful coincidences—is that they are so peculiar that they could not have been created. And they're all about timing—being in the right place at the right time. Consider the possibility that when you are neither forcing nor resisting what's happening or what activity you're currently involved in, but listening to what wants to happen, and responding mindfully, you find yourself more frequently in the right place at the right time and synchronicities abound. In this instance you really do get the experience that all of life and the universe exists for you to have the experience that you're having right now—that it exists to support you to grow and to achieve your goals.

WHAT DIFFERENCE DOES IT MAKE?

THIS ONE is best expressed through the following four quotes:

"We find greatest joy, not in getting, but expressing what we are. Men do not really live for honours or for pay; their gladness is not in the taking and holding, but in the doing, the striving, the building, the living. It is a higher joy to teach than to be taught. It is good to get justice, but better to do it; fun to have things, but more to make them. The happy man is he who lives the life of love, not for the honours it may bring, but for the life itself." — *RJ Baughan*

"I slept and dreamt that life was joy. I awoke and saw that life was service. I [served] and behold, I discovered that service was joy." — *Rabindranath Tagore*

"It is not the critic that counts; nor the man who points out how the strong man stumbles, or whether the doer of deeds could have done them better. The credit belongs to the man in the arena, whose face is marred by dust and sweat and blood; who strives valiantly... who knows the great enthusiasms, the great devotions; who spends himself on a worthy cause; who at the best knows in the end the triumph of high achievement, and who at worst, if he fails, at least fails while daring greatly, so that his place shall never be with those cold and timid souls who know neither victory nor defeat." — *Teddy Roosevelt*

"This is the true joy in life, the being used for a purpose recognized by yourself as a mighty one; the being a force of nature instead of a feverish selfish clod of ailments and grievances complaining that the world will not devote itself to making you happy. I am of the opinion that my life belongs to the whole community and as long as I live it is my privilege to do for it whatever I can. I want to be thoroughly used up when I die, for the harder I work, the more I live. I rejoice in life for its own sake. Life is no 'brief candle' to me. It is sort of a splendid torch which I have a hold of for the moment, and I want to make it burn as brightly as possible before handing it over to future generations." — *George Bernard Shaw*

Perhaps the most important learning you can take away from this chapter is the importance of not ever getting into a comfort zone. Most people live their lives aiming to win some version of a lottery, whether a literal lottery or by selling their start-up for a sum that will enable them to retire. "Usually what happens," says Csikszentmihalyi "is that the person finds himself back at square one, with a new list of wishes, just as dissatisfied as before."

Life doesn't stand still. If you live on your desert island for long enough, eventually the boredom, if not the flies, will get to you. Life is not about the goal, it's about the journey; and remaining in flow, and therefore remaining nonreactive, is a proven way to achieve that. So if you ever win the lottery, take a short holiday, buy yourself a nice house, and then go back to work. It's by mindfully applying the principles of flow that you'll have a different, better experience of life.

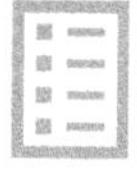

CHAPTER SUMMARY

THIS CHAPTER looks at the application of mindfulness to the subject of flow and high performance. Key content includes:

- Flow is a state that has definite determining factors and so it can be mindfully, consciously created and sustained.
- The factors for generating flow, based on the work of Mihaly Csikszentmihalyi, and the by-products of being in a state of flow.
- Brain imaging technology has provided more objective data on the state of flow that Csikszentmihalyi's initial research was able to. The results strongly support his findings.
- Five motivational states are proposed: rest, ennui, animation, agitation and flow.
- Being aware in the context of flow means being connected to your motivational state and using that awareness to choose actions that will initiate and/or sustain the state of flow.
- A real-life example of a military training challenge that produced a state of flow.
- Being nonjudgemental in the context of flow means letting go of judgements and preferences in order to get over the inevitable

"dip" that either precedes or stands in the way of generating a state of flow.

- Being nonreactive in the context of creating and sustaining the state of flow means not applying force or resistance and not getting into a comfort zone, but rather increasing the level of challenge to match increased skill levels.
- A practice for finding the extraordinary in the ordinary.

10 | Authentic Being & Relating

ET'S IMAGINE that you're late for a meeting. When you arrive, you make the excuse that the traffic was really bad. Perhaps in one instance, everybody accepts your apology and you settle in. However, let's say someone points out that the traffic wasn't so bad, as they travelled the same route and were able to make it on time.

At this point, if you're like most people, you'll add to your story in order to save face. Oh, you might say, the traffic jam must have happened just as you got onto that road. Alternatively, you can take the less common route and own up that you left home later than you should have. Period. No story. Or you may choose to confess, if it's true, that you stopped to pick up a coffee, and stuck to that mission despite the long queue in the coffee shop.

When you choose the first option, you add a second layer to the little white lie—a layer, ostensibly, of protection. You want to save face. This is a reactive state based on the judgement that telling the truth would be bad for you. If you choose the second option, you don't add that second layer. Instead, you allow the truth—which everyone else can see or feel anyway—to come out. It requires a mindful, conscious choice to do this and, when you do, you create presence—and the possibility of completion—for yourself and everyone else.

As you know by now, it's not the thing itself, but your relationship to the thing. Similarly, it's not the little white lies that are the problem. We all cover up, make excuses and tell little white lies. It's a natural human phenomenon, and anybody who insists that they never do that is either very unaware and self-deluded, or doing it.

You can say that the little white lies oil the wheels of social interaction. For example, if you'd been late because you'd eaten too much chilli on your pizza the night before and were stuck on the toilet, well nobody needed to know that. We'd call that "TMI" (too much information) or "overshare".

The problem is that second layer. If the situation requires that you remove that second layer to reveal the truth, can you? How willing and able—and available— are you to do that? Because when you do, you open up the possibility for authentic being and relating to occur.

Imagine a world in which you, the people around you, even your bosses and public leaders, could just remove that second layer. Imagine if everybody could quickly, easily and lightly admit to their faults and mistakes and take the consequences. You can see that things might take a completely different direction. You might have a different, better experience of life.

In this chapter, you'll discover how this is possible when you integrate your mindfulness-based practices to develop a more authentic way of being and of relating to others.

With this chapter you will:

- Gain an understanding of the link between awareness, presence and authenticity;
- Learn how to generate authenticity from being present, aware and non-judgemental;
- Learn to apply mindfulness principles and practices to the relating context (work, personal and public);
- Start to develop an authentic personal or leadership brand using the three key elements of mindfulness.

The "What Is" of Authenticity

THERE IS no hard-and-fast definition of authenticity. Generally, when people define the term, they offer the phrase "being true to oneself". An article on the Association for Psychological Science website (psychologicalscience.org) offers the following: "Authenticity means not only owning one's actions, but also acting in accordance with one's thoughts, desires and needs."

The first part of that definition—"owning one's actions"—refers back to the example given earlier of being late. Owning your actions would mean removing that second layer and admitting the truth about why you were late, even if it's just that you woke up too late and took too long to get ready.

To do this is not easy. Your natural reaction is to defend, to cover up, and to keep defending and covering up. There is a strong self-preservation mechanism that drives this—it's the same mechanism that's at work when you go into the red zone.

The second part of that definition is "acting in accordance with one's thoughts, desires and needs". However, as you've learned, those "thoughts, desires and needs" are like those clouds in the sky. Imagine if you were true to every single thought and feeling that arose. You might do some crazy things! Isn't that exactly what we defined reactivity to be, and the reason why you started on this journey in the first place, to stop buying into every thought and emotion that arises?

As you can see, we need to look at this more carefully.

Perhaps the clue lies in another statement by our friend Csikszentmihalyi, which is that the "self is [effectively] a system that is going round and round". What he means is that the self is constantly recreating itself out of what has already been created. For example, let's say you made a decision, under pressure from your family, to become a lawyer. Now you want to pursue your true passion, which is art. You can make a decision that takes into account your experience and yet puts you on a path to where you want to be. It might be too late to start painting, but perhaps you could become an art dealer. Once there, you might decide to make further changes and become a forgery detective.

So, you're always the sum of all your decisions and actions to date, however, that doesn't limit you. You can still add to what you've become. You can still head off in a new direction.

In the chapter on flow, you saw—and hopefully you've tested it by now!—that you can do an activity, even though you don't feel like it, and then come away having enjoyed it. Part of that enjoyment is that you have the experience of an expanded sense of self. You've grown from having developed your skills. Csikszentmihalyi calls this the expanded self.

This ability that human beings have to set an intention and head off in a new direction, or develop a new set of skills, can apply not only to what you do, but also to who you are as a person. You can develop new beliefs based on new information that is available to you. You can add new facets to your personality. You do not have to be limited to your childhood conditioning, or who you find yourself to be. Studies in neuroscience support this possibility—it's called the neuroplasticity of the brain.

We're going to call this your *intended* self, because it's initiated by a decision to act in line with who you *intend* to be.

This *intended* or *expanded* self is juxtaposed to the *conditioned* or *reactive* self, that which you found yourself to be as a result of your upbringing and all the reactions you carry with you. I gave an example in the previous chapter about how I intended to be a more engaged parent at playtime and then I acted on that. That was being true to my intended self, not to the conditioned, reactive self that I found myself with.

Now, try this on for size: authenticity is "being true to your *intended* or *expanded* self". In other words, authenticity means being, deciding and acting in alignment with your more mindful, conscious self, that which you are working to become, or working to grow into. For example, if you believe that being non-racist is a virtue, then you do your best to bring your thoughts and actions into alignment with that. Similarly, if you wish to be an inspiring leader, or parent, then you bring your thoughts and actions in alignment with that.

Of course, the question becomes, what to do with those pesky thoughts and feelings that arise like those clouds in the sky and which you feel so loyal to? The answer is, you own them, in just the same way as you own your behaviours when you're late. In other words, you admit them to yourself and, if challenged, you admit them to others, however, you don't have to act them out. For example, you might say, I don't feel like being inspiring for my team right now, and I will do it for their sake. You'll find more about this later in the chapter.

As you can see, this is not about suppressing, nor denying, your thoughts and feelings. It's about admitting to yourself—and possibly to others, if appropriate—what you are honestly thinking and/or feeling, and then acting mindfully, nonreactively, according to what's best for the situation.

So now you have a working definition of authenticity. You also have a distinction between authenticity and honesty which enables you to deal with the thoughts and feelings that arise. Below are two key concepts related to the theme of authenticity. Read these, then move on to learn how you can apply the three key elements of mindfulness to the area of authenticity.

| KEY CONCEPT – TAKE NOTE |

Presence and Authenticity

LET'S LOOK at another dimension of authenticity: presence. In the earlier example of trying to save face when you were late for the meeting, you can see that as long as you're doing that, you're not present. You're lost in your story about what happened and occupied by thoughts of defending yourself. If people don't buy your story, you might continue to have the argument in your head long after the meeting is over, as you try to find a way to convince them—and save face.

If you continue to operate in that way, you're likely to build up a whole host of stories that you then have to remember in order to not ever get caught out. With each story, you add an incompletion. You create stress for yourself. You also make it ever more difficult to own up to anything, because the whole house of cards will come tumbling down. You're constantly at Defcon 3.

Similarly, when you act out the thoughts and feelings of your conditioned self— for example, when you're experiencing reactive anger and you let it all hang out— you're also not present.

Conversely, when you become aware of your cover-up, or of your reactive emotional state, you become present to "what is". You become present to both the cover-up, as well as to the facts of the situation. This enables you to deal with the situation as it is, not as you are. It enables you to respond authentically, instead of reacting unconsciously. Everybody else becomes present too, because they're no longer trying to figure out the truth; they're looking directly at the facts.

> *When you become aware of your cover-up, you become present*
> *to "what is". Everybody else becomes present too.*

The Latin root for the word presence is *praesentia*, which can also be translated into *effect*, *force*, *power*, and *strength* and when you describe a person as having presence, you're probably also referring to those qualities. You would probably also think of them as being authentic. They come across as people with nothing to prove, like it's all there for them, just as they are.

This is most clearly illustrated by stories of the rich and famous who conduct themselves well with mere mortals. It's been said of former US president Bill Clinton that he has tremendous presence, and that statement is usually backed up by the description that when he talks to individuals they feel like they are the only person in the room while he's engaging with them. The same was said of Sir Ernest Oppenheimer, founder of the global mining giants Anglo American and De Beers. As a journalist in my youth, I had the privilege of being in the presence of Nelson Mandela and having personal audiences with Richard Branson and billionaire Internet investor and Naspers chairman Koos Bekker, among many others. Mandela's presence was so powerful it made me giddy, and the description of being present, aware and nonjudgemental applied to all of them.

In my experience, people with authentic presence are aware of others and their impact on others. They are nonjudgemental, which is likely to show up as affirming, diplomatic, and ready to see other points of view. Almost certainly, they're not trying to win arguments or prove a point. To this end, they tend to be light, flexible and ready to laugh, especially at themselves, and share from their own experience. This quality enables them to act easily in alignment with their intended self, rather than being deeply immersed and stuck in their reactive self.

You can say that people with presence are focused on the situation and "what is" rather than on themselves and their preferences, or their story about "what is". This doesn't mean that they can't express their preferences, and strongly. The difference is, they tend to be nonjudgemental and non-attached.

They are more likely to get what they ask for, not because they are manipulating for it, or threatening, but for the very reason that they are not doing that. People are keen to comply. It's almost as if other people want some of that presence to rub off on them.

Clearly then, presence is a desirable quality and it's strongly linked to authenticity. It's been said that the attention goes to the person in the room who is most present. How would you respond to a person who walks right up to you and looks you in the eye, with no agenda? Can you do this to somebody else? Try the exercise below and see. There is a tremendous amount of energy in being present in this way with somebody else.

PRACTICAL EXERCISE – DO THIS NOW

Being Present

FIND SOMEBODY who will agree to do this with you: sit face-to-face, knees a few centimetres apart, and make eye contact. Blink normally and try to maintain eye contact.

Avoid the temptation to pull faces, laugh, giggle, talk, or do other activities that break up the energy. Let go of any discomfort or any agenda. Go for as long as you can and record your time. Then repeat and try to go for a longer period.

NOTE You might find that doing the exercise for a ridiculously long period of time—like 20 minutes or more—has greater benefit than shorter stints. You increase the likelihood that you'll enter a state of flow and derive real benefit from becoming desensitized to making eye contact—and therefore being present—with another human being.

KEY CONCEPT – TAKE NOTE

Identity

IN ORDER to apply the three key elements to the context of authenticity, we need to consider the distinction of identity.

We're all identified with being something. It can be: your role (father, mother, provider, boss); your vocation / profession (social worker, accountant); or your standards of value (powerful, funny, kind, different, victim).

An indicator of being identified with something is that the person would rather die than give it up. For example, the mother who gives up her life for her children; the accountant who has a heart attack while working himself to death; the "kind" person who gives it all away rather than have someone think they are "selfish"; the "victim" who lets their pattern repeat endlessly until it destroys his / her life rather than give it up and no longer be able to get attention by complaining.

You can see that these things that people are identified with are not real, but rather ideas they have about themselves. So, you can say that people would rather die than give up some core idea about themselves. For instance, you get people who complain endlessly about their lot and then, when you suggest a change, they say, "Yes, but…", or, "No, because…". They have their identity, and then their story about their identity, all those circular arguments that keep them trapped.

If you observe the way people are about their way of being, it's like, if they gave it up, it would be the end of them. Instead, they defend it with all their might. Not only that, they also judge the world from that vantage point: "Everybody who doesn't see me the way I see myself is wrong." They might expand that into, "Everybody who doesn't see the world the way I see it is wrong."

You can also view your identity as being like that monster on your back that you read about in Chapter 5. It needs to be fed in some particular way and when it doesn't get what it wants, it creates drama in your own mind—all those thoughts that tell you that things have to be a certain way before you can be happy; or that tell you that you can't do something you know you'd really like to do. All those feelings of resistance. All those things that keep you small.

Identity—your core idea or belief about yourself—is the opposite of presence as it is a focus on *me / my / mine* (the anchor for identity) and attachment to your labels and judgements, rather than on the situation and "what is". Most people feel strongly tied to their identity and this makes it difficult for them to change, or develop. They live to justify the way they've always been.

The thing to see is that your identity was set up as a defence mechanism, in the way that was described in Chapter 6, in the introduction to the red zone. Your identity served a purpose once, and it still can serve a purpose. However, it doesn't have to limit you. If you let it go, you won't die. You might even grow up and have a different, better experience of life.

REAL-LIFE EXAMPLE

Working the Room

MOST PEOPLE who attend our workshops are surprised to hear that Colinda and I are the world's biggest introverts. We're much happier at home reading and writing than being out there with people. However, most of our time at work is spent talking to people.

As anybody knows, that can take a tremendous amount of energy, especially when it's people who need your help, or people in large groups. Some people find that energising in itself and don't need any time out from it. They just want more. For people like us, we need to hibernate in order to regenerate.

Before I did what I do now, I worked in the media business, first as a journalist and later as a magazine editor. My wife at the time worked as a television presenter. That combined lifestyle meant being invited out to functions all the time. We could easily spend five nights of the week at cocktail parties or events. We were young, and it was fun, up to a point—the point at which my introverted side needed to take a break.

My reason for sharing this is to highlight the difference between how it was for me back then, and how it is now.

Back then, I had to really work at being "up" for these events. Nobody knew that, of course, because I put on a good show and, as a result, I felt a little fake. Everything and everyone around me felt fake too—that's how it is, we project our stuff onto the world. It often reminded me of Holden Caulfield, the kid in *Catcher In the Rye*, who hates phoniness, but finds himself face-to-face with it wherever he turns.

My response was quite extreme: I would stop going out for months at a time. Eventually, I stopped altogether.

The difference now is that I can get myself "up" very easily and it's never fake. I'm honouring my reason for being there, and consciously stepping into who I need to be, rather than resisting and letting my negative thoughts and feelings—all those judgements about self and others, all those preferences for what I'd rather be doing—have any hold over me.

In addition, I never feel that other people are being fake with me. I know that everybody is putting up a front of some sort, that's how human beings are, so I don't judge people for it. I have empathy, and I read it for what it is. People are often ashamed of telling the truth about some aspect of their lives and the less judgement they experience from you, the less need they have to do that. The more open you are, the more open they are. Except sometimes.

The outcome is that being with people costs me less energy and I can sustain my energy for longer, and without feeling the need to withdraw as quickly or as often.

Applying the Three Key Elements

AT THE centre of the system that is the self, there is that part of you that can notice—or observe—and evaluate what's going on. It can look at your past, assess your situation and your feelings, and decide what next. That part also operates at a micro-level when you meditate. It's the part that notices when your attention has wondered and generates the decision to bring your attention back to your breathing.

You can call this part of yourself the observer, or perhaps, because it also makes decisions—for example, where to put your attention—you can call it the decision-maker. You could also call it the gatekeeper, the guide, the captain of your soul. Whatever you name it, it's that part of yourself that gets activated by awareness and is able to observe, assess, set an intention, and redirect your attention and energy towards that intention. It's dormant when you're being reactive and becomes active the moment you gain awareness.

You've been activating that part of yourself, and giving it some decision-making authority, throughout this process so far. Now, to move into authentic being and relating, you will need to do a big heave-ho and shift the reference point for your personality from your identity, as defined earlier, to your intended self—and give that gatekeeper part of yourself a lot more power to choose between the two.

This will mean loosening the grip that your identity, or reactive self, has over you and making a wholehearted shift to becoming who you intend to be. Of course, you're likely to want to keep a large part of who you are, so this is not about rejecting yourself. Rather, it's about embracing who you are and refining some bits. You can achieve this by applying the three key elements of mindfulness to the subject of authenticity.

Being Aware | Honesty and Authenticity

Being aware in the context of authenticity means being aware of your thoughts, feelings and actions in a way that enables you to evaluate whether they are in alignment with your intended (expanded) self. For example, when you attend a work conference that involves people of different races, social classes or political persuasions, you might be aware of your own prejudiced or biased thoughts towards those who are different from you. You then use that space created by the awareness to do a check and decide what your *intended* values and beliefs are with regards to the situation. You do your best to act in alignment with those.

Note that this is different from suppressing or pretending. Suppressing would mean denying, even to yourself, that those thoughts or feelings exist. That would imply a kind of enforced self-deception, which would not be authentic. When you're suppressing, your only option is to insist—to yourself as much as to others—that your true thoughts and feelings don't exist. For example, you might insist, even in your own mind, that you never have a single prejudiced thought, or you never, ever, tell a white lie. Pretending happens when you consciously or unconsciously hide the truth about what you really think, feel and believe, and what you'd really say if you had half a chance. Here, you'd be busy having racist thoughts, or telling a white lie, and then completely duck the question when someone challenges you.

Being authentic to your intended self is a sincere attempt to realign your actions with a different set of values or ideas than what you inherited, or what you find yourself with, while being honest about having those inherited values and thoughts at the same time. In this instance, you might say something like, "I'm human and I have my prejudices like everyone else; and I do my best to see past them."

The reason why you may have considered this to be fake in the past is that you haven't had this distinction revealed to you before. In that instance, you would naturally have felt a certain loyalty to your thoughts and feelings as they appeared, unfiltered, because you didn't know what else to do with them. You had no other possibility of being. Something in you knew they weren't serving you, but you thought you had no choice, so you just acted them out and sought ways to justify that, or you tried to suppress and deny them and pretend they didn't exist. Mindfulness reveals that you didn't create those thoughts or feelings. They arose from your reactive self, but that's not who you have to be forever. You can change that. You can mindfully choose a new set of values to live into.

There are three levels of being honest about what you really think and feel. The first level is being honest with yourself. The second level is sharing that with someone else, probably someone you trust who won't blab it to everyone or use it against you. The third level is to share it with the person concerned, which you would only do if it's appropriate and beneficial.

> *Being authentic to your intended self is a sincere attempt to realign your actions with a mindfully chosen set of values.*

For example, when the time came to play with my son after a long day at work, I may have admitted to myself that I didn't really feel like it in that moment. I may have shared that feeling with my wife by giving her that look that parents give each other. However, I had no need to share my feelings with him. I just got on with it and played. I got on with being in alignment with my intended self. However, now that he's older, and if he's a father himself one day, then it might be beneficial to share it.

You can share what you honestly think and feel by using statements like the ones that follow:

- I'm scared for my child, *and* I will be brave.
- I'm tired and grumpy, *and* I will be inspiring for my team.
- I'm tired from a long day, *and* I will be engaging when I get home.

Notice the use of the word "and" in those sentences in place of the word "but". The use of the word "and" implies ownership in that it does not negate what comes before. When you use the word "but" you imply resistance, and so you can only achieve the intended behaviour through denial and force. When you use the word "and", you carry the feelings into the room with you, owning them, even while you act in line with your intended self. You'll find that there's a tremendous difference in the energy when you do that. There's no denial, you're in alignment with yourself, you feel lighter—and you soon forget about them as you enter the state of flow with your chosen response.

Here are some typical indicators to be aware of that will tell you when you're likely to be out of alignment with your intended self:

- Behaviours
    - Saying yes when you know you should say no—or saying no when you know you should say yes;
    - Being withdrawn, aloof, condescending or sarcastic at a social event when you know you should really connect with others;
    - Trying to be the centre of attention, when you know you should really give others some space;
    - Being sarcastic when you know you should really just ask for what you want.

- Cognitions
    - Thinking, "Don't rock the boat," when you know you really should;
    - Having internal judgements about others that you know are just a way to make you feel less inadequate about yourself.

- Emotions
    - Feeling sorry for yourself when you don't get noticed or don't get your way, when you know you should just get over it and be present;
    - Being half-hearted or cynical for the same reasons as above, when you know you should give it up and contribute wholeheartedly.

- Physical symptoms
    - Tension—as an indicator of any of the above;
    - Illness and accidents—the identity's survival instinct is strong and you may find that when you try to change a fundamental behaviour, your body resists by getting sick, or your subconscious creates obstacles or even accidents to stop you from making the change.

THE SCIENCE

Consciousness & Intention

"BECAUSE NO branch of science deals with consciousness directly, there is no single accepted description of how it works," says Csikszentmihalyi. He advocates a "phenomenological model of consciousness based on information theory". This means a model that deals directly with events—phenomena—as we experience and interpret them, rather than focusing on the anatomical structures, neurochemical processes, and so on, while adopting principles from information theory.

"With this framework in mind, [being conscious] means that certain specific conscious events (sensations, feelings, thoughts, intentions) are occurring, and that we are able to direct their course.

"Thus we might think of consciousness as *intentionally ordered information*. … We may call intentions the force that keeps information in consciousness ordered.

"The intentions we either inherit or acquire are organized in hierarchies of goals, which specify the order of precedence among them. … Most people … adopt 'sensible' goals. … But there are enough exceptions in every culture to show that goals are quite flexible. Individuals who depart from the norms—heroes, saints, sages, artists, and poets, as well as madmen and criminals—look for different things in life than most others do. The existence of people like these shows that consciousness can be ordered in terms of different goals and intentions. Each of us has this freedom to control our subjective reality."

"One of the main forces that affects consciousness adversely is psychic disorder—that is, information that conflicts with existing intentions, or distracts us from carrying them out. We give this condition many names, depending on how we experience it: pain, fear, rage, anxiety, or jealousy. All these varieties of disorder force attention to be diverted to undesirable objects, leaving us no longer free to use it according to our preferences. Psychic energy becomes unwieldy and ineffective.

"The opposite state from the condition of psychic entropy is optimal experience. When … awareness is congruent with goals, psychic energy flows effortlessly. … The positive feedback strengthens the self, and more attention is freed to deal with the outer and the inner environment.

"The 'battle' is not really *against* the self, but against the entropy that brings disorder to consciousness. It is really a battle *for* the self." By this last statement, Csikszentmihalyi means it is a battle to create your own unique self in the face of all your conditioning and all the social forces that try to force you to conform. He calls this process *differentiation*, which could be likened to Jung's concept of *individuation*.

Csikszentmihalyi warns that differentiation should not come at the cost of disconnecting from society but should be balanced by *integration*. He gives the example of a motor car engine where each part is unique, yet they work together as an integrated whole.

Being Nonjudgemental | Loosening Up

Recall the earlier example of being late. At the level of owning your actions, you can see that choosing to cover up, instead of owning up, is based on the judgement that to tell the truth would be bad for you. Usually, what most people want is just for you to own up. The outcome is seldom, if ever, as bad as you think it's going to be. Your fear is most often an assumption based on past experience.

Letting go of that judgement frees you up to tell the truth and face the consequences. Doing that puts you, and anybody else involved, in touch with "what is"—the facts of the situation and the facts of the consequences. When that's done, everybody can move on with the meeting, or their lives, depending on the level of impact that your white lie is having.

One reason for not being able to remove that second layer could be that you're in the grip of your identity—that monstrous ego—similar to when you're in the red zone. The idea of yourself as being somehow perfect has to be maintained at all costs. In order to achieve authentic being, you may need to loosen that monster's grip on you.

The best way to achieve this is to recognise that you did not create that monster—you did not create yourself to be the way you are. Not entirely. Most of who you are is a reaction to experiences. You either listened to your parents and teachers, or you rebelled against them—or a combination. Either way, the way you find yourself to be was probably created more through reactive decisions than conscious, mindful ones.

If you can see this, you can also see that it doesn't make sense to fight so hard for all those ideas you have about yourself and all those preferences that you never created in the first place. You feel loyal to them simply because they appeared to come up in your own mind. Stubbornness is nothing other than being loyal to a thought simply because it arose in your own mind. When you've observed mindfully how many random thoughts come up in your mind every day, you get to see how insane that is.

At the beginning of this book you learned that being non-judgemental means loosening your grip on *having* to have things go your way. Similarly, you can loosen your grip on having to *be* a certain way, or be identified with a certain career, or way of being, or way of being seen. For example, you don't have to be the perfect mother, the hardest worker, the kindest person, or the poor, suffering victim. That's just a habit. You can change that if you just stop holding onto it so tightly.

This doesn't mean you have to throw the baby out with the bathwater. You may decide that you like 80% of who you are and you'd like to keep that. There may only be a small percentage that you'd like to change. Perhaps there's nothing you'd like to change and your growth path is simply to accept yourself a whole lot more. Both of the above would be an expression of being nonjudgemental in a way that can lead to greater authenticity.

Remember, it's not the thing itself, but your relationship to the thing, that matters. When it comes to being nonjudgemental in the context of authenticity, here are some things you can let go of:

- **All the ideas that you have about yourself that you hold onto so tightly.** Examples of this include being the perfect father, mother, the most successful entrepreneur, the hardest worker, etc. This doesn't mean you can't strive towards being the best possible version of any of the above. It means that while you're striving towards it, you can also recognise, admit to, and accept, your shortcomings. You can let other people see them too. You can let people in and share your thoughts, concerns, challenges, fears, even as you strive towards being the best you can be.

- **Worrying about what others might think of you.** This is the main driver of those cover-ups we looked at earlier, that second layer that you add in the attempt to save face. Worrying about what others think creates separation, destroys presence and is fundamentally inauthentic. We give a lot of power away to what others might think of us. Most often, they're not even thinking that. Firstly, they're more concerned with themselves, and what *you* think of *them*. Secondly, they probably have another perception of you entirely, which you'd find out if you bothered to ask. Most of your fear is your own projection and then you allow that to control you. You create cover-ups that are not even necessary. Give it up.

- **What you want / don't want to have happen.** Most often, when you have an agenda with someone, it's because you're trying to angle things towards a particular outcome. You edit yourself when you speak, you withhold information, or you cover up the truth. This is inauthentic. Stop it. Express your intention and then let things take care of themselves. The person is either going to buy, or not buy, whatever you're selling, even if it's yourself as a relationship partner—because admit it, that's where we do this most often.

- **The labels *me / my / mine.*** It's always easy to see the "truth behind the lie" when you're observing others. You can even talk about it behind their back without feeling anything. But if it's you, or someone in your family, or one of your friends, that's being observed, noticed, talked about, well here comes the cover-up, the defence, and the upset. What if you could hear the truth about yourself, your family, your friends, without judgement, just noticing it? What if you could open up to the information, be objective, admit to it, deal with it, take what's relevant and discard the rest, and move on? Now that would be authentic, and powerful.

- **Your story about the other person.** If you're halfway normal, you most likely expect other people to share your priority of values, perspectives, and ways of doing things. When they don't, instead of just letting them be, you judge them as being wrong. Then you try to force, cajole or manipulate them into seeing or doing things your way. If you're reading this and insisting that you're not that person, then how are you when other people behave in that way? Do you insist that they should be just as allowing as you? Indeed, we all do it in some way. Only the most enlightened—and you may be one of those—manage to escape this trap entirely. Letting go of your story about the other person opens up the possibility for authentically engaging with them as they are.

PRACTICE - SAVE FOR LATER

The Authenticity Check-In Exercise

USE THIS exercise as a regular check-in to spot your own cover-ups and remove the second layer to activate your authentic self.

Complete the sentences:

- I find myself pretending that… [eg. I know what I'm doing at work in my new job].
- The truth is… [eg. I'm floundering and I'm afraid to ask].
- What I need to let go of is… [eg. worrying about what others will think].
- Who I'm committed to be (my *intended* self) is… [eg. eager and willing to learn].
- What I will do is… [eg. make a list of the questions I have and go and ask them].

You'll find that just writing these down brings tremendous relief, because it means you have admitted these things to yourself. At least now you're not fooling, or deluding, yourself.

The second step, if it's relevant and appropriate, is to share them with someone else. By sharing this with another person, you'll release more energy toward feeling and being authentic. This may be a necessary step to check your judgement—and develop your courage—to take the next step.

Step three is the ultimate step, which is to share the truth with the person concerned (if appropriate, it may not always be) and to act according to any decision that arises.

Being Nonreactive | Stepping Lightly

When you're covering up your white lie in order to save face, there is no awareness. You're in a reactive state. Very often, other people can see it, but you continue to deny the truth and insist on the cover up. You're determined to save face and you don't want to hear anything else. Nobody can get through to you.

Another example of this is the often humorously presented example of a man asking a woman, "What's wrong?" and she replies, "Nothing." If he digs deeper, she'll probably insist even harder that it's nothing. She wants him to figure it out.

You can see that when you're being this way, you waste a lot of time and energy—yours and other people's. You lose presence and you destroy the possibility of presence for others. You drive people apart and reduce affinity. Most importantly, you can see that you're not choosing that behaviour, you're just reacting.

Being nonreactive, on the other hand, is defined by the exercise of choice. Letting go of your defences, or removing that second layer, doesn't happen naturally, at least in the beginning. It requires a conscious choice, the choice to act in alignment with your intended self.

When you choose to let go of your defences and just say what you want, or tell the truth about what happened, or how you feel, you become nonreactive. You become present. You create the possibility for others to be present. You generate affinity and bring people together.

If you do this and gather the evidence from your experience, you'll very quickly see the benefits. You'll discover that people are willing to forgive, and more willing to help you out when they know you're being honest. It will become easier and easier to do.

> *If you gather the evidence from your experience, you'll very quickly see the benefits. It will become easier to do.*

In addition, you may have noticed that when you choose to act in alignment with your intended self, you mostly want to do it in a positive direction. You choose to tell the truth rather than cover up. You choose to put your own fears aside to reassure the child who is hurt. You choose to put your personal problems aside to inspire your team. You choose to put your prejudices aside and not say things that would be received as racist.

This intention—to do good, inspire others, or reduce harm—generally seems to be the direction chosen by every person who becomes aware of this possibility. Unless, of course, you're a psychopath. That's not a joke.

Now let's look at some more complex examples.

Let's say you're a woman who is known for her strong feminist views. You get invited by your Muslim friend to visit a mosque, where you discover that the women have to sit separately, upstairs, behind a curtain. Or let's say you're a man for whom honour is important and you overhear someone insulting your wife.

What would mindful, nonreactive authenticity look like in these scenarios?

Once again, we have to go to the key indicator of being nonreactive, which is the exercise of choice. If the woman was to stage her own personal protest by walking out onto the main floor of the mosque during prayers, would she be exercising choice in the direction of doing good, inspiring others, and reducing harm? Or would she be reactive, driven by her identity, and having no choice but to give in to the monster on her back? Likewise, if the man was to punch the other man in the face to defend his honour, would he be exercising choice, or would he be reactive?

It's easy to look at the overt behaviour and say that the woman would be standing up for the rights of all women, so she's good, while the man is being violent, and so he's bad. Certainly, that's the conclusion you'd expect if this was thrashed out on social media.

Looking through a mindfulness lens, we'd say let go of the judgements of right or wrong, good or bad, or what you personally like or don't like, or what you would have done. It is what it is. Each person has to answer to herself or himself: did they exercise a mindful choice in terms of what was appropriate for the situation, or did they simply react? At the end of the day, only they will know.

Here is what they might do if they use the process presented so far. Firstly, they'd admit to themselves how they're feeling. Secondly, they could tell someone what they truly think and how they feel. The woman at the mosque could share honestly what's going on for her with her friend. The man whose wife has been insulted could do likewise. Thirdly, they could tell the person involved. She could speak to the imam—or stage her protest. He could speak to the offensive male. However, as we've said, that part is not essential, and depends on what's appropriate. That's where the ultimate choice lies.

If both parties stopped at the second step, despite their strongly held beliefs, despite their strong emotions in the situation, people will most likely respect them for their self-restraint—perhaps more than if they took the third step. Plus, there's nothing to stop them from doing something after the fact. Each could write a blog post about their experience and perhaps start a debate.

Is this authenticity? Well, yes, if you're answering to your intended self, and not your reactive self. Yes, if you're not trying to prove a point in order to express your identity or save face with your own social grouping. That last one is important and you have to be honest with yourself. Have you identified with some social ideal that you're now trying to force on the world? Even though it may be a good one, when you're trying to force it on the world you're no different from a religious zealot. Remember, we're not looking at the content, but at the behaviour, at who you are being.

When you're being authentic, you remain centred in yourself, anchored to your intended self. To remain centred in yourself you don't have to fight every battle you encounter. Just as the martial arts guru wouldn't pick a fight with every person he encounters who annoys him. Part of his artistry means choosing when to act and when not to act. At the highest level, martial arts training is about not even being there for the fight, because you don't attract it. You rise above the need to fight. This is an image of what authenticity can look like. It's not about showing yourself, or getting your way in the world at every turn. Remember the examples given earlier of people with presence.

If you're acting in the same way, in the same direction, every single time—even if you believe you're fighting for some cause—then there's a good chance you're being reactive, not authentic.

Here are some examples of when you might find yourself being reactive in the name of authenticity:

- Rebelling against the context, eg. refusing to comply with the rules of a place because your views are—or asserting your identity is—so important right here, right now;
- Thinking, "I'll show you," when you know you really shouldn't;
- Needing validation or to "win" or get your point across in some way, when you know that it's not needed by the situation;
- Making somebody, or a situation wrong, and treating it like it's the end of the world, when really it's not.

Here's a quote by academic and author Brené Brown: "Authenticity is not something we have or don't have. It's a practice—a conscious choice of how we want to live. Authenticity is collection of choices that we have to make every day. It's about the choice to show up and be real. The choice to be honest. The choice to let our true selves be seen."

Of course, as you've seen, that "true" self is the mindfully created self, not the reactive self.

To be nonreactive in the context of authenticity means remaining committed to your intended or created self and acting that out completely, without doubt, without giving in to the voice that tells you that this is fake. If you give in to that voice, you're likely to return to the thoughts and feelings of your conditioned self. You're likely to do that thing that you know is wrong, that you know you'll regret.

Think about it like this: if you're watching a movie scene and the actor is playing his or her part half-heartedly, you're not going to buy into the scene. Your attention might even go to the bad acting instead. The actor has to completely become the role. They have to authentically feel the emotions of that character and express them wholeheartedly. They have to give it all they've got. When they do, you buy into it. You experience them as being authentic.

Similarly, when you act in terms of your intended or expanded self, you can't have divided loyalties between that and your conditioned self. You need to buy in wholeheartedly. When you do, without judgement and with full presence and careful attention, you'll create the conditions for the state of flow. You'll become that person—that inspiring leader, or parent—that you intended to be.

When you've done it, you can acknowledge yourself for the shift you've made. You can allow yourself to identify with the person you became during that action or activity. You can use this to reinforce not listening to the voice that tells you it's fake. Each time you repeat this, it will become easier, more natural, until it becomes the new you.

There's an important caveat here: you should not try to become something that you're not. An introvert should not use this to try to become an extrovert. If you're not naturally a funny guy, you should not try to use this to become the local comedian. If you're not an academic, you should not pretend to be one. This is not about pretending to be something that you're not. It's about fulfilling your potential by being the best version of yourself that you can be.

Based on this exploration of authenticity through a mindfulness lens, here's a possible definition of authenticity that arises: *Being and acting in alignment with your intended self, according to what's best for the situation, while remaining honest with yourself and being willing to be honest with others.*

WHAT DIFFERENCE DOES IT MAKE?

THINK ABOUT the frustration you feel when other people won't admit to their faults, but choose instead to defend themselves to the death. Likewise, think about your own tendency to do this. It's no good denying, it, we all do it to some degree—mostly to a much greater degree than we like to admit.

Perhaps the most illustrative example of this tendency that I know of comes from the Biblical story of the disciple Peter. All the canonical gospels recount the story that, during the Last Supper,

Jesus claimed that Peter would "deny me three times" before the cock crowed the following morning. Of course, Peter insisted that he would not and yet, when he was spotted in the crowd and was pointed out as one of the disciples, he did exactly as Jesus foretold, and denied that he knew him.

There is a phrase used in the Landmark Forum trainings that goes like this: "Human beings are fundamentally inauthentic and they're inauthentic about their inauthenticity." In other words, we present ourselves in the best possible way, and when it gets pointed out that we're not being entirely truthful, we start to reach for all kinds of evidence in our favour, rather than just shut up and say, OK, I was wrong, or whatever.

Imagine a world where people were more readily willing to do that. There would be a lot less polarity, many less dictators and corporate cover-ups, a lot of energy saved chasing the truth and denying the reality that's there for everyone to see.

Just bringing this back to the scale of your own life, think about how much energy gets spent on maintaining things in order to look good and not have the truth come out, and on not allowing what wants to happen, to happen.

Being authentic reverses that cycle. The willingness to be honest creates clarity, and the more clarity you create, the more you will begin to recognise what else is inauthentic in your life. Each time you go through the cycle you reduce stress, find it easier to make decisions (because you can be honest), and that in turn makes the flow state more available.

This can be scary at first, but if it's liberation you're after, it will be worth it. Plus, if you wish to see more of it in the world, then you have a duty to walk this path. As Gandhi said, "Be the change you want to see in the world."

As you can see, authenticity has a lot to do with you being OK with who you are. The more you're OK with who you are, the less you need to "prove" anything to the world, the less you need to convince other people to agree with you, even if they're not seeing you as you'd like to be seen. It means recognising that people will see you through their own lens anyway, so if there's work to be done, it's not out there in convincing others, but internally, in checking that you know that you're in alignment with your intended self.

This sense of having a deep-rooted connection to oneself is a hallmark of an authentic person. People can see it and feel it, and generally want to be part of it.

CHAPTER SUMMARY

THIS CHAPTER looks at the application of mindfulness to the subject of authentic being and relating. Key content includes:

- The problem of telling a white lie then adding a second layer to save face, instead of being honest.
- The concepts of presence and identity and how they correlate—one positively, the other negatively—to authenticity.
- Some accepted definitions of authenticity and the problem of having to be true to the reactive self.
- A new possibility of being in alignment with your intended or expanded self.
- Being aware of when you're not in alignment with your intended self. Plus, some indicators to look out for.
- The distinction between honesty and authenticity, and how to work with them to align with the intended self.
- Being nonjudgemental means being able to loosen your grip on identity—or loosen your identity's grip on you.
- Things you can let go of to open yourself up to authentic being.
- An exercise to uncover self-deception—the root of inauthenticity.
- Being nonreactive as indicated by making a choice, rather than having a knee-jerk reaction and acting out.
- Some simple and some more complex examples of what authenticity might look like and how to measure it.
- Being centred, or anchored, to your intended self.
- A new definition of authenticity.

11 | Conclusion

HOPEFULLY YOU can see the possibility for a new way of being. Hopefully you can see how this way of being can benefit more than just yourself, that it can benefit, firstly, the people in your life and then the people in their lives. And, possibly, it can be extended beyond that to the rest of the world.

Life is underpinned by irony and fairness. The irony is that chasing after your preferences for the sake of happiness is the very source of unhappiness. Letting go of your attachment to those preferences is, ironically, the ultimate freedom and the source of happiness.

The fairness is that what you put in, you get out, and what you give up, you gain. In other words, when you live the lottery version of life—*Give me what I want and then I'll be happy!*—you're often not really willing to put in what's needed in order to gain that happiness that you seek. Then, what happens? You don't get it.

It seems like a lot of trouble—and counterintuitive—to have to work to get enjoyment and happiness, and yet that's precisely what happens.

Similarly, the practice of mindfulness itself is not passive. It's a very active process. You have to be constantly aware, nonjudgemental, nonreactive. Yet, the results you get from it become apparent. Life becomes lighter and naturally more enjoyable. Your experience of life transforms, and this reinforces the behaviour.

Similarly, once you've gained balance, it doesn't mean you're going to become a competent or champion bicycle rider. You have to train. Training in mindfulness means not only practicing "on the field" of your daily life, although that's important. It also means practising "off the field" in the form of meditation.

As someone who has exercised a lot throughout my life, I can say that as I've grown older, the benefits have become more pronounced. I feel a lot younger than I am. Similarly, my mental state as a result of meditation is a lot sharper than it might have been. I've often likened that to putting money in the bank instead of spending on credit.

I can also say that a mere twenty minutes a day three times a week can go a long way towards getting you fit and gaining some of the benefits of meditation. Therefore, even if that's all you manage, it's worthwhile. The more you can do— the longer you can sit and the more often—the better.

When you drop off any of these practices, or find yourself having reacted, never mind. What matters is to get back on track. Gently forgive yourself and put yourself back on track. The trackers that are used by airline autopilot systems in fact do exactly that: they spend their time allowing the plane to drift off track and then bring it back on track. It's imperceptible of course, thank goodness, but the principle applies.

When you do this consistently over time, you'll find that your reaction times get shorter and shorter until you get ahead of yourself. Still, you'll find that you revisit areas, but each time you'll notice that you're doing it at a higher level of awareness, and with less reactivity than before. My favourite saying to describe this is that, "Your lows will be higher than your highs used to be."

One more thing to remember is that you're defined by your commitment to the path, rather than by your achievements along the way.

Finally, remember that having a different, better experience of life happens naturally when you make it about the journey, not the destination.

TABLE A: Stress Equation

FOR EACH area of life below, identify your stress demands and resources. For the example marked, there is an acute physical stressor in the form of construction at the office, that is causing irritability. Resources include doing the Sensation Meditation (inner) and buying earplugs (outer).

Area of Life	Subcategory	Demand	Resource
[EXAMPLE] Health	Physical Mental Emotional Spiritual	Acute / Chronic / Hassle Inner *Irritability* Outer *Construction noise at office*	Have / Need Inner *Use Sensation Meditation (lunch)* Outer *Get earplugs*
Health	Physical Mental Emotional Spiritual	Acute / Chronic / Hassle Inner Outer	Have / Need Inner Outer
Support	Emotional Practical Informational	Acute / Chronic / Hassle Inner Outer	Have / Need Inner Outer
Finances	Earnings Savings Debt	Acute / Chronic / Hassle Inner Outer	Have / Need Inner Outer
Relationships	Partner Friends Family Work	Acute / Chronic / Hassle Inner Outer	Have / Need Inner Outer
Work	Formal job Home Studies Other	Acute / Chronic / Hassle Inner Outer	Have / Need Inner Outer

TABLE B: Creating Completion

MARK Y for all those things that are complete. In other words, they're sorted. Mark N for all those things that are *not* complete, that you *need* to get sorted. Then say what you'll do, and by when you'll have done it.

Area of Life	Subcategory	Complete?	Do what, by when?
General Are you sorted (complete) in these areas? If not, what do you need to do, and by when will you do it?	Household clutter Business clutter Digital clutter Physical storage Digital storage Personal admin Personal projects	Y / N Y / N Y / N Y / N Y / N Y / N Y / N	
Support Do you have people you can turn to in these areas?	Doctor(s) Lawyer Accountant Coach Handyman Mechanic	Y / N Y / N Y / N Y / N Y / N Y / N	
Order Areas Are you sorted (complete) in these areas? If not, do what, by when?	Workspace Books Music Clothing Tech equipment	Y / N Y / N Y / N Y / N Y / N	
Relationships All good? If not, what issues do you need to resolve?	Broken promises Changed agreements Unresolved arguments Resentments Unforgiven stuff Withholds	Y / N Y / N Y / N Y / N	
Balance All good? If not, what do you need to put in place?	Time for self Time for family Time for friends Time for work	Y / N Y / N Y / N Y / N	

TABLE C: Priority of Values

Score your priority of values by asking yourself: How much do I prioritise each area by planning and/or spending time and/or money and/or mental energy on this activity? Do I sacrifice time / money / energy spent on other areas for the sake of this area? Score 1 if very low; 10 if very high, then rank them from 1 to 8.

Area of Life	Subcategory
Health / Exercise / Diet / Fitness (Time / money / energy spent keeping fit / healthy) 1 2 3 4 5 6 7 8 9 10	Ranking:
Immediate Family / Significant Other* (Priority given to time with family / partner) 1 2 3 4 5 6 7 8 9 10	Ranking:
Meaningful Vocation* (Priority given work that is your passion, regardless of money earned) 1 2 3 4 5 6 7 8 9 10	Ranking:
Making Money* (Priority given to working for money, regardless of passion for the activity) 1 2 3 4 5 6 7 8 9 10	Ranking:
Social Life (Time and money spent socialising) 1 2 3 4 5 6 7 8 9 10	Ranking:
Spiritual (Time and money spent on spiritual pursuits) 1 2 3 4 5 6 7 8 9 10	Ranking:
Intellectual (Time and money spent learning / educating yourself) 1 2 3 4 5 6 7 8 9 10	Ranking:
Leisure (Time and money spent on leisure activities) 1 2 3 4 5 6 7 8 9 10	Ranking:

*** See notes in main chapter text for scoring these options.**

BIBLIOGRAPHY

Alidina, Shamash. *Mindfulness for Dummies*. Chichester, England: John Wiley & Sons, Ltd, 2010.

Atmosphere Communications. *Kellogg's® All-Bran® launches the Feel All-Bran® New in 5-Days Promise*. Issued on behalf of Kellogg's® South Africa. http://www.fastmoving.co.za/activities/kellogg-s-all-bran-launches-the-feel-all-bran-new-in-5-days-promise-5713, 6 February 2015.

Barlow, David. *Clinical Handbook of Psychological Disorders: A Step-By-Step Treatment Manual*. New York: The Guilford Press, 2008.

Barlow, David et al. *Unified Protocol for Transdiagnostic Treatment of Emotional Disorders*. New York: Oxford University Press, 2011.

Beck, Aaron. *Cognitive Therapy and the Emotional Disorders*. New York: Meridian (Penguin), 1979.

Buchbinder, Amnon. *Out Of Our Heads: Philip Shepherd On the Brain in Our Belly*. https://www.thesunmagazine.org/issues/448/out-of-our-heads, April 2013.

Chatterjee, Debashis. *Leading Consciously*. Boston: Butterworth-Heinemann, 1998.

Csikszentmihalyi, Mihaly. *Flow: The Psychology of Happiness*. London: Rider (Penguin Random House), 2002.

Damasio, Antonio. *Descarte's Error*. New York: GP Putnam Sons, 1994.

Demartini, John. *The Values Factor*. New York: Berkley Books, 2013.

Gershon, Michael. *The Second Brain*. New York: Harper Collins, 1999.

Goleman, Daniel & Davidson, Richard J. *The Science of Meditation*. London: Penguin Life (Penguin Random House), 2017.

Halbfass, Wilhelm. *On Being and What There Is*. Delhi: Sri Satguru Publications, 1992.

Herbert, Wray. *To Thine Own Self: The Psychology of Authenticity*. https://www.psychologicalscience.org/news/were-only-human/to-thine-own-self-the-psychology-of-authenticity.html, 23 January 2015.

Hollis, James. *Swamplands of the Soul*. Toronto: Inner City Books, 1996.

Horney, Karen. *Our Inner Conflicts*. Oxford: Routledge, 1946 (Digital Version, 2007).

Horney, Karen. *Neurosis and Human Growth*. Oxford: Routledge, 1951 (Digital Version, 2007).

Jayasinghe, Romesh. *A Look at the Second Brain—The Brain in the Guts*. https://www.researchgate.net/publication/315726781_A_look_at_the_Second_Brain_-_the_Brain_in_the_Guts, 2017.

Jung, Carl (Ed.). *Man and His Symbols*. London: Picador, 1978.

Kotler, Steven. *The Science of Peak Human Performance*. http://time.com/56809/the-science-of-peak-human-performance/, 30 April 2014.

Krishnamurti, Jiddu. *Facing A World in Crisis*. Cape Town: Spearhead, 2005.

LeDoux, Joseph. *The Emotional Brain*. New York: Touchstone (Simon & Schuster), 1998.

Lehrhaupt, Linda & Meibert, Petra. *Mindfulness-Based Stress Reduction*. Novato, California: New World Library, 2017.

Lehrer, Jonathan. *How We Decide*. Boston: Houghton Mifflin Harcourt, 2009.

Lehrer, Paul M., Woolfolk, Robert L. & Sime, Wesley E. *Principles and Practice of Stress Management (3rd Ed)*. New York: The Guilford Press, 2007.

Linde, Colinda. *A Cognitive-Relaxation-Visualisation Intervention for Anxiety in Cancer Patients*. Rand Afrikaans University (University of Johannesburg), 2000.

McGonigal, Kelly. *The Upside of Stress*. New York: Avery (Penguin Random House), 2016.

McTaggart, John. *The Theme of Transcendence in Georg Simmel's Social Theory*. McMaster University. http://hdl.handle.net/11375/15572, September 1989.

Robbins, Tony. *Awaken the Giant Within*. New York: Simon & Schuster, 1992.

Ruiz, Miguel. *The Four Agreements*. San Rafael, California: Amber-Allen Publishing, 1997.

Ruiz, Miguel. *The Voice of Knowledge*. San Rafael, California: Amber-Allen Publishing, 2004.

Segal, Zindel, Williams, Mark & Teasdale, John. *Mindfulness-Based Cognitive Therapy for Depression: A New Approach to Preventing Relapse*. New York: The Guilford Press, 2002.

Selye, Hans. *Stress and Disease*. Science (122, 625-631), 1955.

Selye, Hans. *Confusion and Controversy in the Stress Field*. Journal of Human Stress (1, 37-44), 1975.

Senge, Peter. *The Fifth Discipline: The Art and Practice of the Learning Organization (Second Edition)*. New York: Doubleday/Currency, 2002.

Singer, Michael. *The Surrender Experiment*. New York: Harmony Books, 2015.

Singer, Michael. *The Untethered Soul*. Oakland, California: New Harbinger Publications, 2007.

Tirch, Dennis, Silberstein, Laura R. & Kolts, Russell L. *Buddhist Psychology and Cognitive-Behaviour Therapy: A Clinician's Guide*. New York: The Guilford Press, 2016.

Tolle, Eckhart. *A New Earth*. London: Penguin Books, 2005.

Yates, John & Immergut, Matthew. *The Mind Illuminated*. New York: Touchstone, 2017.

FURTHER RESOURCES

The Practical Mindfulness program is conducted live in Johannesburg, South Africa and, by invitation, in cities around the world. There is also an online self-study version, which can be branded and packaged for corporate clients, and a global webinar series.

The program consists of six modules. Module 1 is the introduction and covers the essential content of Sections A and B of this book. Modules 2 through 6 unpack the content in Section C of this book—each module correlates to a chapter, eg. Module 2 correlates to Chapter 6, Module 3 to Chapter 7, and so on. Modules can be conducted fortnightly, or together as a two-day workshop.

Details can be found at www.practicalmindfulness.co.za.

Other channels include:

YouTube — https://youtube.com/channel/UCQfC_X5AWpq4Dw_2PSb2ehg

Facebook — https://facebook.com/practicalmindfulnessZA/

Downloadable products include:

Breathing (Clouds-Are-Not-The-Sky) Meditation
http://practicalmindfulness.co.za/product/breathing-meditation/

Sensation Meditation
http://practicalmindfulness.co.za/product/sensation-meditation/

Full Program Home Study Pack
http://practicalmindfulness.co.za/product/home-study-pack/